NO
SAFE
HARBOR

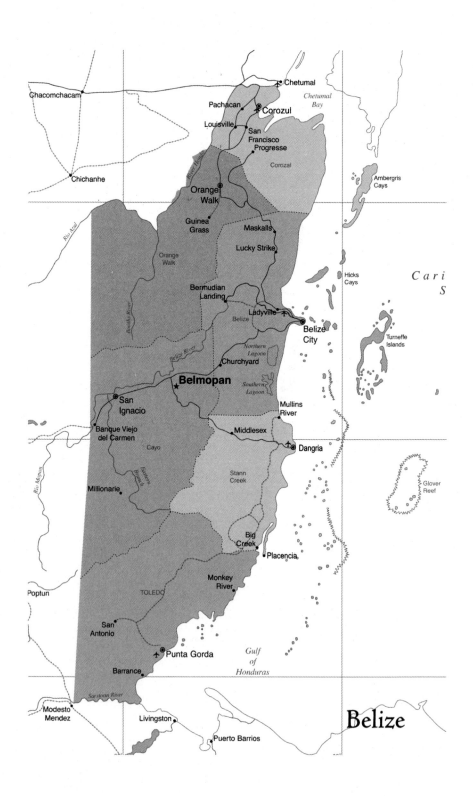

Chacomchacam

Chetumal

Chetumal
Bay

Pachacan
Corozul
Louisville
San
Francisco
Progresse

Chichanhe

Corozal

Ambergris
Cays

Río Azul

Orange
Walk

Guinea
Grass

Orange
Walk

Maskalls
Lucky Strike

Hicks
Cays

Cari
S

Booths River

Bermudian
Landing

Ladyville

Belize

Belize
City

Turneffe
Islands

Belize River

Northern
Lagoon

Churchyard

Belmopan

Southern
Lagoon

San
Ignacio

Mullins
River

Banque Viejo
del Carmen

Cayo

Middlesex

Dangria

Glover
Reef

Río Mojon

Eastern Branch

Millionarie

Stann
Creek

Poptun

TOLEDO

Big
Creek
Placencia

Monkey
River

San
Antonio

Punta Gorda

Gulf
of
Honduras

Barrance

Sarstoon River

Modesto
Mendez

Livingston

Belize

Puerto Barrios

NO
SAFE
HARBOR

The Tragedy of the Dive Ship
Wave Dancer

JOE BURNWORTH

1700 Madison Road, 2nd Floor, Cincinnati, Ohio 45206

For further information, contact the publisher at:

Emmis Books
1700 Madison Road
Cincinnati, OH 45206
www.emmisbooks.com

Library of Congress Cataloging-in-Publication Data

Burnworth, Joe.
  No safe harbor : the tragedy of the dive ship Wave Dancer / by Joe Burnworth.
    p. cm.
ISBN-10: 1-57860-219-X
ISBN-13: 978-1-57860-219-3
1. Wave Dancer (Yacht) 2. Hurricane Iris, 2001. 3. Shipwrecks—Belize.
4. Scuba divers—United States. I. Title.
  GV822.W36B87 2005
  910'.9163'65--dc22
                        2005008479

Edited by Jack Heffron
Interior designed by Carie Reeves
Cover designed by Andrea Kupper

Cover photo of Hurricane Iris hitting Belize courtesy of Marit Jentoft-Nilsen, NASA GSFC and the Earth Observatory webpage.

Photo credits in the insert. Page 3 (top) courtesy of Dave DeBarger; (bottom) courtesy of Tara Williamson. Pages 4-9; courtesy of the Richmond Dive Club; Page 10 (top) courtesy of Dave Mowrer; (bottom) Channel 5 Belize; Page 10-11 (spread) courtesy of Tara Williamson; Page 12, rendering by Carie Reeves; Page 13 (top) courtesy of Channel 5 Belize; (bottom) Dave DeBarger; Pages 14-15 courtesy of Channel 5 Belize; Page 16 (top) courtesy of WWBT-TV Richmond; (bottom) courtesy of Dave DeBarger.

To my wife Linda,

who has weathered many a storm with me on both land and sea.

Foreword

On October 8, 2001 I witnessed the worst accident involving scuba divers in the history of the sport. As a passenger on the live-aboard yacht *Belize Aggressor III*, I watched in horror as Hurricane Iris tore the yacht *M/V Wave Dancer* from its moorings, capsized it, and in a matter of minutes took the lives of seventeen members of the Richmond Dive Club and three crewmembers. After living with the memory of the tragedy for almost a year, I felt compelled to write the story of that night both as a tribute to those whose lives were lost and in the hope that the lessons learned from this disaster will make live-aboard diving a safer sport for the millions of people who want the thrill of diving in lush tropical waters.

The people, places, and dates are factual, and the story is based on my personal recollections, on research, and on interviews with survivors of the accident and with the many people affected by the small but deadly hurricane. Where some specific conversations were not available word for word, I have recreated them based on information gained from interviews of those involved. I used newspaper, television, and Internet resources to support and amplify the interview material, and you'll find those credits at the end of this book. I have written as complete an account of the accident as possible given the information available.

Writing about the accident at Big Creek has been an emotional journey for me. Many times I had to stop—once for two weeks—to collect myself. The vivid image of the partially covered bodies lying side by side on the Banana Enterprise Dock was at times draining and always haunting. Other times I burst out laughing at the antics of Glenn Prillaman, Buddy Webb, and Doug Cox. Over and over as I reviewed my work, I thought about Neil Diamond's song "Done Too Soon." The lyrics mourn great lives ending too soon, as did those aboard the *Wave Dancer*.

"The sea has never been friendly to man. At most it has been the accomplice of human restlessness."

Joseph Conrad

Chapter One

"Yes, I love it. The sea is everything. It covers seven-tenths of the terrestrial globe. Its breath is pure and healthy. It is an immense desert where man is never alone for he feels life, quivering around him on every side. There is supreme tranquility. The sea does not belong to despots. On its surface iniquitous rights can still be exercised, men can fight there, devour each other there, and transport all terrestrial horrors there. But at thirty feet below its level their power ceases, their influence dies out, their might disappears. Ah, sir, live in the bosom of the waters! There alone is independence. There I recognize no masters! There I am free."

Jules Verne, 20,000 *Leagues Under the Sea*

Lisa Powell paused for a moment at the long wooden pier to take in the scene stretched out in front of her. The cloudless sky was strikingly blue, the water a crystal reflection of the sky. Amid the palm and cypress trees, tropical hibiscus bloomed everywhere in radiant red, gold, fuchsia, and purple. Hours before, she had been in Richmond, Virginia, where the air was crisp with an October chill, but now a warm breeze slid through her hair, the temperature hovering around eighty-five degrees. A taste of sea salt lit on her tongue. In the water beyond the pier, two beautiful yachts awaited her and her friends from the Richmond Dive Club, all of whom had come to Belize for a week of diving and relaxation.

Affectionately known as "Mother Nature's Best Kept Secret," Belize is located approximately half way between the equator and Florida. Promotional brochures proclaim it "The Land Where Wildlife Rules and People Come Second." Lisa, a petite, athletic woman with sandy blonde hair, stood patiently as her bags were unloaded from the airport taxi. Within a few minutes she would be on the *M/V Wave Dancer* with nineteen of her diving buddies while the remaining ten members of the RDC would join another eight guests on the yacht *Belize Aggressor III*.

The 120 foot, four-tier *Wave Dancer* stood tall against the horizon. It offered a sky deck on top, where, between dives, guests could meet for some rays or to read a book in the shade of the canvas canopy. The deck below contained the wheelhouse with the captain's quarters, three master staterooms, and the salon used for meetings, guest entertainment, and dining. Four slightly smaller deluxe staterooms occupied the main deck, along with a dive deck equipped with a camera table, individual bins for dive gear storage, and a dive platform. The lower or dolphin deck contained three twin staterooms and staff quarters. All of the rooms had a tinted porthole. With its crisp blue-and-white exterior, chrome railings, and tinted windows glistening in the sun, the *Wave Dancer* looked every bit the pride of the Dancer fleet.

As Lisa stooped to pick up her bags, she heard a hearty male voice from behind her. "Welcome to the *Wave Dancer!*" the man said. "I'm Aaron Stark, your host and dive master."

Lisa looked up to see a handsome young man in a *Wave Dancer* T-shirt, shorts, and deck shoes smiling at her. With his strawberry blond hair blowing in the Belizean breeze, he appeared to be a poster model for the Caribbean scuba diving industry. He held out his arms to take her bags, which she gladly gave him.

"Thanks," she said. "I'm Lisa Powell."

"Let me put these in your cabin," he said. "Then we can tour the boat."

"Sounds good to me," she said.

"And you can leave your shoes with your luggage. On the *Wave Dancer* there will be no shoes, no worries, just great diving and a lot of fun in the sun."

As he led her below the main deck to her cabin, Lisa couldn't help but wish that her fiancé, Mike Bjorson, was here to enjoy this great experience with her. A smile crossed her face as she recalled how in July she had sent him on a scavenger hunt that ended with his diving into a swimming pool and retrieving a wedding band she had placed there earlier. Unfortunately, due to his job in the Navy, he had to report to a new duty station in Seattle and was unable to make the trip to Belize. At thirty-one, Lisa looked forward to settling down into married life, though a spirit of adventure still tugged at her.

She was standing at the doorway of her air-conditioned cabin when she realized Stark was talking to her—describing her accommodations, politely pointing out the twin beds, basin, closet, shower, and toilet. All of the cabins featured a television with a VCR for the guests who wanted to enjoy some private entertainment. The cabin was set up for two people, but Lisa and her friend and roommate, Mary Lou Hayden, planned to use it only for sleeping. They wanted to spend every available minute that week diving and having fun with their friends.

Like the other members of the Richmond Dive Club, Lisa had come to Belize to enjoy and explore a naturally created underwater fantasyland on the second largest barrier reef in the world. She had read the tourism literature, which touted Belize as a destination with "no artificial ingredients, only natural flavors" and a place where you could find "the essence of earth as earth should be." She soon would find out if everything she read and heard about the reefs of Belize was true.

After quickly stowing her unpacked bags in the cabin, Lisa followed Stark upstairs to the dive deck, where he assigned a locker for her dive equipment. Then they went to the salon, where he explained the eating and entertaining arrangements and encouraged her to get a glass of rum punch and go to the sky deck while he assisted other arriving guests from the Richmond Dive Club.

*　　*　　*

The RDC had evolved from the Virginia Divers in 1997 when Glenn Prillaman took over its presidency and changed its direction. Prillaman wanted an active dive club that made frequent trips and that was not associated with just one retail dive shop (as was the Virginia Divers) but would be supported by all area scuba diving merchants. The first RDC gatherings were held at Milepost 5, a seafood restaurant with a small meeting room. Prillaman's engaging personality and philosophy of combining food and drink with the meeting, along with a noted industry guest, increased the membership from thirty to one hundred and seventy in one year. The rapid growth soon forced the club to move to a larger space at the La Siesta Mexican restaurant.

The RDC began to make frequent trips to land-based diving locations in North Carolina, Florida, and the Bahamas. Many members of the RDC were always ready to try something different and exciting. Some of them—such as Jim and Kim Garrison, who owned James Limousine Service—were entrepreneurs. The Garrisons, who in a few short years had developed their business from three to six limousines, used the diving destinations to expand their knowledge of other cultures. Other members were financially successful business people and professionals who had flexible schedules, an independent attitude, and an interest in living close to the edge. Many had heard about live-aboard dive boats through advertisements in the monthly dive magazines but had no first-hand knowledge of them.

In March 2000, Prillaman asked Christy McNiel, the club's activity chairperson, to check into a possible live-aboard trip somewhere in the Caribbean. Christy investigated the Aggressor Fleet, Nekton Pilot, and the Peter Hughes Company. She reported that the *Sun Dancer*, a Peter Hughes boat, located in the Turks and Caicos, was available in October. Prillaman and Christy didn't know what kind of response to expect but immediately filled fourteen of the sixteen spots available on the *Sun Dancer*. Although the fourteen RDC members had never taken a week-long live-aboard excursion, they relished the prospect of diving up to five times a day.

On the *Sun Dancer*, the members of the RDC met Captain Ian Stezaker and his crew—which consisted of a chef, dive master, photo specialist, and stewardess. They also met Ray and Teresa Mars from Maryland, who would soon join the club. The *Sun Dancer* was one hundred and twenty-eight feet long, a beautiful blue-and-white, three-tier, live-aboard dive yacht. The large cabins offered ample storage space, and the salon provided a relaxing place to gather for meals and entertainment. The dive deck included storage bins for dive gear, a camera table, and a platform that made it easy to get in and out of the water. The *Sun Dancer* exceeded all of their expectations for comfort, dining, and service. They were especially impressed with the *Sun Dancer's* ease in getting to the quality dive sites of Turks and Caicos. Captain Stezaker and his crew made such a memorable impression in those few days that the members of the RDC were hooked on live-aboard diving.

As soon as the group returned home, Prillaman asked Christy to call the Peter Hughes Company to get a list of available dates and trip locations. Hughes had been in the live-aboard business since 1991 and owned seven live-aboard boats including the *Wave Dancer*. He also ran a land-based diving operation. Prillaman, a consummate promoter and a man of many experiences, knew that live-aboard diving was going to be very popular with the members of the RDC and would help him further his vision for the club.

In a few days Christy secured the *Wave Dancer* in Belize for October 6-12, 2001. The RDC's only stipulation with the Peter Hughes Company was that the *Wave Dancer* be adequately manned. On the *Sun Dancer* Captain Stezaker had a crew of four when, in Prillaman's and Christy's opinions, he needed a minimum of seven. The crew shortage had created several minor problems that easily could have turned into major ones. At times during the week the crew had been so overworked they napped on the dive deck while divers were in the water. There also was no night watchman.

Nevertheless, the excitement and enthusiasm of the members who went to the Turks and Caicos spilled over to the other RDC members so much that when Christy announced she had secured the twenty-passenger *Wave Dancer* in Belize it sold out in three days. Of the twenty passengers booked on the *Wave Dancer*, fifteen had gone to Turks and Caicos, including the newest RDC member, Ray Mars. Because Christy now had a waiting list, she called the Aggressor Fleet for possible openings for the same date on the *Belize Aggressor*. She was told that there were twelve available spaces on the *Aggressor*, and ten members signed up, including Lisa Powell and Mary Lou Hayden.

Unlike most members of the RDC, Lisa struggled financially. Her job as the manager of The Toymaker of Williamsburg, an upscale toy store, didn't pay well. Because they were late with their reservations, she and Mary Lou could not get the group rate the RDC members received on the *Wave Dancer* and had to pay an additional three hundred dollars on the *Aggressor*. To pay for her trip, Lisa worked a second job one day a week as a hostess at Buckhead's Restaurant. She notified Christy that if someone canceled a reservation on the *Wave Dancer* she wanted to change boats, and three weeks prior to the departure date a couple canceled. Lisa and Mary Lou transferred to the *Wave Dancer*.

Mary Lou had worked in the healthcare industry since 1972, serving as an instructor in the School of Nursing at the University of Virginia's Medical School, and she easily could afford to stay on the more expensive *Aggressor*, but she moved to the *Wave Dancer* to be with her young friend, who reminded her of her daughter, Melanie. Mary Lou thought that if the three of them walked down a street together people would think they were mother and daughters. Mary Lou and Lisa met in 1999 when a group, including Lisa's father, Forrest, went to Bonaire on a diving trip. For a week they ate, dove, and hung out together. Mary Lou saw that Lisa loved people, had an infectious laugh and a magnetic personality. By the time they left, they had formed a friendship that extended to phone calls, e-mails, shopping, and diving trips.

* * *

When Lisa reached the sky deck, she saw two familiar and welcome faces. Glenn Prillaman and Dave DeBarger, the club's vice-president, leaned against the deck's rail, enjoying the sun and sipping the *Wave Dancer's* famous rum punches. They already had changed into comfortable shorts and T-shirts, sans shoes. Both wore sunglasses and looked set for the week's activities.

"Hey, Lisa, you made it!" Prillaman shouted when he saw her. "Let the party begin." A grin stretched beneath his thick, Groucho Marx moustache as he lifted his drink in an exaggerated toast to her arrival, a cigarette burning between his fingers. His eyes darted devilishly behind his dark-rimmed glasses, as if in search for the next bit of fun, a search that inevitably infected everyone around him. Lisa couldn't help but smile.

"How's the punch?" she said.

Prillaman took a gulp, wiped the pink froth from his moustache, and announced, "De-licious." DeBarger, always the conservative straight man to Prillaman's wild antics, raised his glass, though in a more formal salute. While Prillaman looked as if he had slept in his clothes, DeBarger, with his crisp attire and full head of slightly graying well-groomed hair, appeared every bit the distinguished gentleman. Together this odd couple formed the center of the RDC, and no gathering would be quite the same without them.

They met in 1996 at McNeal's Dive Shop while preparing for a trip to Grand Cayman. Because they were the only singles on the trip they shared a room together. Soon they realized how well they complemented each other and became instant friends. DeBarger, a recent widower, was a quiet, serious person who had worked at WCVE-PBS in Richmond for thirty years. He was meticulous in every detail of his life. By contrast, Prillaman lived "large." He liked to get everyone involved in what he was doing. It was said that as he traveled down the highway of life, when he came to a fork in the road he always took the one marked "Fun." In Richmond he was known for the Aristo G Gauge model train layout, affectionately dubbed Acorn

Falls Railroad, which covered his backyard. It delighted many busloads of school children and was one of Richmond's more popular stops during the annual Tacky Christmas Lights Tour.

A restless spirit, he had worked at seemingly every imaginable profession, including selling airplanes and boats and being a radio producer and an EMT. He delighted in handing out business cards that read:

USED CARS • LAND • WHISKEY

MANURE • NAILS • COMPUTERS VERIFIED

WARS FOUGHT • GOVERNMENTS RUN • COUNTERFEITING

HORSE TRADING • BALLOT BOXES STUFFED • REVOLUTIONS ARRANGED

ELECTIONS RIGGED • CALL GIRLS • SHORT FIELD TAKE-OFFS

WHEELS-UP LANDINGS • PARTIES

GLENN PRILLAMAN

804-320-2989

WENCHES • WRENCHES • BANQUETS • MILITARY SECRETS

DANCING GIRLS • BOOTLEGGING • ARTIFICIAL INSEMINATION

SEDUCTIONS • ONE-WAY RIDES ARRANGED • WIRETAPS • BALLS

BLACK MARKET SURPLUS • SUICIDES COMMITTED • ORGIES ORGANIZED

ALSO AN ASSORTMENT OF NUTS AND BOLTS • MOSTLY NUTS!

He had finally landed in real estate sales because the flexible work schedule fit his lifestyle and no one pressed him for production.

He always had a gag of some kind available for everyone's amusement. One of his favorites involved special teeth he had ordered from Drbukk. com, as modeled on the Internet by such celebrities as Jenna Elfman, Edward Norton, and Shaquille O'Neal. The teeth were yellow, gapped enough to hold a cigarette in them, and as crooked as a hound dog's hind leg. He called them his hillbilly teeth. When Prillaman and DeBarger went out to eat, Prillaman would put the teeth in his mouth and attempt to place his order. The waitress invariably laughed so hard she couldn't take the order. Prillaman then demanded to see the manager. When the manager arrived Prillaman attempted to explain the problem and soon the manager was laughing too. Eventually everyone within earshot giggled at his antics. Prillaman and his foil, DeBarger, had received more than one free meal using this gag. In anticipation of another joke-filled voyage, Prillaman brought several of his practical joke items with him to the *Wave Dancer*, including a slingshot normally used for flinging T-shirts into the crowd at a ballgame. On this trip he planned to use the slingshot to wing water-filled balloons at members of the RDC on the *Belize Aggressor*.

On the sky deck of the *Wave Dancer*, Lisa grabbed a drink and chatted with Prillaman and DeBarger. They talked about the exhausting trip that had brought them to this beautiful place and congratulated each other for having made it.

"Here's to a great week," Prillaman said, shooting a mischievous look at Lisa and DeBarger. They laughed at what he might have planned for them, knowing he would keep everyone entertained. After a quick gulp and a quicker wipe of his thick moustache, he said, "And here's to finally making it."

Lisa and DeBarger nodded and lifted their cups.

Though they had been planning the trip to Belize for more than a year, the members considered changing the plan after the catastrophic events of September 11, 2001. When the World Trade Center Towers collapsed, people became very cautious about travel. Unnecessary travel, particularly by air, was abruptly canceled or at least postponed. Three days after the 9/11 attacks, the airline industry resumed limited flights with a mere 10 to 20 percent of normal passenger capacity. People felt nervous about baggage security checks, passenger scrutiny, and flight safety. Passenger check-in and security lines became slow and cumbersome. The airline industry was operating in uncharted territory and was adamant about adopting a "better safe and slow than sorry" approach to the future security of their business.

The members scheduled to leave for Belize in Central America on Saturday October 6 needed to do some individual soul searching about continuing with their plans for the trip of a lifetime. They needed to justify to themselves that the reward of scuba diving in the beautiful Belizean waters was greater than the perceived risk of flying on an airplane so soon after 9/11. They e-mailed each other with their individual concerns, and Christy, who had the group list, sent changes and assurances to each of them. In the end, all but two of the group decided to proceed with their plans. They agreed with the growing sentiment among many Americans that changing their plans or lifestyle in any way would mean a victory for the terrorists.

Prillaman confirmed with Christy that the airlines and dive companies were ready to proceed as planned. Tall and attractive, Christy was affectionately referred to as "Tour Barbie" by her many friends in the club. She first checked with Continental Airlines, the carrier they had chosen, only to find that the first leg of the flight from Richmond to Houston had been canceled. She checked Continental's options available to the RDC but found that they would have to fly out of Norfolk International Airport in Norfolk, Virginia, located ninety miles southeast of Richmond. To travel from Richmond to Norfolk they would need to hire a bus and would have to leave at two in the morning to be in Norfolk by four, the now mandatory two hours before their flight was scheduled to leave for Houston.

Prillaman needed to face the issue of getting his fellow divers through the increased airport security. This wouldn't be easy. For their own underwater safety and protection most of the members carried a scuba diving knife with them. The scuba knives were considered an emergency part of their equipment. In the event that a diver became tangled in some underwater debris, such as nylon filament from fishing lines, he would need to be able to free himself. The knife also provided protection from the unfriendly advances of underwater creatures. However, after 9/11, airport security might not perceive the knives as necessary equipment.

Additionally, many of the divers carried metal containers of spare air called "pony bottles," which are used as an auxiliary source of compressed air that could save the life of a diver or his buddy in an emergency air loss situation. Members of the RDC frequently carried these containers for additional safety during deep wreck diving where they had the potential of an emergency air loss or shortage situation. The pony bottles hold enough air to allow a distressed diver to slowly ascend to the surface and thus avoid the potential of physical trauma caused by rapid ascension. Prillaman wondered if airport security would consider the auxiliary compressed air containers part of an explosive device and thus confiscate them.

To circumvent the security issues, Prillaman contacted Ken Scott, the executive director of Norfolk International Airport, explained the problem, and asked for help. Fortunately, Scott understood the problem and promised to assist the RDC when they arrived at Norfolk International. With the security and airline issues settled, Prillaman and Christy turned their attention to the live-aboard companies. They discovered that there had been no repercussions from 9/11 in Belize, and so there would be no changes with the boats. After many emails, phone calls, and a very long trip, the members finally made it aboard the yachts and awaited their diving adventure.

As Lisa drank the sweet rum punch with Prillaman and DeBarger, she thought again about her fiancé, wishing he had been able to join her in this paradise. She looked at her left hand and noticed for the umpteenth time that she wasn't wearing her engagement ring. Before leaving for Belize she had taken it to her jeweler for sizing. It would be waiting for her when she got back home to Richmond.

Chapter Two

"A method of escaping in tempest and shipwreck at sea. Have a coat of leather, which should have the part over the breast in two layers, a finger breadth apart; and in the same way it must be double from the waist to the knee; and the leather must be quite air tight. When you leap into the sea, blow out the skirt of your coat through the double layers of the breast; and allow yourself to be carried by the waves; when you see no shore near, give attention to the sea you are in and always keep in your mouth the air tube which leads into the coat; and if now and again you require to take a breath of fresh air, and the foam prevents you, you may draw a breath of air within the coat."

Leonardo da Vinci, 1499

At a press conference in May 2001, Max Mayfield, director of the National Hurricane Center, advised the general public of the 2001 hurricane season projections. According to his projections, as many as eleven tropical storms—including five to seven hurricanes—could threaten the Atlantic and Gulf coasts during the season, which runs from June 1 to November 30. The National Oceanic and Atmospheric Administration predicted what it called a normal hurricane season for 2001, but it warned that "normal" did not mean the danger would be any less.

"Although we expect an average level of activity this season," said acting NOAA Administrator Scott Gudes, "residents in hurricane-prone areas can't afford to let their guard down. Just one storm can dramatically change your life."

A normal Atlantic hurricane season typically brings eight to eleven tropical storms, of which five to seven reach hurricane strength. A season also can include two or three major storms. A leading independent forecaster, William M. Gray of Colorado State University, predicted ten tropical storms, of which six would be hurricanes, two of them intense. The "normal" forecast was based on the absence of such influences as the El Niño and La Niña phenomena, in which unusual warming or cooling of the tropical Pacific can affect the weather worldwide. Without those influences, the key climactic factors guiding 2001's expected activity were long-term patterns of tropical rainfall, air pressure, and temperatures of the Atlantic Ocean and Caribbean Sea, according to Jack Kelly, director of NOAA's National Weather Service. "Forecasters will monitor these climate patterns, especially leading up to the August–October peak period of the season," Kelly said.

Mayfield stressed that hurricane-spawned disasters occur even in years with normal or below-normal levels of activity. Hurricanes Donna of 1960, David and Frederic of 1979, and Edna, Gloria, and Juan of 1985 are reminders of the destruction that can occur during seasons with "normal" hurricane activity. Hurricane Andrew of 1992, the costliest hurricane on record, developed during a season of below-normal hurricane activity.

Despite improvements in recent years, predicting where a hurricane will strike the coast three days ahead is still subject to error by as much as two hundred miles. That's half the error margin of twenty years ago, but it still poses serious problems for officials making decisions about evacuation. The forecast improvement has led to one major change: Storm surge slamming ashore is no longer the major killer in these events. People are now warned and, for the most part, they evacuate the area.

During the last days of September 2001 a poorly defined tropical wave moved westward across the tropical Atlantic. An extremely hostile upper-level wind environment caused by a large, upper-level trough with an "embedded low" centered just to the northeast of the Lesser Antilles, prevailed over the Atlantic. As the tropical wave reached 50W on the third of October, the upper-low became detached from the trough and began to move toward the southwest over the eastern Caribbean Sea. This condition resulted in the development of an upper-level ridge over the tropical wave, providing a favorable environment for tropical cyclone formation. While this pattern evolved, satellite imagery indicated an increase in thunderstorm activity and a cyclonic rotation in the mid-level. Gradually, a low-level cloud circulation became more pronounced on satellite imagery and was later confirmed by surface observation.

The National Hurricane Center sent a report regarding the storm to Carlos Fuller, Chief Meteorologist, Belize C.A., at 3:00 p.m. on Thursday, October 4. The report stated: "It is estimated that Tropical Depression #11 with a poorly defined center formed from this system about 85 nautical miles southeast of Barbados at 12:00 p.m. on Thursday, October 4. The depression is moving west-northwest at 18 mph with heavy squalls over the Lesser Antilles." Fuller forwarded the report without comment to the Belize headquarters of the National Emergency Management Organization [NEMO], to the Cabinet Secretary, and to the Ministry of Public Utilities, Energy, and Communications.

On Thursday, October 4, two days before they left for Belize, the traveling members of the RDC met at the home of Jim and Kim Garrison to have a "we're going to Belize party" and review their final arrangements. The Garrisons always enjoyed having a house full of guests. Jim, a very outgoing person, never met an "adult toy" he did not like. He always bought the newest dive equipment with the most recent technology, and then sold his last year's model to one of his friends in the RDC at a bargain price. Nicknamed "Gadget Man," he would buy anything just to try it and render his opinion on its functionality, appearance, and merit.

Kim Garrison—tall, blonde, and beautiful—complemented Jim in both appearance and support of his business venture. She had two young sons, Brandon and Steven, by a previous marriage and was totally committed to Jim and their new family. Jim loved the boys as if they were his own. In fact, the Garrisons were so concerned about the boys' future that they agreed never to travel on a plane together, feeling that if something happened to either one of them the survivor would be able to care for the children. This trip to Belize, they nervously agreed, would be the one exception.

Their home provided an ideal setting for the final trip meeting. The food tables were set up in the family room. The finished garage, with carpeted floor, had two long banquet tables with forms for all to fill out, including release waivers from the Peter Hughes Company, airline tickets, and so on.

The dress for the evening was casual with Lisa, Mary Lou, and Christy wearing warm-up suits while Prillaman wore shorts and an RDC polo shirt. Others arrived similarly dressed, some wearing jeans. Everyone wore a smile. They batted around jokes about who was going to do what to whom. The law of brinkmanship would be the rule of the trip. Ray Mars had traveled two and a half hours from his home in Scaggsville, Maryland, a suburb of Washington D.C., to complete his registration forms and receive his room assignment. He also had a concern with the trip that he wanted to resolve. A supervisor with the Food and Drug Administration, Ray loved a good time, but he didn't want to wake up in the middle of the night with a fire hose drenching his cabin, as had happened to Prillaman and DeBarger on the Turks and Caicos trip. He knew there would be a lot of pranks during the week, so when he found out he would share a room with Buddy Webb, the instigator of the soaking incident, he sought assurances from Christy that there would be no similar antics in his cabin. After several e-mails with Christy, he was convinced that Webb, now referred to as "Fire Hose," and Prillaman were committed to sleeping in dry quarters for the week.

When everyone had eaten, Prillaman and Christy moved the group into the finished garage area, where they sat on the floor and discussed the formalities. Christy, the "Taskmaster," took control and explained when they needed to meet the bus, listing what each person should bring, what to pack, what carry-on items were allowed and which ones were not, such as knives and full pony bottles. She supervised the forms, assigned rooms and roommates, and reviewed the boat layouts.

With the details of the trip out of the way, the group moved back to the family room where RDC member Dave Mowrer had prepared a video of the underwater reefs of Belize. Mowrer, a diving instructor at Dallas Weston Dive Center in Chester, a suburb of Richmond, was also an underwater photographer and videographer, and he had visited Belize in April, staying aboard the *Wave Dancer*. He was very familiar with what his friends would encounter both above and below the turquoise surface. His video proved that everything they had heard and read regarding the fine quality of the underwater reefs of Belize was true. The reef coral, fans, sponges, and sea life shimmered in exotic colors. Everyone gave particular interest to the footage of the Blue Hole.

"The Blue Hole is like a giant pupil in a sea of turquoise," he told them as the video began to play on the big screen television. He stroked his salt-and-pepper beard as he spoke, and his eyes sparkled at the memory of the natural wonder. He explained that it was considered the Landmark of Belize, the most heavily marketed and visited natural attraction of the country. In 1970 the famous underwater explorer Jacques Cousteau deemed it "one of the four best dive sites in the world."

The Blue Hole is a deep, circular and incredibly blue sinkhole in the center of Lighthouse Reef. Its diameter at the coral rim surrounding the site measures approximately a thousand feet. It is four hundred and twenty feet deep. When Cousteau, who many call the father of scuba diving, first attempted to explore the Blue Hole he found it too difficult to navigate. To get his boat, the *Calypso*, to the center, he used dynamite to blow a hole in the outer rim of the reef large enough to accommodate the *Calypso*. Except for two breaks, one natural, on the eastern and northern edges of the Hole, the site is completely enclosed by living coral. It's a strange geological formation that dates back approximately fifteen thousand years when the world was in the midst of an ice age.

As the lecture continued and breathtaking images danced on the television screen, Mary Lou felt pleased to be able to enjoy the sport of diving. She grew up in California and loved the water, especially sailing, but had suffered ear problems so severe she thought she would never be able to dive. Then while visiting Cancun in 1998 she took a ferry to Cozumel, where she tried an introductory dive class and realized she could clear the pressure in her ears. When she returned to the States she took a scuba course and received her certification.

Mowrer went on: "The Blue Hole is a protected area that is unique not only in all of Belize, but in the rest of the Caribbean. In that sense it's similar to great sites like Stingray City at Grand Cayman, the Shark Dive at Walkers Cay, the wreck of the Yongala in Australia, and Blue Corner in Palau. There are certain 'must do' dives on a well-traveled scuba divers list," he said, "and the Blue Hole of Belize is at or near the top of the list."

The party resumed with everyone chatting and enjoying the evening, but the images they'd just seen stayed on their minds. It would be just two more days until they would all be able to see the Blue Hole and the magnificent reefs of Belize for themselves.

On Friday, October 5, at 5:00 p.m. as the members of the Richmond Dive Club finished packing for their trip, tropical Depression #11 became Tropical Storm Iris, moving west-northwest at fifteen miles per hour. The National Hurricane Center, a branch of the Tropical Prediction Center in Miami, warned that Iris was expected to become a hurricane on Saturday.

In Belize, Chief Meteorologist Carlos Fuller sent the center's advisory to NEMO, the Cabinet Secretary, and the Ministry of Public Utilities,

Energy, and Communications. Fuller, advised that the system could pose a threat to Belize the following week, said that he might have to recommend the preliminary phase of Belize's hurricane preparedness program on Monday, possibly as early as Sunday.

From this time forward the NHC would issue an update on Tropical Storm Iris every three hours until the storm dissipated. The report would include the projected direction of the storm as well as its movement, wind velocity, and expected storm surge above normal tide levels. The NHC warnings would also include upgrading the storm, issuing a storm watch for those areas that might be affected, and a warning for those areas that would actually be in the path of the hurricane. These warnings would be accessible through radio, fax, and telephone transmissions. Advisories also would be sent over the Internet and through marine voice frequencies on an hourly basis. At 5:00 p.m. the NHC issued a hurricane watch for Cuba and Jamaica, and their models predicted that Iris would hit land in the Yucatan Peninsula/Belize.

Prillaman and DeBarger were exhausted after the short night's sleep, the bus ride from Richmond to Norfolk, and the mandatory two-hour early arrival at the airport, as well as from the flights from Norfolk to Houston, and Houston to Belize, going through customs and the short bus ride to the Belize port where the *Wave Dancer* and the *Belize Aggressor* waited for them and their dive buddies. But after a clink of their rum punch glasses, like the click of Dorothy's heels, they knew they were not in Virginia anymore, and all of their effort had been worth it.

The only problem they encountered during their trip was at the Norfolk Airport and involved the late arrival of RDC member Jimmy Topping. He lived in Plymouth, North Carolina, owned his own airplane, and elected to fly to Norfolk. When the travelers had gone through security a head count revealed that he was missing. He arrived as the rest of the members of the RDC boarded their flight and had to be rushed by Ken Scott through security.

After her tour of the boat, Mary Lou stowed her dive gear and ambled to the salon, got a rum punch, and headed for the sky deck, where she found her fellow divers clustered in groups. As new roommates, Buddy Webb and Ray Mars chatted next to Lisa, Mary Lou, Prillaman, and DeBarger. They toasted a great week of diving and joked about what pranks might be pulled, Mars reiterating that he wanted to sleep in a dry bed, poking his roommate with an elbow of reminder.

Webb laughed. "Trust me," he said. "I promised. Nothing is going to happen."

Prillaman shook his head and grinned. "Are you really going to believe a guy nicknamed 'Fire Hose'?"

"I know I wouldn't," Lisa said, sneaking a look at Mary Lou.

"You'll sleep like a baby," Webb said. "Not that we won't find a few other ways to make your trip, um, exciting."

The laughter and banter continued as anticipation of the week ahead percolated through every conversation. The sky deck was full as the members broke into groups of two and three, swelling to larger groups and breaking off again. The week had begun. And the club couldn't wait to dive.

The human desire to swim freely underwater is as old as our fascination with flight. The first recorded effort occurred in 322 BC. At that time Greek philosopher Aristotle's *Problemata* describes a diving bell used by Alexander the Great at the siege of Tyre. In the 1500s, Leonardo de Vinci designed the first known scuba gear. His drawings of a self-contained breathing apparatus combining air control and buoyancy in a single system appeared in *Codex Alanticus* and foreshadowed later diving suits.

Several inventors and inventions led to the technology needed to allow man to spend unencumbered time searching for sunken treasure, performing commercial and military duties, or simply enjoying the experience. Englishman William James is given the most credit for developing the first scuba system. In 1825, he created a method of diving that employed tanks of compressed air and a full diving suit with a helmet.

However, it took the field of entertainment to spark the public imagination about the possibilities of spending time in the underwater world. In 1870, French novelist Jules Verne wrote the science fiction classic *20,000 Leagues Under the Sea*. In his novel, the central character, Captain Nemo, uses an underwater breathing device and theorizes about the inevitable next step that would eliminate the diver's dependence on surface-supplied air.

The book became a full-length feature film in 1915 and the remake in 1954—starring Kirk Douglas, James Mason, and Peter Lorre—won two Academy Awards. Other big-screen legends, such as John Wayne, Sean Connery, Nick Nolte, and Jacqueline Bisset, starred in films that popularized the underwater world. From 1958 to 1961, the television show *Sea Hunt*, starring Lloyd Bridges, introduced millions of viewers to the world of scuba.

In 1968, Jacques Cousteau was asked to make a television series based on his many underwater adventures. For the next eight years, *The Undersea World of Jacques Cousteau* introduced the public to a world of sharks, whales, dolphins, sunken treasure, and coral reefs. His encounters with fish and reef creatures in their natural surroundings romanticized the sport of scuba diving, enticing adventurers around the world to "come see for yourself."

With the increased media attention, the evolution of scuba equipment, and the construction of resorts and other dive destinations designed for scuba divers, the number of people becoming certified divers has increased dramatically. According to the Professional Association of Diving Instructors [PADI] the number of members their international organization certified increased annually from 3,226 in 1967 to 854,052 in 2000 worldwide. PADI estimates that two out of three divers are male and also two out of three divers in the U.S. and one out of two in the world are certified by their organization. PADI has new cumulated certifications totaling over ten million since 1967 equating to over twenty million new divers worldwide since that time.

Most of the members of the Richmond Dive club making the trip to

Belize were certified by PADI and had been scuba diving for several years. They owned their own equipment and all but one were considered advanced divers. Several of them were dive masters and two of them were scuba diving instructors. Prior to coming to Belize, each member had checked his or her dive equipment to ensure that the regulator hoses did not leak and all of the gauges and computers worked correctly. As a group, the RDC took a conservative approach to diving. They did not push the limits of safe diving by going too deep or staying down too long because they knew that tomorrow is always potentially another good day of diving.

Chapter Three

"The sea, biologists tell us, holds the key to the mysteries of life. In some unknown time and way a molecule of matter crossed an unknown line and became a living cell. Other scientists believe that the human mind has a dim awareness of long tenuous roots that stretch back into the sea. When we dream of being in water, they say, of diving into it or coming out of it, we are reliving the mysteries of our own birth. Our language reflects the uneasy awe we feel towards the unknown world, which covers most of the planet. When something is beyond our understanding we say it's "Too deep" or that "We just can't fathom it!"

Lil Borgeson and Jack Spiers, *Skin Divers Handbook*

Late that afternoon Prillaman asked all of the RDC members to meet on the sun deck of the *Wave Dancer* so he could make sure their accommodations were acceptable and to resolve any issues before they left Belize City. The *Wave Dancer* would be at sea for six days, so any needs the divers anticipated had to be satisfied before they left port. At the meeting Prillaman said the *Wave Dancer* would leave Belize City at 6:00 p.m. and dinner would be served at 6:30. He added that after dinner the *Wave Dancer's* captain, Philip Martin, would officially welcome them with a briefing about the boat, safety issues, and what to expect in the week ahead.

As he spoke his eyes darted through the crowd. The pitch of his voice made even the mundane announcements seem like fun. While Prillaman was talking, Webb, smiled, thinking "Paybacks are hell." He was not sure what to expect, but he knew that the soaking he and Captain Ian Stezaker had given Prillaman during the Turks and Caicos trip would be avenged. In the category of practical jokes, Prillaman's philosophy was, "you're never even until you're one up." Webb knew that the club's leader, now guiding them through the details of the trip, would soon be a mad avenger, giving better than he got.

Webb, like Prillaman, was a big kid at heart who enjoyed more than anything his weekend camping trips with his two sons, Ben and John Wesley. During the trips the three would get decked out in their paintball gear, layout a course consisting of trees, cars, and any other obstacle they could use as concealment from which to attack each other. The fact that Webb had been a marksman in the Marines did not always work to his advantage, because he was a larger target and somewhat slower than his sons. And, he liked to add to his stories of these weekends, what good dad wouldn't take an occasional paintball hit from his son?

At 5:00 p.m. Saturday, October 6, the NHC announced that Tropical Storm Iris had now become Hurricane Iris and was a level one storm. The direction of the hurricane had shifted to west from northwest, moving in a more southerly direction, speeding along at seventeen mph with winds increasing to seventy-five mph. In the Dominican Republic, Hurricane Iris claimed its first three victims in a mudslide caused by torrential rains that trapped them in their small jungle village.

On Ambergris Caye, the largest and best known of the two hundred islands off the Belize coast, Lori Reed prepared herself and the guests at her small hotel for evacuation. Reed, a Canadian, had owned the small hotel for eight years and realized the safety of her guests came first. She had been through hurricanes Mitch, and Keith, as well as Tropical Storm Chantel, and she had been forced to evacuate herself and her guests from

Ambergris Caye each time. To her, this evacuation, inconvenience, and expense were an inevitable part of living in a tropical paradise.

At six o'clock the *Wave Dancer* and the *Belize Aggressor* departed Belize City for the offshore barrier reefs and the dive trip of a lifetime. Lisa and Mary Lou leaned against the railing of the sky deck, a tropical evening breeze blowing through their hair, and watched the skyline of Belize City melt into the distance. They said little, knowing that the other was content to appreciate the beautiful view in silence. They muttered an occasional "This is incredible" but expected no response. The moment needed no words. In the opposite direction, the sun was setting on the ocean's surface, beckoning them to a new horizon.

The *Aggressor* knifed through the water near them, and they could see some of their friends aboard. A few members waved back and forth to each other from their places on the boats. The *Aggressor* was the fifth boat added to the Aggressor fleet and was designed much like the *Wave Dancer*, though its colors were black and white while the *Wave Dancer* was blue and white. Both yachts could comfortably accommodate up to twenty divers and nine crew members. The *Aggressor* was three tiered with a sky deck on top, but lacked the shade of a canopy. The wheelhouse, captains quarters, and one suite were on the second level along with the bar, lounge area, and hot tub. The main level contained the salon, dining area, kitchen, photo lab, and dive deck. Below the main deck were the balance of the sleeping quarters, laundry facilities, and engine room. The *Aggressor* was ten feet shorter than the *Wave Dancer*, and so its cabins contained bunk beds rather than twins. Aesthetically designed with tinted glass and chrome railings both were yachts that would enhance any harbor.

Prior to leaving Belize City several of the Belizean crew aboard the *Wave Dancer* discussed the approaching storm. From the time they are old enough to read and write, young Belizeans are taught to be cautious of tropical storms, particularly hurricanes, much the same way young Americans are told to be alert when they hear the sound of a rattlesnake. Hurricanes and rattlesnakes have many similarities. They both give a warning before they strike. The strike is sudden, violent, and sometimes fatal.

Bart Stanley, the *Wave Dancer*'s dive master and photo specialist with twelve years of experience in the Belizean waters, had reason to be worried. As a young man his mother had told him about Belize's turbulent history of hurricane activity, including Hurricane Hattie, which in 1961 so devastated Belize City, then the nation's capital, that the government moved the capital farther inland to Belmopan. She showed him old photographs of Belize City with flooded streets and destroyed buildings. She told him of her many friends who had died during Hattie and prayed that a storm like that would never occur again. Although Stanley only knew about Hattie through his mother's recollections, he did remember Hurricane Mitch, which had occurred three years earlier in October 1998. Mitch, he remembered, caused nine thousand deaths in Central America. It also led to the sinking of the 282-foot steel-hulled schooner *Fantome* off the coast of Honduras. Thirty-one people, all crew, died after the ninety-seven passengers and some non-essential crew disembarked in Belize City. These lessons of death and destruction were indelibly etched in his mind.

Stanley and Eloisa Johnson, the Belizean head cook, both had many years of live-aboard experience. On that first evening they went to Captain Philip Martin, told him of their concerns, and suggested that the *Wave Dancer* not leave Belize City until they knew more about the approaching storm.

They did not know that earlier in the day Chief Meteorologist Fuller had began the process of initiating the Meteorological Service's Hurricane Emergency Plan. He had prepared the hurricane roster. He had requested that Deputy Chief Meteorologist Justin Hulse return early from his vacation and work the emergency shift that night. He had also advised the other members of the staff, including Junior Meterologist Dennis Gonguez, of the emergency shift. More importantly, the Belizean crew did not know that one hour earlier the NHC had upgraded Tropical Storm

Iris to Hurricane Iris, a level one hurricane. The radio, which Eloisa always monitored, had been removed from her galley.

Aaron Stark gave the bell next to the salon entry door three clangs, which meant it was time for dinner. Since this was the group's first meal on the *Wave Dancer*, Stark also went through the hallways on each level and the sky deck shouting that hot food and cool drinks were ready and waiting. Although the bell was the official way of notifying all the guests of mealtime or a dive briefing, it was the *Wave Dancer*'s customer-friendly policy to also go through the hallways to make sure everyone was informed that their presence was requested.

A turquoise-and-orange sectional sofa ran along two walls of the salon, creating an L-shaped area in front of the television, which was equipped with an attached VCR and DVD player. Below and next to the television were two sets of bookshelves and a double-door cabinet. The bookshelves contained several paperback and a few hardcover novels left behind by former *Wave Dancer* guests who either did not want to carry them home or preferred to share a good novel with future guests, creating a borrow, share, and return library. Most of the dog-eared novels by well-known authors had been so bleached from the sun they had barely legible bindings. Previous readers had written their names and hometowns on the inside covers.

On one shelf stood second editions of *Reef Fish Identification, Reef Creature Identification* and *Reef Coral Identification,* by Paul Humann. Of all the books, these three would get the most use as divers referred to them after their dives to identify fish, critters, or coral. They would also make notations in their log books that would be reviewed for years to come.

Across the room at a small table, *Wave Dancer* staff members Stanley and videographer Thomas Baechtold reviewed slides for the evening's presentation. The recent slides taken by Stanley and Baechtold displayed the underwater life on the Belize reef and would introduce the RDC members to the variety, color, and size of underwater life they would soon encounter.

Bill and Sheila Kelley moved across the center of the room to the line of guests waiting to fill their plates at the serving counter. Although only six feet long and two feet wide, the counter contained more than enough food to satisfy all persons on board and then some. The small blackboard at the entry to the buffet announced tonight's specials: cream of broccoli soup and sirloin steak or grouper with double layer chocolate cake for dessert. The buffet offered two choices of bread, wheat and white roll, two types of salads, Caesar and tossed, baked potatoes, twice-baked potatoes, corn, green beans, and mushrooms in brown gravy. The drinks included ice water, iced tea, Kool-Aid, coffee, beer, or wine.

Sheila went through the buffet line first and filled her plate with a small portion of Caesar salad, white roll, green beans, corn, and grouper. Bill, a hearty eater, loaded his plate with two white rolls, a baked potato, corn, and a large sirloin. As they looked for a table, Angela Luk, part-time chef and stewardess, asked them what they wanted to drink, told them to sit wherever they wanted, and she would bring Sheila's white wine and Bill's red wine to them.

When the Kelleys found a spot, Doug and Phyllis Cox sat down across from them.

"Quite a spread," Doug said, digging into his food.

"They said we wouldn't go hungry this week, and it looks like they meant it," Sheila said.

Bill echoed her sentiments with a "Mmm-hmmmm."

Doug raised his glass to make a toast. "Before we get too far into this feast," he said, "here's to your anniversary."

The foursome clinked their glasses.

The Kelleys had made the trip to celebrate their twenty years of marriage. The two had been in the RDC for less than a year but eagerly volunteered for committees and offered to help the club in any fashion. Bill, a former U.S. Army officer, didn't stray too far from his military background upon retirement. After finishing his PhD in Secondary Education at the University of Arizona, he accepted a position as the director of instruction at the U.S. Army Quartermaster School at Fort Lee, Virginia.

Sheila, an accomplished scholar as well, received a myriad of honors including multiple Dean's List standings and the editorship of the *Law Review*, in pursuit of her degree from the Salmon Chase College of Law at the age of thirty-seven. Since that time she had operated her own law practice as well as acting as a Judge Protem. She loved volunteer and fundraising work for the Petersburg Symphony Orchestra and told Phyllis how fulfilling it was to her.

When she finished, Phyllis told Sheila that she, too, did a lot of volunteer work for the Leukemia and Lymphoma Society. She told them their oldest son, Michael, died in 1995 from Leukemia, and thus she felt compelled to raise money so other parents may not have to go through such heartache. The realization that she was able to make a difference helped her cope with the loss of their son.

The two couples sat in silence for a moment as Phyllis finished speaking. Then Prillaman called over to Doug Cox from a nearby table: "Hey, enjoy that meal," he said. "You might be wearing your next one." Everyone in the room laughed.

"At least I waited until dessert," Cox shot back. The previous year when a group of RDC members went to Cozumel, Cox paid a waiter in their restaurant to put a cream pie in Prillaman's face. Prillaman had roared with laughter, always appreciating a well-executed prank, even when he was on the receiving end of it. Since then, however, he had sworn to avenge himself with Cox. Prillaman, Cox, and Buddy Webb were considered the club's "Three Musketeers" of hilarity and mischief. Like Prillaman, Cox had a set of Dr. Bukk teeth that he frequently used to liven up parties.

"I just hope for your sake you brought a few horseshoes along," Prillaman said. "You'll need the luck."

"I don't need any luck to handle you," Cox said, puffing his chest in mock bravado.

"Well, maybe while we're here you can drum up a little business," Prillaman answered. Again, everyone roared. Cox worked as a farrier, and

Prillaman, a jack of many trades himself, loved to wonder out loud about how a grown man could make a living shoeing horses.

The pair exchanged a few more salvos before returning to conversation with the people nearest them. The talk turned to food, room accommodations, dive deck, sky deck, and staff. The Kelleys, and Coxes were satisfied with the size, albeit small, of their cabins, and liked the *Wave Dancer* in general and the staff in particular. They all felt this would be a good week of diving and getting to know each other better. The one consensus among the groups was that while they had been diving together on day trips many times they seldom got a chance to really talk, to get to know each other, to share family stories and events of importance to each of them. In many cases they knew and liked each other but some substance to the relationship was missing. They hoped that during the next six days there would be many opportunities to share more intimate stories about their personal and family lives and to create a deeper bond with their diving buddies.

As the Kelleys and Coxes were finishing their double-layer chocolate cake, Captain Philip Martin, who had been in charge of the *Wave Dancer* since March, walked into the dining area of the salon and announced that the orientation briefing would begin in fifteen minutes. Martin was tall, handsome, athletically well built, very clean cut, and had a straight, sturdy demeanor. The four gold stripes on the black shoulder epaulets of his crisp white shirt—the insignia of a captain—left no doubt as to his position on the *Wave Dancer*. His accent was noticeably different from the divers and the crew, but with so much British influence in Belize it was hard to discern the fact that he was actually from New Zealand.

Fifteen minutes later the staff appeared wearing their monogrammed *"Wave Dancer*, Eat, Sleep and Dive" T-shirts (except Captain Martin who wore more formal attire). He opened his large black binder and for the next half hour proceeded to explain the week-at-a-glance to his guests.

Captain Martin's natural smile contrasted his reserved nature and formal approach to the task at hand. As he sat, back straight and feet firmly planted on the floor, he opened his talk by assuring the group that they were first and foremost his and his staff's guests. Lisa and Mary Lou, tired but attentive, sat on the floor with their legs stretched out, leaning against the side of the sofa and into each other for support. The glass of wine with dinner was having a sedative effect on the weary duo. In the back of the salon Webb rested against the wall and listened to the captain, knowing within minutes that he would not have a pranking comrade in arms like Captain Ian Stezaker on the Turks and Caicos trip.

Captain Martin gave his passengers a brief verbal tour of the *Wave Dancer*. He explained each level of the four-tier boat and said they had the run of the ship with few exceptions including the engine room, staff's quarters, and fore deck, where the week's accumulation of trash would be stored. He told them they were welcome in the wheelhouse to ask questions about the operation of his ship as long as he or his second mate, Frank Wouters, was there. He then played a fifteen-minute video that explained the safety procedures of the *Wave Dancer*, including location of the fire alarms, points of emergency exit, location of life jackets and lifeboats. He went on to say that it was a Peter Hughes Company policy that weekly safety drills be conducted by the crew and include guest participation. These drills, intended to assure that the crew maintained peak performance skills, would include such scenarios as man overboard, fire at sea, abandon ship, unconscious diver, lost diver searches, and more.

He explained that the *Wave Dancer* had its own reverse osmosis water maker, which would supply everyone on board with fresh potable drinking water they could enjoy without fear of some vacation-upsetting bug. Martin also mentioned that this was the water the chefs would use in food preparation and that all showers would use fresh water instead of the saltwater from the Caribbean.

"Although we make our own water and normally there is plenty of it," said the captain, "please do not waste it."

"There is also a photo E6 processing lab on board for your underwater slide processing. Also, if you need to rent any scuba gear, video or 35mm cameras, we have a limited supply on board. For those of you who use an electric razor, curling iron, or hair dryer, there is U.S. standard 110 volt electricity in every cabin and in the salon. Bart Stanley will tell you more about the dive platforms, photo table, dive gear set-up, and all related items at your first dive briefing at 8:00 a.m. sharp tomorrow morning."

Martin then reviewed the various forms each passenger had completed and signed. They included a two-page release from liability and indemnity agreement holding the Peter Hughes Company harmless from any action, accident, act of God, etc. Other forms involved status of personal health, including prescription medications taken, questions about heart ailments, surgeries, anything that could be an impediment to diving safety, certification, and level of diving qualifications. Captain Martin acknowledged that he had personally reviewed each person's qualification and information sheets and felt that each guest aboard was in good standing and that this would be a good week for health and happiness.

With the necessary orientation material covered, Martin said, "This is the time when I normally have you, our guests, introduce yourselves and tell us where you are from so you could get to know each other during the next few days. But, since you are all members of the Richmond Dive Club I assume you already know each other. So, I will bypass that portion of my agenda and introduce my staff. I will start by telling you their names and then invite each person to say something." Some members were struck by the formality of his diction and gestures. Though this was a pleasure boat, the captain clearly took his work very seriously.

Second mate Frank Wouters was introduced first. With his outgoing nature he was a good counterpart to Martin and popular with the crew. He told his listeners that in addition to assisting Captain Martin, he was the ship's engineer and as such was in charge of keeping the engines running. He also served as a dive master and would assist in the water.

Eloisa Johnson stepped forward. Of Mayan heritage, she was small in stature but big in heart. She knew the slogan of the live-aboard industry was "Eat, Sleep and Dive" and wanted to make sure the eating part of the motto was well represented. On every trip she asked each new guest if they had any special dietary needs so she could accommodate them. This time only DeBarger, who didn't like seafood, would require her special attention. She announced that the galley would open each morning at 6:00 a.m. for coffee, breakfast would be served at 7:00 a.m., there would be a snack served between morning and afternoon dives, lunch at 12:30 p.m. and dinner at 6:00 p.m..

"And by the way," Eloisa said, "there is always something available in the refrigerator for anyone who wants a midnight snack."

The group hooted its approval. Then she continued, "Tomorrow morning between dives Bart Stanley and I will entice you to the sky deck with fresh chocolate chip cookies and cool drinks to listen as we tell you about our favorite country, Belize." She concluded by saying she "was happy to see so many nice people," then introduced her assistants, Brenda Wade and Angela Luk, who both stepped forward, acknowledged their introduction with a slight smile and wave of the hand, then without saying a word stepped back.

Next up: Thomas Baechtold, a tall blond whose good looks and friendly Swiss accent had already caught the attention of several female members of the group. He gave everyone a big smile and introduced himself. He told them that during the week he would be in the water making a video of the divers, the reef, fish, and special dives such as the Blue Hole and night dives. He said he would also be shooting special video footage of each guest.

"So," he said, "when you see me smile, wave, and pose for the camera. Let's make this fun! At the end of the week, before you depart," he said, "I will make copies of your week underwater available to you for the meager, paltry, almost give-away amount of only forty dollars each. After this trip of a lifetime you will surely want the video recording to show your family and friends. Otherwise they will never believe the beautiful reef, fish, and critters you saw on your special week aboard the *Wave Dancer*." His hands moved in energetic gestures as he spoke, and everyone responded to his charm and passion.

Bart Stanley, a young Belizean, stepped forward. "This week belongs to you," he said. "I will do anything I can to assist you with your photo needs, so if you have a problem with your camera or want tips on underwater photography come and get me. I have a repair kit, batteries, and film at your disposal. Also, I will be your head dive master this week. If you have any problems with your dive gear, buoyancy, or whatever, see me.

"For those of you who want to spend some time improving your skills this week I have several classes available—advanced open water, deep diver, and underwater navigation. I also have two classes to assist you in identifying reef fish and reef creatures. Each class comes with a Paul Humann book.

"You can learn to extend your decompression time by taking the two enriched air or nitrox classes. You all will have some extra time this week, so this is a great opportunity to upgrade your skills in a most pleasant environment. At noon tomorrow Aaron Stark, my new and most knowledgeable associate, will give those interested an introduction to the benefits of nitrox. Take it away, Aaron."

On cue Stark explained that he was a dive master from the San Francisco Bay area. He'd been on the *Wave Dancer* for just two weeks but was a quick study and felt that he now knew his way around the Belizean reefs pretty well. "Last week I spotted a rare seahorse on a dive at Lighthouse reef," he told the group, "so if you want someone to point out special hard-to-find reef creatures for photos or your personal pleasure just let me know."

"Last but not least is Chico," said Martin. "He's our night watchman." Chico, carrying a large Maglite and wearing a light windbreaker, was truly a man of few words. He stepped forward, gave a slight smile and wave to the guests, and stepped back.

"Regarding this week's itinerary," Martin went on, "presently we are heading southeast about sixty miles around the Turneffe Atoll to Lighthouse Reef. We have smooth seas with a gentle prevailing breeze so the trip will take us between six and seven hours. We'll tie up to one of our moorings on the reef and stay there tonight. Tomorrow morning when you get up and finish your 8:00 a.m. briefing with Bart, you will have two morning dives. Then, while you are eating lunch, Wouters and I will move the *Wave Dancer* to a new location where we'll have two afternoon dives and the night dive.

"We'll repeat that pattern each day, moving to our next dive site while you are either eating or sleeping. The only day the schedule will change is Friday, when we have to head back to Belize City after the morning dives so we can prepare for our next guests. You will be on your own for dinner Friday night and you can stay on board the *Wave Dancer* until 9:00 a.m. Saturday. At this time, you will need to board the bus so you can be at the airport in time to catch your outgoing flight.

Prillaman raised his hand. Though the group expected some type of joke or silliness, he asked when they would do the Blue Hole.

Martin nodded quickly, a formal acknowledgment of the question, and then answered in his stiff diction, "Presently, I plan to do that on Monday morning," he said. "Additional dive information will be given to you tomorrow by Stanley. He will fill you in on everything you need to know to have a safe week of diving."

"One last thing before I leave you for the evening. You have heard reports of a tropical storm named Iris brewing east of us. Just to let you know, I've been in contact with the home office and as of eleven this morning the storm was 210 miles south-southeast of the Dominican Republic. It is moving north and west of where we are going to be diving, and while we may get a day of rain and some rough seas, it is nothing that we should get overly concerned about. We will continue to monitor the storm and will move on the leeward side the reefs and islands to insure you have a smooth ride and good diving. Enjoy the slide show, have a good evening, and sleep well." With that, Captain Martin and most of his crew left the salon.

Despite outward signs that all was well with Captain Martin and his crew, more than a storm was brewing. The crew felt Martin was belligerent and had unnecessarily criticized them in front of guests. His aloof attitude and "need to know" approach indicated that he did not respect them or their opinions. On two separate occasions during previous voyages Stanley had been forced to take control of the helm because Martin was steering the *Wave Dancer* into the reef. Stanley's quick actions had saved an accident that endangered both the reef and boat. These close encounters had been reported to Peter Hughes, and he had concluded that Martin, with limited piloting experience, lacked the navigational talent necessary to run a vessel with the complexities of the *Wave Dancer*. Unbeknownst to the RDC divers, their voyage aboard the *Wave Dancer* was scheduled to be Captain Martin's last charter with the Hughes Company.

As soon as Martin left the salon, Stanley told all the guests to take a ten-minute break, get a glass of wine or a beer, and come back for their world-famous slide show. When the *Wave Dancer* guests were re-seated, the lights went out, and Stanley began describing each slide. He introduced the program by saying that the slides were designed to give the divers a preview of the variety of fish, coral, and critters they could expect to see in the coming week. He went on to explain that the water around the reefs of Belize was considered a marine park and everything within this area was protected.

"This means you can see and enjoy it but don't touch or remove anything," Stanley warned. "Everything you'll see in the water, whether living or an inanimate object, serves a purpose and should be treated with respect. Finally, in Belize diving gloves are not allowed. As good divers, you are expected to control your buoyancy without using your hands. So, keep your hands in front of you or at your side—anyplace except on the coral."

Stanley began the show by saying, "I'm going to show you slides of social schooling and hiding fish, which include angel fish, tarpon, and spotted drum. Also, there will be slides of large fish including grouper, barracuda, and sharks." Every week during the slide show the mention of sharks sparked approval. He would assure his guests that they would see sharks on almost every dive, which would add excitement and adventure to the week.

Toward the end of his show, Stanley showed slides of sea whips and fans and used them to emphasize safety issues. "These are one of your key indicators of the direction and intensity of the current," he said. "Take notice of them and begin your dive going in the opposite direction of the current. That way, toward the end of the dive, when you may be a little tired, you will be coming back with the current and will not have to work as hard at getting back to the boat.

"One last thing before we leave. For those of you who will be taking underwater photos, we will develop your film into slides after the second afternoon dive while you are having dinner. So the slide show tomorrow night will be of your making. At the end of the week we will have a contest where you will pick your one or two best slides and we will vote a winner. The winner will receive a free, guaranteed-to-fit, monogrammed *Wave Dancer* 'Eat, Sleep and Dive' cotton polo shirt. Good Luck! Have a good night's sleep, and we will see you on the dive deck at 8:00 a.m. tomorrow morning."

Chapter Four

"The sea was the cradle of Primordial Life, from which the roots of our own existence sprouted. Billions of years of evolutionary development brought forth an enchanting variety of forms, colors, lifestyles, and patterns of behavior."

Werner Gruther, *Life in the Sea*

While Stanley conducted his slide show about fish and the reef on the *Wave Dancer*, Captain Jerry Schnabel, a seasoned boat captain, concluded his orientation briefing on the *Belize Aggressor*. His plan for the week resembled Captain Martin's, but Schnabel, having learned that Tropical Storm Iris was now Hurricane Iris, informed his guests that a level one hurricane moved north and west of them. He said he had been through two hurricanes and a tropical storm and felt confident they could avoid Iris. Schnabel explained that the storm might require him to move the *Aggressor* around a little more than normal to stay out of the perimeter wind and rain. He would stay in close contact with his offices in the U.S. and Belize to keep abreast of the latest information.

Each year an average of ten tropical storms develop over the Atlantic Ocean, Caribbean Sea, and Gulf of Mexico. Many of these storms remain over the ocean and never affect the coastline, but six become hurricanes. According to the NHC in Miami, a hurricane watch is issued when the Tropical Prediction Center's models indicate a costal area could experience hurricane conditions within thirty-six hours. This watch is intended to trigger a disaster plan for those within the hurricane's path. Protective measures should be initiated, especially those actions that require extra time, such as securing a boat, leaving a barrier island, and so on.

A more heightened state of awareness, a hurricane warning, is issued for coastal areas when there is an indication that sustained winds of at least seventy-four mph are expected within twenty-four hours or less. When this warning has been issued, those in the path of the hurricane should complete protective actions and choose their safest location.

The ingredients of a hurricane include a pre-existing weather disturbance, warm tropical oceans, moisture, and relatively light winds aloft. If the right conditions persist long enough, they can combine to produce the violent winds, incredible waves, torrential rains, and floods we associate with this phenomenon.

A hurricane is a type of tropical cyclone, which is a generic term for a low-pressure system that generally forms in the tropics. The cyclone is accompanied by thunderstorms and, in the northern hemisphere, a counterclockwise circulation of winds near the earth's surface. Tropical cyclones are classified as tropical depressions, tropical storms, and hurricanes.

The progression of the storm system from the early development stage of a rogue wave to the highest level of destruction and sophistication begins with a tropical depression. This is an organized system of clouds and thunderstorms with a defined surface circulation and maximum sustained winds of thirty-eight mph or less. The next level in the progressive storm cycle is a tropical storm, which is an organized system of strong thunderstorms with a defined surface circulation and maximum sustained winds of thirty-nine to seventy-three mph. The ultimate—most sophisticated and destructive—level of the tropical storm system is a hurricane. The hurricane is an intense tropical weather system of strong thunderstorms with a well-defined surface circulation and maximum sustained winds of seventy-four mph or higher.

Hurricanes are categorized according to the strength of their winds using the Saffir-Simpson Hurricane Scale, which is a one-to-five rating system based on the hurricane's intensity. This scale is used to give an estimate of the potential property damage and flooding expected along the coast from a hurricane landfall. Wind speed is the determining factor in the scale, as storm surge values are highly dependent on the slope of the continental shelf in the landfall region.

A category one hurricane is the entry-level storm, which has winds of seventy-four to ninety-five mph and a storm surge generally of four to five feet above normal tide levels. This storm normally does not cause damage to building structures. Its main effect is felt by unanchored mobile homes, shrubbery, and trees, although some damage will occur to poorly constructed signs. Also, it can cause some coastal road flooding and minor pier damage. Hurricanes Allison of 1995 and Danny of 1997 were category one hurricanes at peak intensity.

The Saffir-Simpson Hurricane Scale rates a category two hurricane as one with winds ranging from ninety-six to 110 mph with a storm surge generally six to eight feet above normal tide levels. A category two hurricane will cause damage to roofs, doors, and windows of buildings and can cause considerable damage to mobile homes, poorly constructed signs, piers, exposed shrubbery, and trees. During a category two hurricane coastal and low-lying escape routes will flood two to four hours before the arrival of the hurricane center and small craft in unprotected anchorages will break their moorings. Hurricane Bonnie of 1998 was a category two hurricane when it hit the North Carolina coast, while Hurricane Georges of 1998 was a category two hurricane when it hit the Florida Keys and the Mississippi Gulf Coast.

During a category three hurricane the winds will reach between 111 and 130 mph with the storm surge ranging nine to twelve feet above normal tide levels. This level of storm will cause some structural damage to small residences and utility buildings with a minor amount of window wall failures. The damage to shrubbery and trees is extensive with foliage blown off trees and large trees blown down, while mobile homes and poorly constructed signs are destroyed. Low-lying escape routes will be cut off by rising water three to five hours before arrival of the hurricane's center. Flooding near the coast destroys smaller structures with larger structures damaged by battering of floating debris. Terrain continuously lower than five feet above mean sea level may be flooded inland eight miles or more. Evacuation of low-lying residences within several blocks of the shoreline may be required. Hurricanes Roxanne of 1995 and Fran of 1996 were category three hurricanes at landfall on the Yucatan Peninsula of Mexico and in North Carolina, respectively.

The more vicious and deadly category four hurricane dispenses sustained strong winds ranging between one hundred and thirty-one and one hundred and fifty-five mph with a storm surge generally thirteen to eighteen feet above normal tide levels. More extensive curtain wall failures with some complete roof structure loss will occur on small residences. All shrubs, trees, and signs are blown down. There is complete destruction of mobile homes with extensive damage to windows and doors of other structures. Low-lying escape routes may be cut by rising water three to five hours before arrival of the hurricane's center. Major damage to lower floors of structures near the shore will occur. Terrain lower than ten feet above sea level may be flooded, requiring massive evacuation of residential areas as far inland as six miles. Hurricane Luis of 1995 was a category four hurricane while moving over the Leeward Islands and Hurricanes Felix and Opal of 1995 also reached that status at peak intensity.

The master of destruction, disaster, and distress is the category five hurricane, with winds greater than 155 mph and storm surge greater than eighteen feet above normal tide level. A category five hurricane will cause complete roof failures on many residences and industrial buildings, some complete building failures with small utility buildings blown over or away. All shrubs, trees, and signs are blown down with complete destruction of mobile homes and extensive damage to windows and doors of other structures. Low-lying escape routes are cut by rising water three to five hours before the arrival of the hurricane's center. Major damage will occur to lower floors of all structures located less than fifteen feet above sea level and within five hundred yards of the shoreline. Massive evacuation of residential areas on low ground within five to ten miles of the shoreline may be required. Hurricane Mitch of 1998 was a category five hurricane at peak intensity over the western Caribbean. Hurricane Gilbert of 1988 was a category five hurricane at peak intensity and is the strongest Atlantic tropical cyclone on record.

At 8:00 p.m. on October 6, the NHC in Miami reported a hurricane warning in effect along the south coast of the Dominican Republic and along the south coast of Haiti. A hurricane warning also remained in effect for Jamaica and parts of Cuba. According to the NHC, Hurricane Iris was moving west, away from the Dominican Republic, where the hurricane warning was lifted that night. At the same time, the Cayman Islands upgraded from hurricane watch to hurricane warning.

The center of Hurricane Iris was located near latitude 17.0 north longitude and 74.0 degrees west or about 190 miles east-southeast of Kingston, Jamaica. Iris was moving toward the west at a steady seventeen mph according to the NHC models. They predicted it would move between the west and west-northwest during the next twenty-four hours. On this track Iris would pass over or near Jamaica during the next twelve hours. Maximum sustained winds held at seventy-five mph over a small area near the center with higher gusts. Forecasters expected Iris to strengthen during the next twenty-four hours.

Hurricane-force winds extended outward up to twenty-five miles from the center and tropical-force winds extended outward up to one hundred and fifteen miles. The latest minimum central pressure reported by the C-130 hurricane reconnaissance plane was 992 MB. Coastal storm surge flooding of four to five feet above normal tide levels along with dangerous battering waves was expected to continue to affect the southern coast of Hispaniola through the night and Jamaica on Sunday. Rainfall accumulations of four to five inches with isolated higher amounts were expected near Iris's path.

Doug Cox grabbed a beer and headed to the sky deck to enjoy the clear star-filled sky. He and Phyllis had watched the beautiful sunset on the horizon and witnessed for the first time in their lives the elusive green flash that occurs on rare occasions when the sky is perfectly clear with no obstructing clouds or haze. This phenomenon occurs when the red-orange sun starts to set and appears to melt into the blue ocean water. At the very last instant the combination of the red-orange with the blue creates a small green flash that lasts a split-second. It is truly a magical moment, one that is never forgotten by those who are fortunate enough to witness it.

After the long day of travel, Phyllis opted for her bed rather than a beer, so Cox headed alone to the sky deck, where he found Prillaman, DeBarger, and Lisa Powell leaning against the chrome rail separating them from a twenty-five-foot drop into the dark water below. They each held a bottle of Belikin beer, which is brewed, bottled, and consumed exclusively in Belize. Prillaman had found the only place on the *Wave Dancer* where he was allowed to smoke. He seemed to be taking particular pleasure in it, tilting back his head to exhale the smoke with tired delight.

DeBarger said to Prillaman, "You know Margo is never going to marry you until you quit smoking."

Prillaman nodded with a rueful grin. "I know. I know. She's told me that a hundred times."

"So why don't you quit?"

Prillman shrugged. "I just love them both," he said. "What's a man going to do?"

Lisa, now wearing a navy blue windbreaker given to her by her fiancé, stood downwind of Prillaman to avoid the secondhand smoke from his cigarette. "Glenn, you need Margo more than you need those smelly things," she said.

The threesome drifted into a discussion of Captain Martin's orientation talk as Cox moved into their group. They were all curious about what the others thought of Martin and his crew and were getting more excited about their next six days aboard the *Wave Dancer*.

Prillaman asked Cox, the only registered scuba diving instructor from the RDC on the *Wave Dancer*, what he thought of the crew, boat, and diving facilities.

"I checked out the dive deck and they seem to be ready for us," Cox said. "I can't think of a thing they don't have that we'll need."

The three nodded their agreement. The *Wave Dancer* seemed to be a first-class operation.

Cox said, "I like the aluminum dive platform. Lots of elbow room. You can have several people getting ready at the same time, and the two ladders will help us get everyone out of the water faster. And Stanley and Stark both seem pretty helpful."

"I agree," said DeBarger. "They seem capable."

"And experienced," Cox added. "We exchanged some dive stories about places we've been in the past. Stanley hasn't been out of the Belize area, but he sure knows the water around here."

"I'm comfortable with them," Lisa said as she tightened the jacket around her in the cooling night breeze. "They know what they're doing."

"They said that everyone on the boat except the cooks dive," Cox said. "So we're going to have a lot of people in the water. That's good."

Webb walked over to the group carrying five frosty Belikins. Like everyone else, he was exhausted from the long day's activities but was too wound up to sleep. He felt that after some light conversation and one more Belikin he would sleep like a baby. Cox graciously accepted the beer saying, "This is going to have to be my last one. As tired as I am I don't want to overdo it."

DeBarger swatted at an imaginary mosquito and took a gulp of his beer.

"I read about some divers in Mexico," Cox said. "They were doing a shore dive, so they didn't have a dive master. The group, about four of them, had been out the night before and partied a little more than they should have to be diving the next day. One of them was a woman. She got in trouble. She must've been either tired or hung over because when they were at sixty feet she vomited in her mask and bolted for the surface. Her buddy raced after her and found her unconscious. They couldn't speak Spanish, couldn't find anyone who spoke English. They finally flagged down some help, but by the time they got her to the hospital she died. So the moral of my story is moderation, friends, moderation. See you in the morning."

Lisa followed Cox, leaving Webb, Prillaman, and DeBarger by themselves. Webb said, "I thought our boats were going to be together this week. I haven't seen the *Aggressor* since we left Belize City. Are we going to meet up tomorrow?"

"I don't know what's going on," Prillaman said. "I'll talk with Martin tomorrow morning and find out what the plans are."

When they'd finished their beers they stood quietly and enjoyed the tropical evening for a few more minutes. Then they slowly headed toward their cabins, all of them anxious for sleep and for the day ahead.

"Some tub, huh?" Prillaman said. Webb and DeBarger muttered their agreement: the *Wave Dancer* was, indeed, quite a boat.

The live-aboard industry had come a long way since its official inception in 1972. Many of the early live-aboard boats were converted fishing and shrimp boats. The early divers were mostly men who slept in hammocks, shared a shower and toilet, and the food was usually carried aboard and prepared by the divers. Though accommodations were sparse, the diving was spectacular, and so the word spread about this new form of reef exploration.

The pioneers of the live-aboard diving industry soon realized that if they provided better accommodations and quality food service the appeal would broaden, creating a larger market. With the addition of more services came more revenue, and soon they were making money. American investors of the live-aboard concept could operate in foreign countries, thus avoiding income tax on their profits.

This practice, already adopted by other ship owners in the maritime industry, proved to be the deciding factor in building and retrofitting more and newer boats for the fledgling live-aboard industry. With the expanded services, the live-aboard owners increased the cost of a weeklong trip from a few hundred dollars to as high as three thousand dollars per person, depending on location, boat, and specials. This fee included food, lodging, and unlimited diving, leading to the catch phrase "eat, sleep and dive". From the pioneering days of Paul Humann and his *Cayman Diver*, the live-aboard industry expanded to 105 vessels worldwide, grossing in excess of 150 million dollars a year.

The modern live-aboard is the scuba diver's ultimate fantasy: wake up at a new dive site, suit up, walk about twenty feet, and jump into amazingly clear water. Virtually alone, the live-aboard is moored at a pristine dive site over a coral reef garden resplendent with reds, blues, and yellows and an abundance and variety of marine life.

When the diver ascends to the boat, the live-aboard staff assists him with his gear and refills the dive tank, preparing the equipment for its next use, while its owner trades experiences with other occupants of the floating hotel. After a hardy meal prepared by the staff, the diving process is repeated up to five times a day.

Each day the live-aboard moves to one or two new prearranged sites, which are geared to provide a wide variety of world-class diving experiences. This form of effortless vacation sport diving with its all-inclusive economic value per dive has become so popular that the live-aboard industry has exploded in growth at the rate of 35 percent per year over the past few years.

The increased quality of live-aboard accommodations has led many divers to try other locations around the world and to revisit favorite sites.

Internet Web sites are full of rave reviews about good times and unforgettable experiences. Among them is one by Wyland, the internationally renowned artist, famous for his massive wall murals depicting underwater environment scenes. He says: "Diving is the ultimate adventure, and a live-aboard dive vessel is the very best way to experience the wonders of the sea. I prefer the live-aboard experience primarily because of the personal attention to detail provided by two of the biggest and best dive operators on the planet: Wayne Hasson's Aggressor Fleet and the Dancer Fleet operated by Peter Hughes. Each of these organizations sets the highest standards in diving, comfort, service amenities, and the dive experience itself, with vessels at many of the world's most sought-after diving sites. Once you've been on a Peter Hughes boat or an Aggressor boat, you'll want to repeat the experience again and again."

In the salon, Jim Garrison, Bill Kelley, and Rick Patterson huddled around Baechtold and Stanley. Garrison and Kelley had brought their underwater cameras to the slide show hoping they could get some tips from the crew. Three days prior to the trip, "Gadget Man" Garrison purchased a new Cannon D10 digital single lens reflex state-of-the-art camera with a wide-angle lens, digital flash system, and custom underwater case. It looked more like a professional setup than something a three-times-a-year novice needed, but then that was Garrison. Kelley's smaller 35mm Nikonos, which cost a few hundred dollars, probably a fifth of Garrison's, took excellent photographs as well.

Patterson, not an underwater photographer, was curious by nature and wanted to learn more about this part of the sport. A shy person, he enjoyed sitting on the periphery of a group conversation and interjecting a comment only when he felt the need arise. As a senior field engineer for Medrad, Inc., he consulted on the services of electronic medical equipment with hospitals and clinics, so he enjoyed technical conversations like the one he knew Garrison would have with Baechtold and Stanley.

Showing them his camera, Garrison said, "I just bought this and may need some help getting use to it."

"That's a real nice outfit," Stanley said, admiring the expensive equipment.

"Do you think I'm going to need a filter on these dives?" Garrison asked.

"It depends on how much you plan to use your flash," Stanley said. "Personally, I'd use my flash the first couple of times, and see how my shots turn out. Then, if I felt a filter would help, I'd make that adjustment on the next dive."

Kelley, devoid of technical questions, asked, "I want to find a spotted drum and a sea horse. Will I see any on these dives?"

"Spotted drums are common, and we'll probably find a few this week," Stanley said. "Sea horses are a different story. I see one once in a while, but they aren't real common." Patterson listened quietly as Garrison and Kelley asked many questions, trying to learn more about the reef and, as photographers, about what special fish and critters were indigenous to the area.

The group also was curious to know more about Peter Hughes, a legend in the live-aboard world. They were told that the president and owner of Peter Hughes Diving, Inc., had been an innovator in the dive industry for nearly thirty years. His interest in scuba diving and related fields began in the mid 1960s, when he learned to dive at a youth camp while living with his family in Tobago. He left Tobago for Anthony's Key Resort in Roatan, Honduras, where he worked as a dive guide and also met his wife, Alice. In 1975 they moved to Bonaire and the Flamingo Beach Resort, where Dive Bonaire had its beginnings. By 1985, Dive Bonaire had become the largest and most highly acclaimed dive shop in the Caribbean. At that time Hughes and DIVI Resorts joined to open a chain of luxury resorts/dive operations in Cayman Brac, Barbados, and the Bahamas in addition to the existing operation in Bonaire.

In their first year together, the concept of a luxury live-aboard dive vessel was developed, and the *M/V Sea Dancer* was created from a former oil rig crew boat. The *Sea Dancer* took her first divers into the waters off Grand Turk in January 1987. The boat was moved to St. Martin, Saba, St. Kitts, and St. Eustasias to test the live-aboard marketability of other areas.

But the Turks and Caicos waters and customers beckoned, and in March of 1990 the *Sea Dancer* returned—this time to Providenciales, where she is still permanently docked.

Peter Hughes Diving, Inc. was formed in 1991 when Hughes purchased the *Sea Dancer* from DIVI Resorts. The *M/V Wave Dancer* joined the *Sea Dancer* to begin the evolution of the Dancer fleet. Formerly an oil rig crew boat and a fishing boat, the *Wave Dancer* was purchased on August of 1991 and taken to Morgan City, Louisiana, to be refitted as what was then the world's highest standard for luxury live-aboard dive boats. Running divers out of Belize City to the Turneffe Islands as well as to Lighthouse and Glovers reefs, the *Wave Dancer* entered service in February 1992 and enjoyed success. In October 1996, the *Wave Dancer* was redecorated in the jungle motif of Belize and equipped with a nitrox membrane system.

Hughes added a new destination or vessel to his worldwide fleet of dive operations every year since 1991. In addition to his interests in Ocean Encounters, a land-based operation in Curacao, he operates live-aboards in the Turks and Caicos Islands, Belize, the Silver Bank of the Dominican Republic, and Los Roques in Venezuela, Palau, Papua New Guinea, the Galapagos Islands, and Bali.

While Garrison, Kelley, and Patterson discussed photography and Peter Hughes with Baechtold and Stanley, Captain Martin reviewed his latest weather fax from the NHC. During the past several hours, he had been preoccupied with his arriving guests and making sure everything on the *Wave Dancer* was ready. As a result, he had not looked at any weather updates. Although he personally had no knowledge of tropical storms, he trusted the Peter Hughes organization, with their many years of experience, to steer him through any weather-related problems during the trip.

After checking the weather fax, he went out on the bow catwalk. Leaning against the railing, he finally had a moment to himself. Although he enjoyed the gentle evening breeze blowing around him, he couldn't help but be concerned about the tension between himself and the Belizean crew.

He wasn't sure why it was happening, but as the captain of the ship, he knew that all matters concerning the crew were his responsibility, and he would not allow any insubordination. Although the crew members seemed polite and acted like they were listening to him, something about their attitude suggested they were not happy with his decision to leave port.

Chapter Five

"Why the ocean? An alien would have no trouble answering that question. He'd look at the planet and if he wanted to understand how this world works, he'd dive in the ocean because that's where the action is. We terrestrial creatures are a minority."

Sylvia Earle

What a great way to wake up in the morning, thought Cox as he walked to the sky deck with a cup of Belize's finest dark-roasted coffee. The gentle rocking of the *Wave Dancer* combined with his complete exhaustion from the previous day's travel had given him his best night's sleep in a long time. He walked out on the top deck and gazed at the beautiful blue Caribbean Sea with the white beaches and lightly swaying palm trees of Long Caye in the distance.

Fifteen minutes later, at 6:15, Kelley, DeBarger, and Prillaman joined Cox on the sky deck. They also had enjoyed a good night's sleep. Prillaman in a T-shirt that looked like he had slept in it, exhaled his first puff of the day.

"Great day for diving," he said. "I love these live-aboards. Best invention since sliced bread." They all agreed with him. The four of them began to feel a mental and physical adjustment from the hectic pace they had left behind in Richmond. Now they were truly on island time—the phrase used to characterize the relaxed attitude, motion, and pace of life common in the tropics. Having enjoyed other dive trips to the Caribbean, the passengers on the *Wave Dancer* knew that the sooner travelers reach the euphoric state of island time, the more fully they enjoy themselves.

With coffee in hand, they discussed their schedules for the day.

"Since Sheila and I are celebrating our anniversary, I think we'll probably only do three dives," said Kelley. "We don't want to overdo it the first day. And we sure don't want to be too tired for the night dive. We both really like night dives."

DeBarger chimed in, "I'm with you on the night dive thing. That's my favorite, too. I'm going to see how I feel as the day goes on. If the dives are all as good as I think they'll be I may do all of them, but I definitely want to do the night dive."

Without reaction, Prillaman and Cox let the conversation about the number and types of dives flow past them. They would let the day decide what and how many dives they would do.

The bright sun was only slightly obscured by the fluffy white clouds left behind by the previous night's moon in its decline. Soon, with morning heat and light growing stronger, the remaining clouds would burn away to expose a perfect sunny day. The light morning breeze created barely a ripple on the blue Caribbean waters. With exaggerated sighs the four unanimously agreed: this was going to be a great day!

Cox excused himself to go to the dive deck to check out and set up the dive gear for himself and his wife. Like a good dive instructor, he wanted to be a step ahead of everyone in case the other divers needed his assistance setting up or checking their equipment. When Cox got to the dive deck he took Phyllis's equipment out of her locker, slipped her black and yellow buoyancy compensator device, or BC, over the compressed air tank, and securely fastened it with the two attached Velcro belts. Next, he hooked up her open circuit regulator to the scuba tank and her BC. He turned on the rubber-coated pressure valve of the scuba tank and instantly the pressure gauge jumped to 3000 psi. Good, he thought. He always wanted to start a dive with at least 3000 psi. He partially inflated the BC to insure it was properly connected and there was no sign of an air leak. He then shut off the valve to the scuba tank and bled the air from the regulator and BC.

Satisfied that the gear worked as it should, he scanned her BC to check the integrated weight belt and emergency equipment, waterproof flashlight, serrated knife, whistle, and safety sausage. He made sure her mask and fins were in her locker, and then turned his attention to his own gear. He knew the boat's dive masters checked out everyone's equipment, but, like all good divers, he accepted responsibility for his own gear.

Chief Meteorologist Fuller was up early, too. He knew he and his associates would get very little rest for the next few days until the threat of Hurricane Iris was over. He had been a meteorologist in Belize for twenty-nine years. A graduate of Florida State University, Fuller, along with all Caribbean area and Central American meteorologists, met for one week each year at the NHC in Miami to discuss the latest changes in detecting, analyzing, and reporting tropic storms in their part of the world. His forecasters also attended a two-week workshop once a year at the NHC in Miami. At these meetings the fledging forecasters trained in the latest techniques for front-line weather forecasting. They also met face-to-face with the people to whom they would be sending notices, memos, warnings, and watches during the next hurricane season.

Fuller noted that, after moving to the west and even wobbling south of due west, Iris once again had resumed a west-to-northwest track. At six on Sunday morning it was centered near 17.3 degrees north and 76.9 degrees west or about forty-five miles south southeast of Kingston, Jamaica, and 745 miles east of Belize City. Iris clearly posed a threat to Belize, so he contacted the cabinet secretary and apprised him of the situation. Fuller estimated that on its present track Iris would make landfall near Corozal Town in northern Belize early Tuesday morning, which meant Iris first would cross over Ambergris Caye.

San Pedro Town, on Ambergris Caye, with its romantic atmosphere of Key West in the 1950s, draws more tourists than any other area of Belize. Its location within a few hundred yards of the barrier reef would need special attention to insure the safety of its guests and residents.

Lori Reed, a resident of Ambergris Caye, watched the advancing path and strength of Hurricane Iris. She prepared herself and the guests of her hotel and would need to make a decision soon about evacuating. She and many of the residents of Belize watched Fuller's weather report Saturday and listened to his projections for Iris, which were later broadcast over LOVE 95, the local radio station.

Fuller had updated his reports and projections for Iris. Noting the increasing strength of the hurricane he estimated it would reach category two or three level hurricane and recommended that Belize declare the preliminary phase of the National Hurricane Emergency Plan. He also recommended that Belize declare a hurricane watch for the northern half of the country. The cabinet secretary requested that this information be sent in writing to adequately brief the Prime Minister. This order was carried out and transmitted to him at 7:45 a.m. in Iris Bulletin No. 1.

Fuller also advised the NHC of Belize's intentions and asked that they include a phrase to that effect in their 9:00 a.m. advisory. This joint storm reporting effort between the NHC, Belize, Caribbean, and Central American countries had been in effect for several years. Its goal was to avoid confusion with the quality and accuracy of their reports both internally and externally. During a tropical storm—brewing or active—a check-and-balance system between the affected countries and the NHC was imperative, and only one jointly agreed upon report was made public. This public report of the advancing storm was issued by the NHC, with one exception.

The one exception applied to Belize, which is the only Caribbean or

Central American country with its own radar system. Because of the quality
of equipment at the Belize Meteorological Center, and the training, skill,
experience, and knowledge of the chief meteorologist and his staff, when
a tropical storm moves within the range of its radar, Belize takes over the
reporting responsibilities. Like all previous reports submitted prior to
any official report from the chief meteorologist on any storm, it had to be
approved by the NHC.

During the past few years the quality of hurricane forecasting had
become very accurate. With advances in technology, satellite image reporting,
and the improved analysis of models, the affected geographic report area
margin of error had been narrowed significantly. Employing these updated
reporting techniques, the NHC and its cooperating countries could now
forecast the affected area of a tropical storm to within 150 miles of a specific
location with a forty-eight-hour notice, and eighty miles with a twenty-
four-hour notice.

Lisa and Mary Lou Hayden arrived at the salon for breakfast dressed in
bright, tropically patterned shorts and T-shirts. Other members of the group
already were filling their plates and bowls with pineapple and watermelon
slices, French toast, scrambled eggs, bacon, sausage, toast and bagels with
mango jam, orange juice, milk, or cold cereal. After filling their own plates
with a little taste of everything, they agreed that they never ate such a big
breakfast at home—but when someone else was fixing it, what the hell! And
they were going to do a lot of diving this week and would need extra energy.

They joined Christy McNiel and Cheryl Lightbound at a table.

"How did you two sleep last night?" Christy asked.

Lisa said, "Great! The only time I woke up was when I thought I
heard the engines running, but it was the generator. Other than that, I
slept like a baby."

"I was sleeping like a log when Christy got up to use the bathroom and
stubbed her toe on something," Cheryl said. "Her yelp woke me, but then I
fell back to sleep."

Mary Lou said, "I was afraid that may happen to me too, so I brought a small flashlight to keep next to my bed. I used it once without waking Lisa."

"You did?" Lisa said. "I didn't hear you at all."

"Thanks to my trusty light," Mary Lou said. "FYI, if you don't have one you can use your night dive light, but mine is a miniature Maglite. It works great!"

"Mary Lou," said Lisa to the others. "Always prepared."

Not surprisingly, the breakfast conversation drifted to the first dive of the day. Everything above the crystal clear water in Lighthouse Reef looked great. It was time to find out if there was an equal treat below the water.

Christy and Cheryl finished their breakfast first and decided to go to the dive deck to check out and set up their dive gear. Both single, about the same age, and close enough in size they could easily have exchanged wardrobes, they had been diving buddies for two years and had gone on many dive trips together. The only exception was a six-month period during the "millennium celebration" when Cheryl, a computer administrator, had taken a sabbatical from her job to tour the world. They were both skilled divers, who, while always very careful in their many adventures, believed in living life to its fullest.

Cheryl in particular cut a wide swath of adventure, admired by many but equaled by few. At thirty-eight, the native of Calgary, Canada, had participated in skydiving, bungee jumping, cycling, kayaking, and now scuba diving. She liked pushing the limits in everything she did, which was apparent to all. Her favorite T-shirt read, "If you're not living on the edge, you're taking up too much space." Christy and Cheryl set up their dive gear and, when finished, watched as Stanley drew a diagram of their first dive site, Black Beauty, on the erasable briefing board.

Stark clanged the bell three times to signal it was eight o'clock and time for the first dive briefing of the week. This time, however (and probably the only time this would happen all week) Stark did not have to go through the hallways and salon shouting that a briefing was about to begin. Everyone from the RDC was already on the dive deck.

Captain Martin appeared looking less formal than the night before, wearing swim trunks and a *Wave Dancer* "Eat, Sleep and Dive" T-shirt. His diction and demeanor, however, were only slightly more relaxed. He still moved and spoke with an air that said "I'm in charge." He began the morning's briefing by saying, "Welcome to Lighthouse Reef. This is one of the most beautiful areas on the Belizean coast. Before we start the briefing, I want to orient you to the dive deck." He went on to explain the procedures surrounding the use of the camera table, rinse tanks, availability of warm clean towels, and shower heads.

A longtime diving aficionado, he began his career in New Zealand and had worked as a deck hand on luxury yachts in the Mediterranean. He had taken the course to become a boat captain in England and, after passing the tests, accepted a position in Belize, ultimately landing with Peter Hughes.

He finished his comments by saying, "When you are ready, put on your BC, carry your fins to the dive platform where one of the dive masters will assist you. They will do a final equipment check, make sure your air is on, and clear you for entry. All of our dives this week will be off the back of the *Wave Dancer*, so make your entry with a giant stride. On your entry give me the OK sign, inflate your BC, go over to the mooring ball, and float around until everyone is in the water so we can all go down at the same time."

Martin knew that scuba diving, unlike riding a bike, is not a "natural event." Even when a person does not ride a bike for a while, he can usually get on one, and if it veers to the right he merely steers to the left. By contrast, most scuba divers know, with or without scuba gear, the natural instinct is to hold one's breath upon entering water that is over the head. Thus, scuba diving is an "unnatural event," which means the natural instinct to hold one's breath upon entering the water instead of free breathing must be consciously relearned if it is not done on a frequent basis. Otherwise, the action can lead to perception narrowing, which, if not monitored, can cause the diver who is so focused on remembering to breathe underwater to forget other skills.

That is why the first dive of the week is always a check-out dive.

"While you are cruising around getting used to your equipment and the underwater environment," Martin said, "Stanley, Stark, Wouters, Baechtold, and I will be in the water with you. If you have any problems with your equipment, ears not clearing, or whatever, signal to one of us and we will assist you. We want you to have a good week of diving. Having a safe first dive is the best way to start."

The group mumbled their agreement. Though they had been through this process many times, they all gave Martin their attention.

Martin went on to say, "After the dive is over, I want you to do a safety stop. You can hang on to the deco safety bar if you want or just hover between fifteen and twenty feet for three to five minutes. When you are ready, come to the rear of the boat, two at a time, take your fins off, and come up one of the ladders. One of the dive masters will be there to help if you need it. When you get back to your assigned seat, take off your BC, shut off your air, and remove your first stage from your tank. Between dives one of us will come around and refill your tank, reattach your first stage, and you will be ready to go again. All of your tanks should have at least 3,000 psi in them to start. If they aren't full, let me know. Also, you should know where the boat is when you have 1,000 psi and be on the boat with a minimum of 500 psi. If for some reason you are low on air, there is an emergency regulator on the deco safety bar. Any questions? If not, Stanley is going to describe our first dive site, Black Beauty."

The members of the group had been well trained in the basic elements of scuba diving as set out by the Recreational Scuba Training Council [RSTC] through PADI. The minimum course content for open water diver certification in the United States and recognized world wide was set up by the RSTC and approved by YMCA Scuba Program [YSCUBA], International Diving Educators Association [IDEA], Professional Diving Instructors Corporation [PDIC], Scuba Schools International [SSI], and PADI. Every certified diver in the U.S. and two thirds worldwide are scuba trained using one of these sets of standards. With the exception of Byron Johnston, they all had taken advanced diving classes, passed additional skill level tests, had many open-water dives to their credit, and were competent divers.

Johnston, a chemical engineer with a PhD in chemistry, had been nurturing an interest in diving because his wife, Shirley, certified since 1994, had been increasing her interest in the sport and encouraging him to get involved. Shirley's commitment to diving began when she took additional classes, both above and below water, to receive her Advanced Diver's Certification. While on a diving trip to Grand Cayman, she took an underwater photography class from internationally recognized aquatic photographer Cathy Church. Shirley's increased enthusiasm for the sport and display of her underwater art was becoming contagious in the family, but Byron's travel schedule and inability to swim kept him from becoming involved. Finally, in the summer of 2000, with the patience only a loving wife can display, Shirley taught Byron how to swim. Byron was now ready to begin the PADI Open Water Diver Certification program from Shirley's longtime mentor, Dallas Weston.

When he completed the training, Byron went with Weston to Lake Rawlings for his two supervised open-water check-out dives. The five-foot visibility and cold water of the lake took some adjustment, but Byron completed his dives and received his PADI Open Water Certification. Shirley was so appreciative of Weston's help with Byron and of the support he had given her over the years, she gave him one of her favorite photographs, a framed and matted picture of Devil's Grotto, a special dive site in Grand Cayman. Weston proudly displayed it on the wall of his dive shop.

Byron, the only person to qualify for the AARP over-sixty discount on this trip, and Shirley were now very excited about being able to dive and travel together. As with many empty nesters, they sought activities they could enjoy together. They had more free time to travel, were financially sound, and wanted to do new and interesting things. When several members of the RDC returned from the Turks and Caicos with glowing reports of good diving, food, fun, and camaraderie aboard a luxury live-aboard yacht, the couple jumped at the chance to take such a trip.

They exchanged a brief glance at each other, very pleased to be there, as Stanley began his briefing. Stanley pointed to his colorful depiction of the underwater formation of the reef dive site known as Black Beauty. He gave the depth of the water under the *Wave Dancer* as forty feet, noted the direction and strength of the current, the make up of the reef formation, and told them what they could expect to see. He mentioned goldentail and moray eels, grouper, schooling fish, stingrays, and sharks.

"This is a real nice dive site to start your week," he said. "I expect you'll see colorful reef fish, eels, and stingrays all swimming around the coral heads. As for sharks, they are not common at this site, but you may see one at a distance as you cross over The Wall."

The word "shark" sent a thrum of anticipation through the group.

"Our first dive," Stanley continued, "will be more controlled than any other dive this week. As Captain Martin said, this is a check-out dive, and for that reason I prefer that you don't take your cameras with you. We'll start out under the boat together. From there you and your buddy can explore on your own, keeping a dive master in sight at all times. Does everyone have a buddy? If not, I will assign one for you."

The members of the group nodded, each trying to listen patiently to the instructions, though with blue skies overhead and clear blue waters below, all anyone wanted to do was begin their carefree week of diving.

Chapter Six

"I can only think of one experience which might exceed in interest a few hours spent under water, and that would be a journey to Mars."
                        William Beebe, *The Arcturus Adventure*

Stanley did not know but soon was told that the members of the RDC were required by their board of directors to sign a Safe Diving Statement of Understanding, which included a commitment to the buddy system as a prerequisite for the trip to Belize. The statement noted that diving was a highly cooperative activity. Everyone needed to look out for everyone else, which was the essence of the buddy system. Each person was responsible to and for a buddy and in the larger sense was responsible to and for the group.

On dives, the dive master and boat captain were in charge of all diving and boating activities and responsible for keeping everyone within reasonable safety limits. Anyone's diving privileges could be suspended if he or she chose not to comply fully with the directions and general guidelines of the dive master, boat captain, or trip leader. Members of the group nodded as

Stanley made his point about the buddy system. He then asked them to check their computers before descending.

"After entry, if you find you are having trouble clearing your ears, need additional weight, or anything else I'll be available to assist you," he said. "See you at the bottom. The pool is open!"

Christy and Cheryl chose Stark to be their first dive guide. Though he was relatively new to the reefs of Belize, he knew them better than they did, so he surely could point out some interesting fish, creatures, and features to them. Christy and Cheryl had shared a Belikin with Stark on the sky deck after the slide show and felt comfortable with his knowledge and skills as a dive master. They also found him attractive, and in their minds it was good to have both a smart and good-looking dive guide.

When Stanley dismissed them, Christy and Cheryl along with the other members of the RDC went to their respective areas on the dive deck. They raced to see who could get in the water first. With the sun shining in a clear blue sky, everyone felt energized. Their thoughts embodied the RDC slogan, "Let's Go Divin'!" as they pulled off their T-shirts and opened their lockers. Twenty people shuffled around and bumped into each other as they got ready. Locker doors slammed and across the deck gentle grunts and groans could be heard as they slipped on their wet suits and weight belts then sat down on the seat in front of their BCs and attached their scuba tanks, slipped them around their bodies, secured them in front, and grabbed their masks. Christy and Cheryl squeezed a few drops of defogger in their masks while Cox did it the old-fashioned way—spitting into it. They put on their booties, then their fins, and moved to the dive platform.

DeBarger mentally reviewed his preparation list: air on—check. Fins and mask—check. Regulator in mouth—check. Inflate BC—check. Secondary regulator—check. Weight belt—check.

As if reading DeBarger's mental list, Prillaman, standing next to him, said, "Don't forget your belt, Dave."

"Got it," DeBarger said a bit ruefully. He had forgotten it on three successive dives in the Turks and Caicos. Each time he jumped in without it he couldn't submerge. Embarrassed, he had returned to the boat where a helpful dive master handed it to him.

Two by two they took a big stride and splashed into the emerald water. Christy and Cheryl bobbed back to the top after their entry. Looking back at the dive deck they placed the fingers of one hand on the top of their head, giving the platform dive master the OK sign, and moved toward the mooring line. Finally, when they were all in the water, Stanley signaled to start their descent. They let the air out of their BCs and slowly started sinking.

Through their masks they could see the underwater glory of the great Belize reef. As the drifted lower, they released a huge amount of pent-up excitement. Finally, they had arrived. After 9/11, changes in travel plans, trip exhaustion, and anxiety, to be diving at one of the greatest destinations in the world made them all feel well rewarded. While descending into this breathtakingly beautiful underwater wonderland, the last thing on anyone's mind was Hurricane Iris.

It was easy to see what Captain Martin meant by the possibility of a diver temporarily forgetting his or her skills. Looking around as they drifted lower Christy and Cheryl saw the reef coming into focus. Fish fluttered and slid past them on all sides, some coming close for a look while others darted away seeking shelter. The shock of such beauty forced them to concentrate on breathing, clearing their ears, removing excess water from their masks, and checking their buoyancy.

Prior to entering the water, Byron Johnston told Captain Martin he would use the mooring line to slowly descend as he sometimes had difficulty clearing his ears. Johnston understood the physics of diving but sometimes the practical application wasn't easy for him.

In the United States, pressure is typically measured in pounds per square inch, or psi. Under water, two kinds of pressure affect a person, the weight of the surrounding water and the weight of the atmosphere over the water. A diver must be in pressure balance with the forces at any depth and must compensate for the pressure exerted by the atmosphere, by the water, and by the gasses being used for breathing under water. This compensation must always be thought of in terms of attaining and maintaining a balance between the pressure inside the body and the external pressure. The three pressures are called atmospheric, hydrostatic, and absolute.

Atmospheric pressure is the pressure exerted by the earth's atmosphere. It decreases with altitude above sea level. At sea level, atmospheric pressure is equal to 14.7 psi or one atmosphere (atm). The higher the altitude above sea level, the lower the atmospheric pressure. At sea level, atmospheric pressure is considered constant and universal; that is, anywhere on the earth at sea level, the pressure is 14.7 psi. The pressure inside a person's lungs is the same as the pressure outside.

Pressure due to the weight of the water is called hydrostatic pressure. The weight of water is cumulative so the deeper the dive, the greater the weight of that water. This weight affects a diver from all sides equally and increases at a rate of 0.445 psi per foot of seawater. Thus, at a depth of thirty-three feet of seawater the hydrostatic pressure is 14.7 psi, or one atmosphere, the same pressure as atmospheric pressure at sea level.

Thereafter, for every thirty-three feet of additional depth in saltwater, the hydrostatic pressure increases by one atmosphere. The sum of atmospheric pressure plus hydrostatic pressure is called absolute pressure. Absolute pressure can be expressed in many ways, including pounds per square inches absolute, atmospheres absolute, feet of seawater absolute, or millimeters of mercury absolute. To understand the effects of absolute pressure on a diver, consider this: the feet of a six-foot tall man standing under water will be exposed to pressure that is almost three pounds per square inch greater than that exerted at his head.

Understanding the physics of diving did little when it came to Byron Johnston being able to equalize the pressure and clear his ears as he descended under water. It remained a struggle. However, he was becoming more relaxed with each dive and hoped that soon he would be as comfortable as the other members of the RDC. He was far from being alone in this regard. To many aspiring members of the scuba community, the ability to descend under water and equalize the pressure against the eardrum is one of the most difficult parts of the sport. Since water pressure increases relative to middle ear pressure, it creates an uncomfortable relative vacuum in the middle ear. This "middle ear squeeze" can be mitigated by yawning, swallowing, or gently blowing against a closed mouth and nostrils, which allows air from the throat to enter the middle ear through the Eustachian tube. By not adequately relieving the pressure, the diver can suffer severe pain in the inner ear, rupture a blood vessel resulting in bleeding in the ear or nose, and even rupture an eardrum. Johnston knew he needed to descend at a slow rate and watch his depth gauge to insure he was using his clearing technique at the correct intervals. He might be the last one down to the dive origination site, but the clearing process would continue to become easier for him with each dive until he would be able to descend at the same speed as Shirley.

Christy, Cheryl, and Stark met at the base of the mooring line. The thick braided rope was looped through an eyelet anchored in concrete. The clear water offered visibility of one hundred to 150 feet. This would be a good day for diving. The twenty members of the RDC and the five crew members created congestion at the meeting site, but two by two with a kick of their fins they swam away. Prillaman and DeBarger left first, then Webb and Mars. Stanley and the Kelleys were next, then Lisa and Mary Lou. Within a minute they dispersed, giving each other a lot of space to navigate their area without running into each other. Christy and Cheryl checked their compass to get their bearings. To the east and south they saw the sandy area under the boat, and to the west and north were the coral heads and several fish. A curious French angel fish swam in their direction. The friendly saucer-sized fish with black scalloped scales each with bright yellow rims, ventured close as Stark wiggled his fingers, creating a welcoming sign. It came within two feet, looked them over and swam around them. Christy and Cheryl emulated Stark by wiggling their fingers to keep its attention.

After a few moments the fish grew bored and swam away. The three looked at each other and gave an OK signal. Then the young dive master gave them a directional motion sign with his right hand and they started off on their dive. Stark barely kicked his fins as he moved west. He was a relaxed and competent diver, which instilled confidence in Christy and Cheryl. They both adjusted to the underwater environment and started to absorb its natural beauty. Cheryl had traveled all over the world and visited many great wonders, but the combination of the beauty of the reef and marine life was far and away her favorite. Now, in eighty feet of pristine water, drifting over the reef, feeling as weightless as an astronaut on a tether, she knew she was living the ultimate life of adventure.

On Placencia, a small, open-beach resort with a population of 750 year-round residents located fifty miles south of Belize City, Frank Gagliano's first mate, Susan, a twenty-year-old lively Belizean, prepared the *Talisman* for a daylong charter trip. Gagliano, a fifty-two-year-old Mel Gibson look-alike, had recently purchased and outfitted the fifty-two-foot sailboat to do personal daylong and weekly charters for up to ten people. He preferred weeklong charters, which allowed him and his guests to sail the full length of the barrier reef and drift down by Guatemala to Honduras past Nicaragua and Costa Rica before returning back to Placencia. During that time Gagliano, Susan, and his guests would snorkel, fish, and occasionally go ashore, tour an area, and get necessary supplies. They needed only basic supplies for meals, which of course included Belikin beer and wine. The main course for most meals—fish, lobster, and conch—was caught and prepared along the way.

Gagliano was a gourmet cook, so along with feeling like they were floating on a cloud all week, his guests would eat like royalty. Gagliano had immigrated to Belize from Montana, after spending several years developing apartment communities. Now he was living the laid-back, good life in an affordable area of the world where the sun shone every day and he could work as hard, or not, as he wanted. Today he, Susan, and their four guests would sail out to the barrier reef, find a good place to snorkel then later, if the fish were not biting, swim into the shallows with their spear guns and get some fish and lobster the old-fashioned way.

As the *Talisman* passed by Whipray Caye, Gagliano blew three times into a conch shell to alert Julian Cabral that he was coming to visit. He, Susan, and their guests would go ashore to stretch their legs and visit with Cabral, a local fly-fishing guide. Gagliano knew Hurricane Iris was headed in their general direction and wanted to make sure Cabral, the only permanent resident of the resort, was aware of the storm and prepared to evacuate. Cabral liked to say that bragging rights are born in Belize, where the tarpon perform impressive aerial acrobatics as they dance across the flats. Bonefish and permit are plentiful, and a good fly fisherman, guided by himself of course, could score a "grand slam"—a bonefish, permit, and tarpon—in one day. When a guest cast for his or her quarry in Belize, Cabral was so confident of his environment he would bet that person's favorite fly or lure that he'd land something.

A Belizean and one of eleven children, Cabral was very personable, handsome, and, as Gagliano was soon to discover, waiting for his fiancée to join him at Whipray Caye. Beverly, the soon-to-be-bride, came into Cabral's life eight years earlier, when he was her tour guide on a snorkeling trip. When she stepped on a camouflaged scorpion fish, he had acted quickly, treating her wounds and saving her from what could have been a serious accident. She told him, "You saved my life and according to Chinese tradition I am yours forever." For the next several years the two sent each other an occasional letter and periodically Beverly would go to Belize where they would have a chance meeting. During these chance meetings they would discover that one or the other was in a relationship at the time.

The moons apparently were aligned when Beverly visited Belize in March of 2001, because neither she nor Cabral was in a relationship at the time. After spending a week together that neither wanted to end, they decided to marry. She returned to Pennsylvania, sold her business and house, then turned her attention to her son, who had recently graduated from high school and was preparing to attend Pacific University in California. She told him she hated to leave him, but she felt that moving to Belize to be with Julian was what she wanted to do. He had lovingly told his mother, "Enjoy the rest of your life—but remember to send money!"

Christy, Cheryl, and Stark returned to the mooring line. After forty minutes of cruising around the reef they were a little tired. Most of their dive had been spent investigating the reef between forty and sixty feet while Stark pointed out a variety of Caribbean fish. Now it was time to ascend slowly so their bodies would adjust to the decreasing pressure. They watched their depth gauge as they began to ascend to insure that they didn't go up too fast and get the bends.

Prillaman and DeBarger, Webb and Mars, and the Kelleys, along with Stanley, Stark, Christy, and Cheryl were all slowly moving up the mooring line. When the depth gauge read twenty feet each diver would either go to the hang bar, which was extended down from the *Wave Dancer* fifteen feet or would hover, maintaining neutral buoyancy between fifteen and twenty feet for three to five minutes. This would allow their bodies to adequately decompress. Christy, Cheryl, and Stark all elected to hover, as did Prillaman, DeBarger, Webb and Mars. To hover, sometimes in brisk current, between fifteen and twenty feet was the sign of an accomplished diver, and as advanced divers, they thought, why hang on to a rope when you can just slightly move your fins one way or the other to catch the current and maintain your depth? After all, fish do it.

Dive masters seldom use the mooring rope for their ascension, so as Stark moved away from the mooring line, making more room for other returning divers, Christy and Cheryl followed him. The three of them— along with Prillaman, DeBarger, Webb, and Mars—hovered fifteen feet under the *Wave Dancer*, in "spread eagle and vertical with arms crossed" positions, letting the Caribbean water flow around them while periodically checking their depth and time gauge to control their decompression stop.

Christy was particularly watching her submersible pressure gauge [SPG]. According to her SPG, after the forty-minute dive at the maximum depth of one hundred feet, she had 1300 psi left in her tank and was sure she had more air left after the dive than any other diver, including Stark. A careful but competitive person, Christy liked to challenge the other divers, especially the men, to see who would end the dive with the most air left in their tank.

Two by two the divers left the hang bar or their hovering positions to move to the back of the boat, where the twin ladders await their arrival. As they slipped off their fins and moved up the ladders, they found Stark and Stanley on board ready to help them with their gear. As each diver shed the forty extra pounds of gear they were carrying, Eloisa and Brenda handed them a clean warm towel and pointed them toward the open-air shower on the dive platform.

It was a great first dive. In her lightweight, neoprene full-body dive skin, Cheryl thought the Caribbean Sea was as warm as bath water and, with its colorful and panoramic visibility, far more interesting. Stark had pointed out several varieties of fish and odd-looking coral formations and had taken them into a tunnel at sixty feet of depth, where they swam to a small light in the distance that opened into the side of The Wall at one hundred feet—a breathtaking entry into one of the great wonders of the world. One moment they were cruising along the edge of the coral reef at sixty feet; then it dropped precipitously from its uppermost edge to the ocean's floor four thousand feet below. The majestic vision of seeing the Grand Canyon under water almost created sensory overload. Christy and Cheryl could only absorb enough to get a general overview of The Wall. They would come back on the second dive to take in the many spectacular features.

At 9:00 a.m. on Sunday, October 7, the Prime Minister of Belize, based on Chief Meteorologist Fuller's recommendation, declared a preliminary phase warning and a hurricane watch for Belize. With that declaration, the nation of Belize was put on alert. Solid red flags were flown on all public buildings, warning of the impending storm. Carlos Fuller made the formal announcement on television, which was immediately picked up and transmitted over LOVE 95 radio, and the buzz that can only be appreciated by people who have suffered through a hurricane, began. In a matter of minutes the conversation about the recent success of the soccer team changed to talk of hurricanes. Cab drivers standing around waiting for a fare, village merchants, and resort operators alike turned their conversation to the now-threatening Hurricane Iris predicted to hit the Belize mainland in thirty-six to forty-eight hours

Belizeans had barely missed the full effect of Hurricane Mitch in October 1998, as it changed direction at the last minute and moved back toward Honduras. They had been preparing for the worst as Mitch evolved into a category five hurricane, threatening their coastal towns. The storm spread fear throughout the region as it increased in strength with wind speeds of up to 180 mph and gusts of 200 mph. Eventually, Mitch became the fourth strongest hurricane of all time, rated behind the Florida Keys Labor Day hurricane of 1935, Hurricane Camille, and Hurricane Gilbert. Mitch dumped twenty to twenty-five inches of rain in Honduras and Nicaragua, flooding many coastal towns and nearby mountain villages and creating massive mudslides resulting in nine thousand deaths and leaving an additional sixty thousand people homeless.

In the aftermath of Mitch, the government of Belize established the National Emergency Management Organization [NEMO]. In April of 1999, the National Disaster Plan for Belize was put into effect, and this was followed in May with a Countrywide Simulation Exercise dubbed Exercise Millennium Breeze, which was designed to test the newly developed plans

NEMO, with the Prime Minister as the permanent chairperson, activates its immediate response program through the ten operational committees: education, communications, and warning; medical and relief measures; housing and shelter; search, rescue and initial clearance; collection control and distribution of food and material; assessment and evaluation of damage; foreign assistance; transport; environment; and utilities. The NEMO mission, in cooperation with the respective emergency management committees and all public and private agencies, is to preserve life and property throughout the country of Belize in the event of an emergency, threatened or real, and to mitigate the impact on the country and its people.

NEMO is responsible for emergency management countrywide and the coordination of all international assistance in the event of a disaster. During non-crisis periods, the NEMO secretariat is responsible for the development, refinement, and exercise of all emergency plans. Training occurs throughout the year in all aspects of disaster preparedness. The main emphasis of NEMO's training program is to "train the trainers," thereby enabling the district emergency committees to set up their own training teams. This is achieved by working with international, regional, public, and private sector organizations. It entails conducting workshops, seminars, and conferences in all districts and towns countrywide. Local and regional business owners were encouraged to support the efforts of NEMO by establishing a standard operating procedure for their business in the event of a hurricane.

In 1999, the Turkish absentee owner of the Princess Hotel and Casino, at the request of a NEMO representative, prepared an SOP as an emergency general guideline for implementation by the general manager of his resort. The Princess Hotel and Casino was the largest and most complete resort destination in Belize. The Las Vegas-style casino was the only one in the country, complete with blackjack, roulette, Caribbean stud poker, and over four hundred slot machines. It stood on Belize City's picturesque waterfront, only a few minutes from the business district and the international airport. During the day, the hotel offered scuba diving, deep-sea fishing, and trips to the Mayan ruins and the pristine jungle. At night, hotel guests could enjoy seaside dining, live music, disco dancing, fabulous Las Vegas-style floor shows, two movie theatres with current releases and, of course, the casino.

At 10:00 a.m., members of the hotel staff told Doncho Donchev, the general manager, that the preliminary phase warning for approaching Hurricane Iris had been issued. Donchev, a Bulgarian citizen, had arrived in Belize three weeks earlier on September 14 to manage the operation and as well as a planned restoration. He had no previous experience with, or knowledge of, hurricanes. He immediately referred to his operations manual for guidance. As he began initial preparations for the advancing storm, Donchev noticed a flurry of activity on the dock in front of his hotel and adjoining properties as people from the outlying islands began arriving and depositing their worldly possessions on the docks, beaches, and lawns. To him, it was beginning to look like a giant yard sale.

With the threat of Iris still more than thirty hours away, it was too soon to force the evacuation of his thirty guests, but Donchev ordered his staff to alert them. The guests would be allowed to stay Sunday night but would need to relocate to a shelter on Monday morning until the threat subsided. It was Donchev's responsibility, under his SOP guidelines, to evacuate the hotel and casino of all guests and unnecessary staff at least eight hours prior to the expected arrival of a hurricane. From now until the threat was over, he could not, for liability reasons, accept any new guests to the hotel.

However, tonight would be business as usual. They would all eat, drink, and party until the wee hours and deal with Hurricane Iris tomorrow. As with most Caribbean destinations, October was the slow season for Belize, so the evacuation and building preparation likely to occur Monday morning would not be difficult.

Chapter Seven

"The reason I love the sea I cannot explain—it's physical. When you dive you begin to feel like an angel. It's a liberation of your weight."

Jacques-Yves Cousteau

Leaning against the rail of the sky deck, Prillaman, Webb, and Christy sipped cold lemonade and discussed their first dive of the day. Cheryl sat in the shade of the canopy on a blue canvas lounge chair within listening distance, writing the particulars of the first dive in her log book. Like most of the divers, she kept a history of buddy, date, time, location, climactic conditions, water temperature, current strength, depth of dive, length of dive, and notable items seen during the dive. A meticulous record keeper, she later transferred all of the information in her logbook to a computer disk that contained the details of all of her previous dives. She used this information for her own reference as well as for recounting her adventures with family and friends.

As she finished her final entry, she heard the others talking about how comfortable the first dive had been and how Stanley's briefing had prepared them well for it. They also compared the various fish, sea life, and corals each of them had seen.

"There's a lot of fish at this site," Prillaman said. "It kind of reminded me of the Aquarium in Grand Cayman." He puffed his between-dive cigarette, his eyes darting as he spoke. The bottom of his T-shirt was soaked where it clung to his wet his swim trunks, but he did not seem to notice. Instead, he talked excitedly about the dive.

Christy, leaning her back against the top rail, had pulled a T-shirt over her blue bikini. "Stark's an excellent diver," she said. "He made sure we stayed close. He took us over the reef through this tunnel that dropped down about forty feet and pointed out a lot of cool fish."

"Some great fish," Prillaman agreed.

Christy nodded, then added, "But, to be honest, nothing really different or unusual."

Webb, working on his tan, stood bare-chested as he listened to the others describe their dives. Always the gentleman, he waited until everyone else had spoken before he added that he and Ray Mars had enjoyed a good first dive. He said the site was above average, and that they saw three lobsters, a barracuda, and a free-swimming, four-foot-long green moray eel. After they all recounted their tales of the first dive, they moved on to talk about "The Wall."

Extending the full 185-mile length of the reef, The Wall is where the edge of the reef suddenly and dramatically disappears into an abyss, and the crystal clear waters seem to turn black. Divers approach The Wall at sixty to one hundred feet below the surface. To that point they have enjoyed many underwater sights; then there is nothing under them except complete darkness that may fall away for four thousand feet. The Wall is a sheer drop-off with a great deal of color-enhanced corals and sponges extending from it. Though big critters—such as sharks and eagle and manta rays—gather there, it is the most visited place on dive trips in the area.

Underwater adventurers often report getting a "high" when hanging out away from the reef with four thousand feet of abyss beneath them. It feels eerie not knowing what is below and not being able to reach out and touch anything solid. The diver feels totally alone, free floating through the "outer space" of water. Prillaman, Webb, Christy, and Cheryl had experienced these sensations while hanging out next to The Wall and were looking forward to the next dive, when they hoped to relive it.

Prillaman said, "I think this wall is more dramatic than Turks and Caicos. It's actually comparable to Grand Cayman." He turned to Christy. "What do you think?"

Having seen all three, Christy initially agreed, but then said she would reserve her final opinion until she had visited The Wall again.

Eloisa, the head cook, arrived on the sky deck accompanied by Stanley, Brenda, and Angela. They brought warm chocolate chip cookies, ice, and soft drink refills. They also wanted to share with their guests a bit of the history and the highlights of their country. Prillaman, Christy, Cheryl, and Webb were quickly joined by Lisa, Mary Lou, and DeBarger, who nabbed the last of the deck chairs. Everyone else, except Jim and Kim Garrison, who discussed Jim's new camera with Baechtold, gathered around on the floor. DeBarger offered his seat to Sheila Kelley, but she declined, remaining seated on the floor and holding hands with Bill, her number one man for the last twenty years.

Eloisa and Stanley weren't sure whether to attribute the turnout to the chocolate chip cookies, their enthusiasm about the subject, or simply curious courtesy. In any event they eagerly shared their stories with everyone. They brought with them two copies of *Destination Belize*, the official tourism guide, which they passed among their listeners and occasionally used as a reference for their presentation.

"The people of Belize know a lot about your country," said Eloisa, "so we want you to know a little about ours." She told them that Belize is the second smallest and most sparsely populated country in Central America, with a population of 250,000, a third of which lives in Belize City. It's a multi-cultural society with 60 percent Creole, 15 percent Mestizos [Latinos] and 15 percent Garifuna [blacks with mixed origin]. The balance is made up of Mayan Indians, Mennonites, and expatriate Europeans and North Americans.

"English is the official language of our country," she said. "It is taught in our schools, so you will be able to communicate almost anywhere you want to go."

"It seems like paradise to me," Prillaman said, and some of the others voiced their agreement.

"Even better than the Garage Mahal?" Webb called

Some in the group laughed at the reference to Prillaman's garage. He shared a home with his longtime girlfriend, Margo, who insisted that he not smoke in the house. He converted his two-car garage—complete with a phone line, refrigerator, and cable television—into his own hang-out, where he could smoke, play poker with his friends, and work on his model railroad. Margo had christened it "the Garage Mahal."

"That's a tough choice," Prillaman said. "But this place seems perfect."

"Of course, we do have hurricanes," Eloisa said. "Belize is in the hurricane belt, and so that's always a concern—from June to November, anyway, though mostly from August to October. As you know, a new one is supposed to arrive in thirty-six hours."

At the mention of Hurricane Iris, Lisa turned, made eye contact with Mary Lou, and gave her a weak smile. This was the first time anyone had mentioned the hurricane since Captain Martin's off-handed reference to it the previous evening. Rick Patterson, uncomfortable on the floor, quietly got up, and went to lean against the rail next to Webb and Mars. Doug Cox headed to the tray of cookies a few feet away and got two, one each for him and Phyllis.

"Captain Martin has promised to keep us all up to date on Iris," she said, as if sensing the note of alarm she may have struck with her comment. After a few minutes, she turned the discussion over to Stanley, who continued with more history of Belize. He told them that Belize was a small independent nation about the size of New Jersey, 70 percent of which was covered by forest and tropical jungle. He spent a few minutes talking about the evolution of his country from the time of the Mayan Indians, through the occupation by the Spaniards and early settlers, to the country's independence in 1989.

Jimmy Topping, on the other side of Mary Lou, legs stretched out and using his arms behind him as a brace, shifted to an upright sitting position and held up his cup signaling that he wanted a refill. This prompted Prillaman to hold up his cup as well. Brenda filled the cups, surveying the group to see if anyone else needed a refill. Meanwhile Stanley talked about the growth of ecotourism and the fact that over three hundred thousand visitors return each year to dive, hike, and raft to explore rivers and caverns and jungles. He was willing to go on but realized he was beginning to lose his audience.

The floor of the sky deck was hard and uncomfortable, which caused some of his listeners to fidget. Also, the mention of the hurricane had shifted the mood of the group, at least for the moment. When they looked around, it seemed impossible that a large, violent storm lurked nearby. The day was bright and clear, the water calm and a brilliant blue.

The bell clanged three times on the dive deck signaling the start of the second dive briefing. The group gathered on the dive deck in a semicircle in front of the briefing board, eagerly awaiting their instructions from Stanley. Several divers huddled at the camera table doing final tune-ups, battery tests, seal checks, lens cleaning, and so on. Everyone treated the equipment with great care, from Cox's five thousand dollar video camera to Kelley's much cheaper Nikonos 35mm slide camera.

To insure quality slides and photographs, Charlie and Cindy Pike had invested a few thousand dollars in their 35mm camera. Charlie, vice president of special projects at Timmons Engineering, and Cindy, a Chesterfield Towne Center staff member, had two photographic goals for this trip. They wanted to win the "best slide of the trip" contest and to have another trophy shot enlarged, which they would add to the collection on Charlie's office wall at

Timmons, where he had worked for twenty-nine years. His office had become a showcase of enlarged underwater photos from dive trips to Mexico and the Caribbean. He also displayed a map full of multi-colored push pins denoting each site visited. The photographs, map, and pins helped ease the stress of his job. When things got too hectic, he could close his office door and escape to the serene depths of the ocean.

After their children had grown, the Pikes opened their home to foster children. They had taken in several kids and enjoyed making a difference in sometimes troubled and less fortunate lives. Through their photographs, slides, and diving stories, they enlarged the children's view and appreciation of the world. They helped them feel special, as if they were connected with exotic travels.

Their 35mm camera had a special pressure-protective housing and double-flash light bar. The light bar extended up to four feet and with the protected camera apparatus in the center, the assemblage looked like a two-legged spider. By being able to extend the light bar and adjust each flash to the subject correctly, they could take clear photos, while a single flash often reflected particles of sediment, which looked like miniature stars in the final photo.

Stanley asked everyone to gather around him for the briefing. He said, "There is nothing new to tell you about this site. Whenever we move to a new site, someone will give you a briefing before the first dive. After that, you'll be on your own to enter the water at your leisure. You must—and I repeat must—check in and out with the dive master in charge on the dive deck both before and after the dive and always let your dive buddy know where you are. We do not want you to be left behind or drift away. There are many stories, and I am sure you've heard a few, about dive boats leaving people behind who later died from exposure or were found floating adrift by a rescue team."

As Stanley issued his warning, Prillaman whispered to Webb, "It wouldn't be hard to get left behind."

"I read an article about this couple," Webb said, "I think their name was Lonergan. They were left behind somewhere in Australia. Never heard from again. *Undercurrent* said it was assumed that sharks got them."

The other members of the RDC nodded their heads in agreement with Stanley. A hallmark of their club had always been strict adherence to safety.

Stanley continued, "This morning when you came back you gave Stark your length of dive and maximum depth. You must do that after every dive. This helps us keep track of you, your number of dives, time and depth of dives, all of that. We can make sure you have good surface intervals and are not pressing the decompression limits."

The divers nodded, understanding the rationale for this system.

Stanley then said, "Baechtold is going to be in the water with his video camera shooting this week's historic adventures of the RDC on the reefs of Belize. So, flash him a smile, make a face, or whatever you like when you see him pointing the camera in your direction. For those of you with cameras, put on your dive gear, get in the water, and I'll hand you your camera. By the way, the crew loves to dive, so if any of you want someone to point out interesting fish, critters, or reef formations let us know. And for anyone interested, Aaron Stark is giving an "introduction to nitrox" class after this dive. I noticed several of you already use nitrox, but the rest of you'll find Stark's information enlightening. Questions? If not, the pool is open!"

Baechtold didn't wait for the divers to enter the water to begin his video. As soon as Stanley dismissed the group, Baechtold began panning the dive deck. He asked Christy to smile as she took off her T-shirt and began to put on her wet suit. He then panned the camera table, where Garrison and Kelley rubbed a Vaseline-like substance on the rubber gasket of their camera housing to insure it wouldn't leak. Then he moved to the back of the dive deck and shot each buddy group as they left the boat.

As Lisa and Mary Lou started to put on their masks and do a giant stride, Baechtold, in his best Austin Powers voice, said, "Smile ladies. Yeah, baby!" They flashed him a smile and with a giant stride and a big splash, they began another underwater adventure on Belize's barrier reef. Just as the animals left Noah's ark after the great flood two by two, so, too, did the RDC divers leave the dive deck of the *Wave Dancer*. Each time Baechtold would say, "Smile!" as they prepared to jump in. Doug Cox flashed his best 'watch me' gesture and did a mid-air summersault entry, eliciting a "That was really cool, baby!" from Baechtold.

As she bobbed up to the top, Shirley Johnston swam to the back of the boat where Stanley waited with her camera. Taking it, she kicked away in a bicycle-riding motion, toward the mooring line, making room for Charlie Pike, Jim Garrison, Bill Kelley, Doug Cox, and Glenn Prillaman to get their cameras. Shirley was anxious to begin shooting. Guided by Byron, her favorite marine-life spotter, she planned to shoot her subjects so she would win the shot-of-the-week contest. Her main competitor for the honor, Charlie Pike, had thrown down the gauntlet, claiming he and Cindy would win.

After submerging, Shirley was awed by the clarity of the water. She could see the reef, its colors, formations, and surroundings better than during any of her previous travels. When she reached the bottom of the mooring line she found Bryon thirty feet away already scouting for photo-ops. They gave each other the OK sign and were off. On the top of the coral reef at forty feet of depth Byron looked to his right and saw, about twenty feet below them, a French angel fish. He thought this would be a first good shot for Shirley, so he motioned to her and pointed in the direction of their subject.

Byron advanced slowly toward the angel fish, which seemed unconcerned with his presence. As Stanley had suggested, he put out his right hand and wiggled his fingers. It was clear the angel fish had seen this trick before, but it still showed enough interest to move toward Byron and Shirley. Hovering, like good photographers do, Shirley waited patiently while the fish moved next to a yellow sea whip, which would complement the black angel fish with a yellow scallop on each scale. At just the right moment she clicked the shutter. That was almost too easy. Is the rest of the week going to be like this, she wondered, and then swam on.

Still at sixty feet Byron saw a large barrel sponge. The hollowed-out sponge looked like a barrel without a lid. It had a smooth finish on the inside, but the outside had rows of ridges, where juvenile fish and shrimp could find shelter. It appeared to be five feet tall and two feet around, although, as Byron knew, everything under water appeared 25 percent larger than its actual size. Still, it was huge. He pointed it out to Shirley, who motioned him to move next to it so she could use him as a size reference. When she had him positioned next to the barrel sponge she clicked her second shot. The sponge appeared a rusty brown at sixty feet, but the bright flash of the camera's lights would bring out its natural orange color. She and Byron were off to a good start. Two "keeper shots" in their first ten minutes!

Baechtold entered the water focused on finding interesting yet familiar fish and critters for footage to weave into the video production he would record for this week's group. It was important to shoot new footage each week rather than use a canned version, because the divers would be able to identify things familiar to them. As he cruised around the reef he saw Shirley and Byron at about eighty feet taking a photo of a medium-sized Hawksbill turtle, approximately two feet in diameter, resting on the reef while dining on a sponge. It was feeding time for the turtle, and it did not care who watched. The three of them closed within two feet of it. After taking two good shots, Byron and Shirley started to swim away. Baechtold, however, motioned for them to move back next to the turtle so he could video them with it.

He decided to cruise along the wall, suspecting most of the divers would be there. He saw Prillaman with DeBarger, who shined his flashlight on the reef in search of interesting subjects, also using it to point to objects for Prillaman to photograph. When Prillaman saw Baechtold, he swam toward the crewman's camera. When he got within fifteen feet, he kicked his fins and moved his arms, tucking and rolling into a 360 degree turn. When he was once again facing the camera, he gave an OK sign with each hand. DeBarger merely waved, knowing he could not top Prillaman's antics.

A hundred feet away, Webb and Ray Mars closed in for some camera time. They went out over the abyss and did a double-spread formation. On the video they would appear to be skydiving into the deep blue background. Seeing no one else hanging around The Wall, Baechtold ventured up to sixty feet and found Bill and Sheila Kelley photographing a Nassau grouper at a cleaning station—a coral formation that was home to two cleaner shrimp. As the grouper opened its mouth and extended its gills the shrimp jumped from the coral into the grouper's mouth and began to clean particles of leftover food and parasites from its mouth and gills. After they finished their photo-op, Baechtold motioned for them to get together and smile for the camera. It didn't take much prompting for Bill and Sheila to embrace, take their regulators out of their mouths and give each other a sweet but salty kiss.

Baechtold had liked the Kelleys from the moment they boarded the *Wave Dancer*. He noticed they doted on each other like newlyweds, which he thought ironic. With his short-cropped hair, square chin, and firm body, Bill could have been a model, thirty years ago, for a Marine recruiting poster. He did not look like a sensitive guy, but clearly Sheila found his soft spot.

Baechtold moved on, leaving the aquatic love birds to their adventure. As he taped some nice filler footage of a purple-tipped anemone and an arrow crab, Christy and Cheryl swam by, took their regulators out of their mouths, blew him a bubble-filled kiss, waved a big "hi" and swam on.

When the dive was finished, Baechtold headed back to the boat to get footage of the divers climbing up the ladders. At the base of the mooring line, several divers were taking Stanley's suggestion of riding on the deco bar during their safety stop. The current was strong, the bow of the *Wave Dancer* was stationary at the mooring ball, and the stern of the boat was briskly swinging from north to south and back again, carrying six deco bar riders.

After they boarded the boat and removed their gear, Webb told Baechtold to grab his camera. Something was about to happen. Taking Webb's cue, Baechtold taped Prillaman under the dive deck shower shampooing the saltwater out of his hair. Webb positioned himself directly over the showerhead so when Prillaman attempted to rinse his hair Webb added more shampoo from a second bottle. After his third attempt to rinse, Prillaman realized something wasn't right. He opened his eyes to see that he was being taped as the victim of Webb's practical joke. Everyone laughed, even Prillaman, who knew there was plenty of time for payback.

At the camera table Pike, Cox, and Kelley joined Shirley in the post-dive ritual of cleaning the cameras, checking the seals, removing the exposed film, putting their names on the containers, and giving it to Stanley for processing. They discussed their various shots, sharing insights with each other while secretly hoping to have taken the best one.

Stark mingled among the divers, reminding them that his nitrox lecture began in five minutes. He noticed that only five divers were not already using the enriched gas mixture, so his class would be smaller than usual, thus his commission for teaching a full-blown class that week would not be large.

Only four divers attended the class—Bill and Sheila Kelley and Byron and Shirley Johnston. Stark opened by saying, "Nitrox, or the use of enriched gas, is the wave of the future. The enriched gas mixture is more forgiving than regular compressed gas, and with its proper use there is less chance of getting decompression sickness."

He told them that the crew of the *Wave Dancer* stressed the use of nitrox because of the repetitive diving. On most one-day trips, people dive one or two times, but on a live-aboard they can do up to five dives a day. By using nitrox, a diver can, within limits, stay down longer and have shorter decompression stops. He said that almost 80 percent of recreational decompression sickness cases result from repetitive dives and most could be eliminated through the use of nitrox. Using his PADI *Enriched Air Diver Manual* for reference, he explained that diving frees us to move through a third dimension.

"On land, we largely function in two dimensions," he said, "but underwater we also float up and over, and down and under. For many of us, the freedom to move in three dimensions is one of the primary appeals of diving. Of course, underwater we're constrained by what physicists call a fourth dimension: time."

While the nitrox class wrapped up, Lisa and Mary Lou went to their cabin to shower, put on some make-up, and dress for lunch. They put on tropical-themed blouses with coordinated shorts and went to the salon. When they arrived they noticed Christy and Cheryl, too, had dressed for lunch and sat together on the sofa writing in their logbooks. Lisa and Mary Lou filled their personally marked *Wave Dancer* drinking mugs with ice and fresh lemonade, pulled up two chairs, and joined them. The four discussed the dives, particularly the clarity of the water and the surprising number of fish and critters.

Baechtold came into the salon, video camera in hand. He pointed it in their direction and said, "Smile, ladies!" In his Austin Powers voice he said, "That's it. What beautiful ladies you are." Christy and Cheryl held up and pointed to their logbooks. Mary Lou toasted him with her mug, and Lisa put one hand behind her head and thrust her body forward, giving him her best Hollywood Diva pose.

"Oh yeah, baby!" he said, "Hot, hot, hot. You are lovely today!" When he moved on to his next subject, the women looked at each other and laughed. Baechtold was just too funny.

After completing his morning dives Prillaman went to his cabin, shaved, showered, and put on a T-shirt and shorts. Before lunch he wanted to check with Captain Martin to find out why they weren't tied up next to the *Aggressor* and why all of the members of the RDC weren't diving together. He went to the wheelhouse and found the captain at the helm. When Prillaman asked about the status of the other boat Martin said that Schnabel, captain of the *Aggressor*, had his own itinerary, but that the group would be diving together before the end of the week. Prillaman asked Martin about the status of the hurricane and was told that there was no change. The storm was staying north of them and wouldn't affect their plans for the week. The home office, monitoring the reports from the National Weather Service, would apprise them of any changes. In short, Martin implied that Prillaman should join the others and leave running the ship to him.

*   *   *

The National Weather Service [NWS] uses several tools to monitor hurricanes to assist the NHC in their storm projections. While hurricanes are still far out in the ocean, satellites are the primary observation tool, though ships and buoys also provide information. When the storms come closer to land, forecasters use more direct measurements—such as reconnaissance aircraft, radiosondes, and Automated Surface Observation Stations. Within two hundred miles of the coast, radar provides indirect measurements. Computer models used to forecast storm intensity and movement require a great deal of data about the atmosphere. Lack of observations, especially over the ocean, and errors and inconsistencies in the data are major sources of forecast errors.

The primary observing systems used by the NWS in the tropics are the Geostationary Operational Environmental Satellites [GOES]. With satellite images, forecasters can estimate the location, size, movement, and intensity of a storm and can analyze its surrounding environment. Instruments on the satellites measure emitted and reflected radiation, from which atmospheric temperature, winds, moisture, and cloud cover can be derived. Satellite images provide basic day/night cloud imagery, observations of land surface temperature data, sea surface temperature data, winds from cloud motions at several levels, hourly cloud-top heights and amounts, and rainfall estimates for flash flood warnings.

Ships and buoys provide information about the wind speed and direction, pressure, air and sea temperature, and wave conditions within the hurricane. Ships and buoys are the only routine source of measured waves in areas unobstructed by land and are often the only way to take direct measurements when a tropical storm is still at sea.

Reconnaissance aircraft flown into the storm provide the most direct method of measuring the winds. Those measurements are limited, however, because they cannot be taken until the hurricane is relatively close to shore. In addition, they are not taken continuously or throughout the storm, so they produce only a snapshot of small parts of the hurricane. Nonetheless, that information is critical in analyzing the current characteristics needed to forecast the future behavior of the storm.

The U.S. Air Force Reserve uses specially equipped C-130 aircraft to conduct most operational reconnaissance. Pilots, known as "Hurricane Hunters," fly into the hurricane center to measure winds, pressure, temperature, and humidity, as well as to provide an accurate location of the eye. The National Oceanic and Atmospheric Administration [NOAA] also flies—usually P3 Orion aircraft and state-of-the-art high-altitude aircraft—into hurricanes to help scientists better understand these storms and to improve forecast capabilities.

A radiosonde is a small instrument package and radio transmitter that is attached to a large balloon. As the balloon rises through the atmosphere, the radiosonde measures air temperature, humidity, and pressure, and the data is relayed to a computer at the surface, providing an important vertical profile of the hurricane's environment. Radiosondes are generally only released over land, which leaves a large data gap over the oceans. Dropsondes, a variation of the radiosonde, are attached to a small parachute and dropped into the hurricane from reconnaissance aircraft. The dropsondes help forecasters understand and predict hurricane behavior.

When a hurricane nears the coast, it is monitored by land-based weather radar, which provides detailed information on wind fields, rain intensity, and storm movement. As a result, local NWS offices can provide short-term warnings for floods, tornadoes, and high winds for specific areas. Sophisticated mathematical calculations give forecasters important information derived from the radar data, such as estimates of rainfall amounts. However, these radars cannot "see" farther than approximately two hundred miles from the coast, and hurricane watches and warnings must be issued long before the storm comes into range.

At 11:00 a.m., while the members of the RDC and crew of the *Wave Dancer* enjoyed their second dive of the day, the NHC issued its twelfth advisory on Hurricane Iris and its accompanying discussion. Dennis Gonguez received the report at the National Meteorological Center in Belize and immediately took it to Carlos Fuller. The report read:

BULLETIN

HURRICANE IRIS ADVISORY NUMBER 12
NATIONAL WEATHER SERVICE, MIAMI, FL
11 A.M. EDT, SUN OCT 07 2001
...IRIS PASSING NEAR THE SOUTHWEST COAST OF JAMAICA...
HEADING FOR YUCATAN...

A HURRICANE WARNING REMAINS IN EFFECT FOR
JAMAICA AND THE CAYMAN ISLANDS.

AT 11 A.M. EDT...1500 UTC...THE GOVERNMENT OF
MEXICO HAS ISSUED A HURRICANE WATCH FOR THE
EAST COAST OF YUCATAN FROM CABO CATOCHE SOUTHWARD.

A HURRICANE WATCH MAY BE REQUIRED FOR
PORTIONS OF BELIZE LATER TODAY.

AT 11 A.M....1500 UTC...THE GOVERNMENT OF CUBA HAS
DISCONTINUED THE HURRICANE WARNINGS AND WATCHES FOR CUBA.

AT 11 A.M. EDT...1500Z...THE CENTER OF HURRICANE IRIS WAS
LOCATED NEAR LATITUDE 17.4 NORTH...LONGITUDE 77.9 WEST OR
ABOUT 85 MILES...135 KM WEST-SOUTHWEST OF KINGSTON, JAMAICA
OR 260 MILES...420 KM...EAST-SOUTHEAST OF GRAND CAYMAN.

IRIS IS MOVING TOWARD THE WEST NEAR 17 MPH...
28 KM/HR...AND THIS MOTION IS EXPECTED TO CONTINUE
DURING THE NEXT 24 HOURS. ON THIS PATH...IRIS WILL BE HEADING
TOWARD THE YUCATAN PENINSULA.

MAXIMUM SUSTAINED WINDS ARE NEAR 85 MPH... 140 KM/HR... IN A SMALL AREA JUST NORTH OF THE CENTER...WITH HIGHER GUSTS. SOME STRENGTHENING IS FORECAST DURING THE NEXT 24 HOURS.

HURRICANE FORCE WINDS EXTEND OUTWARD UP TO 25 MILES... 35 KM...FROM THE CENTER...AND TROPICAL STORM FORCE WINDS EXTEND OUTWARD UP TO 115 MILES ...185 KM.

ESTIMATED MINIMUM CENTRAL PRESSURE IS 989 MB...29.21 INCHES.

COASTAL STORM SURGE FLOODING OF 4 TO 5 FEET ABOVE NORMAL TIDE LEVELS...ALONG WITH DANGEROUS BATTERING WAVES...IS EXPECTED TO AFFECT JAMAICA TODAY.

RAINFALL TOTALS OF 3 TO 5 INCHES...WITH HIGHER AMOUNTS OVER MOUNTAINEOUS AREAS...ARE EXPECTED OVER JAMAICA. THESE RAINS COULD CAUSE FLASH FLOODS AND MUD SLIDES.

REPEATING THE 11 A.M. EDT POSITION...17.4 N...77.9 W. MOVEMENT TOWARD...WEST NEAR 17 MPH. MAXIMUM SUSTAINED WINDS...85 MPH. MINIMUM CENTRAL PRESSURE ...989 MB. AN INTERMEDIATE ADVISORY WILL BE ISSUED BY THE NATIONAL HURRICANE CENTER AT 2 P.M. EDT FOLLOWED BY THE NEXT COMPLETE ADVISORY AT 5 P.M. EDT.

FORECASTER AVILA

HURRICANE IRIS DISCUSSION NUMBER 12, NATIONAL WEATHER SERVICE, MIAMI, FL
11 A.M. EDT, SUN OCT 07 2001

LATEST RECON REPORTED A MINIMUM PRESSURE OF 991 MB FROM A DROPSONDE AND AN EXTRAPOLATED PRESSURE OF 985 MB. IT APPEARS THAT THE DROP DID NOT HIT THE CENTER BECAUSE SURFACE WINDS WERE MEASURED AT 28 KNOTS. SO WE ARE USING 989 MB IN

THE ADVISORY... BASED ON PREVIOUS MEASUREMENTS. FOR A WHILE THE CLOUD PATTERN BECAME A LITTLE RAGGED...BUT DURING THE PAST HOUR OR SO...HIGH RESOLUTION IMAGES ARE SHOWING THE DEVELOPMENT OF AN EYE FEATURE. THIS MEANS THAT IRIS COULD BE STRENGTHENING AS WE SPEAK. ONCE THE CIRCULATION OF IRIS GETS AWAY FROM JAMAICA...IT WILL BE MOVING OVER THE NORTHWESTERN CARIBBEAN WHERE THE UPPER OCEANIC HEAT CONTENT IS VERY HIGH. THIS...IN COMBINATION WITH LOW SHEAR...WILL PROVIDE A FAVORABLE ENVIRONMENT FOR DEVELOPMENT. HISTORICALLY...A LARGE NUMBER OF HURRICANES HAVE BECOME MAJOR HURRICANES IN THIS REGION.

IRIS CONTINUES TO BE STEERED BY A STRONG AND PERSISTENT MID-LEVEL RIDGE TO THE NORTH. THIS PATTERN IS NOT EXPECTED TO CHANGE..KEEPING THE HURRICANE ON A GENERAL WESTWARD TRACK THROUGH THE FORECAST PERIOD.

IRIS COULD REACH EASTERN YUCATAN OR NORTHERN BELIZE AS A MAJOR HURRICANE IN ABOUT 36 TO 48 HOURS.

FORECASTER AVILA

After reading the report, Fuller told Gonguez to find his assistant, Justin Hulse, for a meeting in the operations room. Fuller showed Hulse the report, which noted that Hurricane Iris had the potential of becoming a major hurricane by the time it reached Belize. He said he was going to recommend to NEMO that a "Hurricane Watch" for their country be put into effect within the next two hours. The two discussed the SOP for a "Hurricane Watch," which included an upgraded national alert. Fuller stated that from this time until after the threat of Hurricane Iris ended they would not leave the meteorological center except to attend NEMO meetings. He further stated that they would meet every three hours to review the latest report from the NHC.

Chapter Eight

"I think anybody who has spent a lot of time in the water, especially diving, understands this great feeling you get, like being born again."

Wyland

"Hey, Buddy," Prillaman called to Webb. "How do I get a job like yours?"

Webb, a successful commercial HVAC entrepreneur, turned to see Prillaman standing farther back in the line for food. He cocked an eyebrow. "Haven't you had enough jobs already?" he asked.

A snicker ran through the line as the group waited with plates in hands, for the buffet Eloise, Brenda, and Angela spread on the long food table.

"But I want a job like yours," said Prillaman, who often teased Webb about being a glorified plumber. "My only question is why you need such a big truck to carry around a dinky little can of Drain-o."

Lisa rose from her thoughts of Mike, her fiancé, and looked at Mary Lou standing next to her. They grinned and shook their heads, knowing that pranks and boyish banter played a part in all RDC trips.

"You're just mad because you couldn't get the shampoo out of your hair." Webb shot back at Prillaman.

"I'm mad because I can't make a hundred bucks an hour dumping a four-dollar bottle of Drain-o down somebody's sink."

Everyone in line laughed. Webb, for once lost for words, just shook his head and began filling his plate. He filled two plates, one with salads and one with a sample of everything else. The crew had prepared a garden salad, pasta salad, cold cuts, cheeseburgers, baked fish, and French fries. There was also fresh fruit, butterscotch pudding, and leftover chocolate chip cookies.

While the guests enjoyed their lunch, Stanley pulled Wouters into the lounge area of the salon to tell him of the crew's growing concerns about the approaching hurricane. He spoke in a low voice, reminding Wouters that almost a year ago to the day Hurricane Keith hit Ambergris Caye, less than sixty miles from their present location, killing five people who stayed on their catamaran.

"Nobody in their right mind messes with a hurricane, and that's what Martin is doing," Stanley said. "Our lives are at risk because of him—or Peter Hughes, or Ryan Vernon, or maybe all of them together." He felt that, of the three, at least Vernon, the Belize-based manager for the Hughes company, ought to know better. "Vernon's lived here all his life. He should know."

Wouters shrugged. "Martin's the captain," he said. "What can we do?"

"Get Vernon to talk with Martin or Hughes," Stanley said. "Martin won't listen to me. He doesn't like me."

Wouters nodded, knowing Stanley was right. Ever since Stanley took the wheel from Martin to keep the *Wave Dancer* from crashing into a reef, Martin had been aloof and dismissive to Stanley.

"You talk to him," Stanley said. "Tell him that while we're out here having fun people are evacuating the outer islands. See if you can get through to him."

Wouters asked Stanley what he thought Martin should do. Stanley replied that in 1998, when Hurricane Mitch threatened the coast of Belize and Honduras, the luxury schooner *Fantome* stopped at Belize City and let off the passengers and non-essential crew before trying to outrun the storm.

"You may not know this," Stanley said, "but Mitch caught up with the *Fantome*, and everyone on board was killed."

"I know about it," Wouters said. They did not have to mention that if a hurricane could sink a 282-foot steel-hulled, four-masted ship, the *Wave Dancer* had little hope of surviving.

"We should go to Belize City, evacuate the guests and some of the crew, and head for the safest place we can find," Stanley said.

"But he's the captain," Wouters said, though with less conviction than before.

"You've got to tell him."

After a quiet moment, Wouters agreed. He headed to the wheelhouse to talk with Captain Martin, who at that time was navigating the boat to the next dive site, Front Porch. The site was less than five miles from Black Beauty, and the *Wave Dancer* would arrive there for the next dive a half hour after lunch. Wouters, a polite seaman who respected the chain of command, asked Captain Martin about Hurricane Iris and the plan to protect the *Wave Dancer*. Martin told Wouters that he had been in contact with the home office and that in their last conversation they told him Iris was moving in a west-northwest direction, heading toward the Yucatan. It would make landfall well north of their position.

Captain Martin respected Wouters, his knowledge of the sea as well as of the live-aboard industry. And Martin liked him. Wouters was easy-going, they were close to the same age, and they shared many of the same interests. Being together for a week at sea with few distractions had a tendency to either bring people close together or move them further apart. Martin felt he and Wouters were close.

"Some of the crew members are worried," Wouters said.

In a pleasant but clearly dismissive manner Martin said, "It is my intention to stay at Lighthouse Reef and give the divers what they came to

Belize for. They paid a lot of money to come here, and I intend to make sure they get their money's worth."

Wouters raised the points he had discussed with Stanley, but Martin made it clear that the issue was settled. Torn between his loyalty to his superior and the emotional plea of his crew, Wouters left the wheelhouse confused, knowing that Stanley and the others would not appreciate the captain's message.

After lunch the guests scattered in various directions. It was a typical subtropic day. The sun shot piercing rays down from the cloudless sky, and the temperature nudged into the low nineties. Everyone left the exposed area of the sky deck, knowing they would be forced to miss some dives if they got a bad sunburn. They sought shade wherever they could find it, many of them in the air-conditioned salon or in their cabins.

Cindy Pike and Jimmy Topping found two vacant lounge chairs in the shaded area of the sky deck and caught up on family news. Topping, who lived in Plymouth, North Carolina, was Cindy's cousin. Because of the distance between them, they did not see each other often. The week together gave them time to renew their family bond and talk about their favorite subject, their children. Three clangs of the bell interrupted their conversation, and they headed to the dive deck for Stanley's briefing on the next site, Front Porch.

Standing in front of his well-prepared, reef-simulated dive-briefing board, Stanley said, "Some dive sites are named for their interesting backgrounds. This morning you dove at Black Beauty, named for its black coral. Front Porch gets its name from a pleasant encounter with a local Lighthouse Reef resident. If you look off to the right you'll see a little house on the beach with a porch on the front of it."

The group turned in unison to see.

"Several years ago a dive boat operator was looking for new sites along this reef," he told them. "An old man sitting on that front porch waved at him, got his attention, and told him about this place. He said he and his friends fished at this spot and always had good luck, so there must be something under the water that attracted all the fish. Well, the dive boat operator dropped his anchor, dove in, and liked what he saw so much he named it to honor the old man. Good story, eh?"

"Charming," Lisa said, and the others agreed, turning back to face the briefing board. Stanley told them that the depth of the water at the base of the mooring line was forty feet. A mild current moved from north to south, and the reef began twenty to thirty feet east of the mooring line.

"As you can see on my board," he said, "The Wall is another hundred to 150 feet beyond that. You'll find this a very interesting site with all of the usual reef fish, eels, grouper, schooling fish, you name it. I have designated a couple of swim-throughs along The Wall. If you want to see sharks, this is your spot. There are almost always a few reef sharks cruising along The Wall at about eighty to a hundred feet. They're shy and cannot be approached, but you can watch them from a distance. I've seen a hammerhead and a few bull sharks here too. You can probably find some nurse sharks resting under a ledge along the base of the reef. Is everybody comfortable diving with sharks?"

"Oh, yeah," a few of them responded. Many members of the RDC had been to Cozamel, Turks and Caicos, and the Bahamas, where reef sharks abound, but their most frequent encounters occurred on their trips to the Outer Banks at Cape Hatteras, North Carolina. A few times each year a group chartered *Captain John's Bayou Runner*, a forty-two-foot Coast Guard-certified vessel and for two days enjoyed some of the best Atlantic coast wreck diving available.

There they find German U-boats, modern vessels, and historic sites. The sunken vessels serve as artificial reefs where beautiful corals, sponges, and anemones flourish. They also are home to other invertebrates and fish. The warm water of the area, along with the many nooks and crannies in the sunken vessels, provide breeding grounds and hiding places for all sizes and varieties of fish—a smorgasbord that attracts the large predators.

Stanley continued, "I see you're all smiling, so you must be comfortable with sharks, but I am obligated to tell you not to bother, touch, pull the tail, or otherwise mess with the nurse sharks you will encounter. Unlike most other sharks, they lie immobile on the bottom as they rest in secluded areas of the reef. There are many stories of stupid divers pulling on the tail of nurse sharks. A couple of years ago a sixteen-year-old kid in Florida found a two-foot nurse shark lying on the bottom. He pulled its tail to see what would happen. Well, he found out. It bit him on the left pectoral muscle and would not release its grip. The kid and the attached shark were pulled onto a boat and taken to the hospital, where they surgically removed the shark. The kid lived, the shark died. People, when nurse sharks bite, they don't let go. So, my message loud and clear is leave the sharks alone!"

He scanned their faces as they nodded in agreement. They were experienced divers and had heard the stories about shark attacks.

"Okay," he said, "the Front Porch is one of my favorite sites. It has everything. Since we'll be here for two afternoon dives and the night dive, I recommend you go to The Wall for the first dive then enjoy the shallow reef and sandy area under the boat for the second dive. That way you'll see different environments and be more familiar with the whole reef area when you do the night dive. Baechtold will be in the water with his video camera again. Stark, Wouters, and I will be in the water too, if you want a guide. Like I said before, for the rest of the week there will be no briefing for the second dive at a site. You're expected to monitor your own surface intervals and can dive or sit out at your discretion. That's it. The pool is open!"

The divers scrambled to their lockers. Two by two they moved to the dive platform and, after getting the once-over by Stark, who made sure the air was turned on, they took a giant stride, gave the OK sign, and slowly began to sink to the bottom of the mooring line. The divers who used cameras entered last, as usual. Cox and Garrison, along with Prillaman, Webb, and DeBarger, had planned to meet at the bottom, drift over to a nice spot where they could kneel in the sand, simultaneously take out their regulators, and videotape a performance of an underwater serenade to the ladies.

While they videotaped an underwater version of "I'm Forever Blowing Bubbles," Prillaman, undetected, slipped a fuzzy lime-green disc into Webb's BC pocket. Prillaman had brought a tennis ball with him on the dive, and as he submerged the increased atmospheric pressure on the ball decreased the size of its molecules, flattening it into a disc. When Webb ascended, the ball would pop back to its original shape creating an instant bulge in his BC. The surprise attack would remind Webb not to let his defenses down.

After finishing their performance, the men returned to the mooring line to reclaim their buddies and begin the dive. Jim and Kim Garrison headed directly for The Wall. They planned to get to deep water as soon as possible, watch where the majority of divers went, and go the opposite way. They knew from years of experience that divers with their regulators, fins, and equipment make a lot of underwater noise, barely audible to them, but as loud as a teen garage band to the marine life. After a few minutes of cruising at ninety feet, their decision was rewarded by the sight of a spotted eagle ray cruising in their direction about thirty feet below. Estimating the ray's wingspan at more than six feet, Garrison thought he'd found a perfect star for his trip's highlight film. A pronounced head, numerous white spots against a dark body, and a long whip-like tail made the ray a sight to behold. With the grace of a soaring bird, it moved closer to them. Garrison and Kim knew rays were wary of divers, so they froze in place, their only detectable motion the movement of the panning camera. As the ray swam directly under them, Garrison got some wonderful footage. After it passed, they took a long delayed breath of air, looked at each other, and gave a thumbs-up sign. They moved on, looking for the next opportunity, certain none would top what they had just seen.

Doug and Phyllis Cox also had a plan before they entered the water. They decided to stay on the top of the reef for about ten minutes, taping some of the local inhabitants before going to The Wall and allowing some space between the other divers and themselves. Too many people in one place at the same time created underwater stress that could be sensed by the reef occupants. As they moved around a coral head looking for an interesting subject, Phyllis, who always enjoyed nook-and-cranny searches, looked inside a small coral head and found a juvenile spotted drum. It was the cutest thing, she thought, just like the one in Stanley's slide show, only better. It was about an inch long, white with a black nose, two dominant black bars on its body, and a third from its long dorsal fin to its tail. The dorsal fin flowed an inch above its body and back to its tail, giving it the appearance of a trailing wedding veil. A nocturnal feeder and easy prey, the drum swam during the day in a twelve-inch circular motion, never venturing beyond its safety zone.

After reveling in her find and having her husband videotape it, Phyllis gently moved away from the coral head to find her next subject. Then Cox tapped her on the shoulder and pointed in the direction of The Wall and off they went. A six-to seven-foot black tip reef shark rewarded their patience by swimming casually into view. It was one hundred feet from them and around fifty feet below. Cox inverted and, keeping his camera in front of him, began to swim toward the shark, getting some distant footage of it before, unconcerned, it moved out of sight. As he turned around to look back at Phyllis to give her a "that was cool" look, Cox realized Baechtold was videotaping them. Baechtold zoomed in a little tighter, gave them a thumbs-up, and swam away.

Since leaving the *Wave Dancer* Baechtold had shot a lot of good background footage for this week's group, so he headed back to the boat. At the mooring line, he saw Prillaman, Webb, Cox, and Garrison putting on a show—a contest to see who could blow the best air rings. Prillaman's method involved taking a deep breath of air, removing the regulator from his mouth, using his tongue to create the center hole, and exhaling. The first few attempts did not come out well, but after that his rings floated in tight circles to the top, growing larger until they broke the surface. Baechtold captured the contest with his camera before surfacing.

Back on board the *Wave Dancer*, Cheryl took some light-hearted kidding from Webb about her new boyfriend, Billy, a five-foot barracuda that shadowed her from the time she left the mooring line until she returned fifty minutes later. It watched every move she made during the dive, but always stayed a safe ten feet off her left shoulder. It swam close enough to Cheryl that Baechtold got the two of them together in his video.

"Do you think a long-distance affair can work?" Webb asked Cheryl.

She laughed. "I think we'll have to be just friends," she said.

Prillaman, standing nearby, noted that the snaggle-toothed barracuda had a better smile than her last boyfriend. Cox and Christy added their hearty agreement.

Cheryl walked away in a feigned huff, saying over her shoulder, "I can't imagine Sylvia Earle put up with this kind of abuse." Earle, the acknowledged queen of scuba, was Cheryl's hero. Cheryl admired Earle's accomplishments and had read extensively about her career, from her first dive in 1953 while a marine biology student at Florida State University to her induction in 2000 into the National Women's Hall of Fame. Always living on the edge herself, Cheryl respected Earle's endurance and tenacity.

While the guests and crew aboard the *Wave Dancer* ate their relaxing lunch, the NEMO committee met in Belmopan to discuss the advancing threat of Hurricane Iris. Chief Meteorologist Fuller recommended a cautious approach, placing Belize, from Belize City northward, on a Hurricane Watch. NEMO approved his recommendation, and at 1:00 p.m. Fuller appeared on national television to warn his country of the heightened alert. An hour later the following report from the National Weather Service reflected Belize's changed storm status.

BULLETIN
HURRICANE IRIS INTERMEDIATE ADVISORY NUMBER 12A
NATIONAL WEATHER SERVICE, MIAMI, FL
2 P.M. EDT, SUN OCT 07 2001

...Iris moving away from Jamaica...
NOAA plane scheduled to check the hurricane soon...
A hurricane warning remains in effect for the east coast of Yucatan from Cabo Catoche southward.

At 2 p.m. edt...1800 utc... the government of Belize has issued a hurricane watch for Belize from Belize City northward.

At 2 p.m. edt...1800z the center of Hurricane Iris was located near latitude 17.5 north...longitude 78.9 west or about 205 miles...330 km...southeast of Grand Cayman.

Iris is moving toward the east near 19 mph...31 km/hr...and this motion is expected to continue during the next 24 hours. On this path...Iris will be heading toward the Yucatan peninsula.

Maximum sustained winds remain near 85 mph...140 km/hr... in a small area just north of the center...with higher gusts. Satellite images suggest that Iris may be strengthening and a NOAA plane will check the intensity this afternoon.

Hurricane force winds extend outward up to 25 miles... 35 km...from the center...and tropical storm force winds extend outward up to 115 miles...185 km.

Estimated minimum central pressure is 989 mb...29.21 inches. Coastal storm surge flooding of 4 to 5 feet above normal tide levels...along with dangerous battering waves... is expected to affect Jamaica today.

Rainfall totals of 3 to 5 inches...with higher amounts over the mountainous areas...are expected over Jamaica. These rains could cause flash floods and mud slides.

Repeating the 2 p.m. edt position...17.5 n...78.9 w. Movement

TOWARD...WEST NEAR 19 MPH. MAXIMUM SUSTAINED WINDS...85 MPH.
MINIMUM CENTRAL PRESSURE...989 MB.

THE NEXT ADVISORY WILL BE ISSUED BY THE
NATIONAL HURRICANE CENTER AT 5 P.M. EDT.

FORECASTER AVILA

After reviewing the report, Fuller and Hulse met to discuss the storm and its path. They agreed that Iris had shown no signs of growing. The fact that its winds only extended outward twenty-five miles from the eye of the storm made it small compared to Mitch and Keith. Their main concern was the potential increase in its intensity and a change in direction. The last two reports indicated that Iris was going to increase in intensity, but by how much they didn't know. The 5:00 a.m. report stated that the storm had wobbled a little south, but since that time it was moving directly west. If it remained on the westward track it would hit northern Belize, but if it drifted south it could hit Belize City, thus becoming more of a danger to the country's population. They both agreed that Iris was moving fast and when it hit land, wherever that might be, it would probably do major damage in a short amount of time and then move on.

Cheryl and Webb headed to the air-conditioned salon to hear Wouters lecture on coral reefs. Bill and Sheila Kelley joined them, along with Jimmy Topping and Ray Mars. The other divers, although environmentally conscious, had their own agendas for the afternoon, which in most cases meant some quiet rest and relaxation.

Wouters explained how coral reefs were formed, and he outlined steps they could take as divers to protect the reefs. Covering less than 1 percent of the earth's surface, coral reefs and their associated mangroves, sea grass, and other habitats are the most biologically diverse marine ecosystems.

"Nearly 80 percent of the world's reef systems have been damaged and are in decline, compared to 90 percent of the reefs in the United States," he said. "Pollution and destructive fishing practices damage the delicate corals. Nutrients in runoff from agricultural areas cause large algae blooms, which smother coral. Scientists find heavy damage from more than a dozen coral diseases. It takes hundreds of years for coral to grow just a few feet but only minutes to be destroyed."

He handed out a pamphlet from the National Oceanic and Atmospheric Administration [NOAA] that listed twenty-five things people can do to help, from supporting reef-friendly businesses to adding vocal support for the reefs. He mentioned a company in Decatur, Georgia, called Eternal Reefs that manufactured concrete cast artificial reefs that combined a cremation urn, ash scattering, and burial at sea into one meaningful and permanent tribute to the environment. "Think about it," he said. "Your own reef. Pretty cool, eh?"

During the reef lecture, Lisa and Mary Lou sat on the twin beds in their cabin and talked about Lisa's future. After the engagement Lisa wondered if her job at the toy store would keep her from being with Mike after the marriage. Over the past three months, she and Mary Lou discussed the nursing profession and the mobility it offered. Mary Lou assured her that a degree in nursing would allow her to move anywhere the Navy assigned Mike. With Mary Lou's support, Lisa investigated nursing school, learning she could get a degree in two years. She applied to a school but still needed to decide if a particular area of nursing would suit her well, one in which she could make a difference. As they sat in the cabin, Mary Lou listened to Lisa's ideas, finally suggesting an area relating to children.

"Children," Lisa said, as if trying out the idea by saying the word.

"You would be great," Mary Lou told her. "You are so loving, so compassionate. I think it would be a great fit for you."

"I don't know," Lisa said, though the tone of her voice clearly told Mary Lou that her young friend found the idea very appealing. Lisa flopped back on her bed and looked at the ceiling. "Children," she said again.

"Think about it," Mary Lou said. "You've got plenty of time."

As Lisa and Mary Lou discussed career objectives, Prillaman, DeBarger, Mars, and Patterson hung out in the shade of the sky deck, talking about their day of diving. Stark interrupted to tell them that the boutique was open and anyone who wanted to buy *Wave Dancer* T- and polo shirts, hats, or shorts could so for the next hour. In unison, they got up and followed Stark down the stairs to a corner of the salon, where the souvenir clothing had been laid out. Most of the other guests had already rummaged through and purchased the attire. Prillaman playfully bumped into Kim Garrison as she held up a pair of shorts for Jim's approval. After a mock apology he tried on and purchased a new baseball style cap, DeBarger a navy blue polo, while Mars and Patterson each got a T-shirt. Eventually, everybody bought something with the *Wave Dancer* or "Eat, Sleep and Dive" logo on it.

As the crew and guests of the *Wave Dancer* enjoyed a calm, sunny afternoon on the water, Jan Neel, the assistant general manager of the Turtle Inn, and her family unloaded the last of their belongings into their new home.

In early 2000, Francis Ford Coppola purchased the Turtle Inn, his second resort in Belize, in the small seaside community of Placencia. After the purchase, Coppola quickly renovated and refurbished it in a manner similar to his other resort, the highly acclaimed Blancaneaux Lodge in western Belize. Made Wijaya, a recognized authority on tropical gardens and Southeast Asian architecture, teamed with Coppola to upgrade the resort, which reopened in December 2000. To ensure the success of his venture, Coppola hired Neel. She and her family moved from the U.S. to the tropics, looking forward to the new opportunity, a myriad of adventures, and a laid-back lifestyle.

The Neels temporarily rented a house in downtown Placencia while they built a home. They knew the hurricane history of the area, so they had contacted a company in Oregon that designed, packaged, and sent them a home that would sit thirteen feet above land and could withstand a category five hurricane. Jan had pushed her inefficient contractor to finish the home and finally told him they were moving in come hell or high water on Sunday, October 7. While unloading the last of her personal belongings, she heard the radio reports that Hurricane Iris was staying on its projected path toward northern Belize. Her family would be safe in a new hurricane-proof home.

As Eloise delivered nachos and salsa to the sky deck, she noticed that very few of her guests sunned themselves on the deck or relaxed in the shade of the blue canopy. Even fewer lounged in the air-conditioned salon. She had seen this pattern of first-day afternoon inactivity on almost every dive trip. The guests arrived travel weary, slept moderately well the first night, woke up the next morning with energy and enthusiasm, enjoyed both morning dives and the first afternoon dive, then crashed. They took an afternoon siesta during the hottest part of the day in their air-conditioned cabins and then awoke refreshed for the first night dive.

With half of her guests napping, she could freeze more water into ice chips and not have to apologize for being unable to chill the drinks. She worried about the poor maintenance on the *Wave Dancer*. It seemed as though something always broke down, and she had said so directly to Peter Hughes. Among other things, neither of the two commercial ice machines had worked for several weeks. She and her staff had to make ice on a tray then chip it with an ice pick, and they had to give up valuable freezer space needed for the week's provisions. But her complaints seemed to fall on deaf ears. Although she did not know who was responsible for the poor maintenance, she saw it as another strike against Captain Martin.

Though not a member of the crew, Webb had offered to fix the ice machines, but Captain Martin told him the parts, ordered weeks earlier, had not arrived from the home office. Webb told Captain Martin that he and his friends had suffered through a similar situation on another Peter Hughes boat in the Turks and Caicos the previous year.

"At least one of the two commercial icemakers on the *Sea Dancer* worked," Webb said. "I told Captain Stezaker I could fix his icemaker, but he told me the same thing. Parts hadn't arrived. This sounds like a company issue to me."

After the icemaker conversation with the captain, Webb met Prillaman and DeBarger in the lounge to discuss the issue, along with other rumblings he'd heard about maintenance on the *Wave Dancer*. He asked Prillaman and DeBarger what they thought of the boat and its staff. DeBarger said he noticed a general uneasiness in some of the crew. They seemed to gather in small groups at times, but other than that, nothing. Prillaman said he hadn't noticed anything but would ask the RDC members aboard the *Belize Aggressor* about their boat and its crew when they got together. Webb brought up his concerns about the boat. As a group, they began to wonder what issues were hidden behind the polished veneer of the Peter Hughes Company.

Christy and Cheryl asked Stark for assistance in locating interesting critters in the shallow areas of the reef on their next dive. They enjoyed their first dive with him but had ventured out by themselves on the next two dives. On those dives they focused on The Wall, so they now wanted to do some nook-and-cranny searching. Unlike the wimps who had to take a nap before the night dive, Christy and Cheryl were not about to pass up a dive on such a clear sunny day. They planned not to miss a single dive all week.

They realized, however, they must not overdo it. If they pressed the multiple dive table limits, they risked getting the bends, and that would ruin their week in this diver's paradise. Like their RDC companions, they had joined DAN [Divers Alert Network] for its special insurance that covered expenses should a diver get the bends and have to be transported to a recompression chamber. Although the crew of the *Wave Dancer* was trained in first aid and accident management, they could not help anyone who got decompression sickness. If a decompression accident occurred, a diver would be taken to the recompression chamber at Ambergris Caye. If the chamber was unavailable or the diver needed more comprehensive treatment, the U.S. Coast Guard or a private jet would airlift the victim to

Miami. The recompression treatment at Ambergris Caye or Miami could cost several thousand dollars, so joining DAN for twenty-nine dollars annually was a bargain.

Christy, Cheryl, and Stark developed their plan, got into their gear, took a giant stride off the platform, and submerged to the reef forty feet below. They had agreed to go east from the mooring to the shallow reef and look around the coral heads for interesting fish and critters. Then, depending on the current, they would move north for ten to fifteen minutes, west and then south for about the same amount of time, covering the area in a box-like pattern. This plan gave them a lot of coral and sand variety and maximum exposure to underwater inhabitants.

As they floated over a coral head, Stark pointed to a sergeant major, a small silvery fish with five black vertical stripes on its body, swimming in a circular motion over some pink-like substance in a shallow crevasse. As Stark approached he was charged by the diminutive fish, which obviously was protecting its eggs from hungry predators. Cheryl and Christy enjoyed the David and Goliath confrontation. Moving away from the sergeant major, Stark scanned the area in front of him and spotted something on a waving fan. He moved toward it and pointed to a small snail-like animal clinging to the face of the fan. The flamingo tongue looked like it had little orange spots all over, but when Stark lightly touched the outer shell, its exterior mantel retracted, exposing a lustrous reddish and cream-colored shell. He then pointed to a two-and-a-half foot rainbow parrotfish, which was scraping algae and coral polyps off the reef with its powerful jaws, taking large amounts of coral along with it. As it swam away, the fish secreted clouds of chalky residue, thus creating sand, which would end up enhancing the area's beaches.

They moved to the sandy area of the reef and saw a field of pencil-thin garden eels swaying in the current, their dark brown color in stark contrast to the white sand. As the divers approached, the eels retreated into their individual cavities. When the divers passed, the eels reemerged in unison to continue catching morsels of food as it floated by.

As they ventured farther into the seemingly barren sandy area, they saw Byron Johnston taking a photo of Shirley, as she appeared to be pointing to something in the sand. As the Johnstons swam off to look for their next subject, Stark motioned for Christy and Cheryl to drop down to where Byron and Shirley had been. With his knees in the sand he put out his finger, just as Shirley had done. Barely visible from more than ten feet away they saw a transparent corkscrew anemone sheltered by two small sediment-covered rocks along with three Pederson cleaner shrimp and an arrow crab. Stark coaxed one of the inch-long Pederson shrimp onto his fingertip. As Stark held out a steady hand, the shrimp jumped from the shelter of the rock and anemone to Stark's fingertip and started cleaning around his cuticle. It tickled. Christy and Cheryl put their fingertips close to the anemone and in a few seconds they, too, had a Pederson shrimp cleaning their cuticles.

When they finished the dive, they ascended together. As they climbed the dive platform steps, Cheryl, holding her fins in one hand and taking off her mask with the other, turned to Stark and thanked him for guiding them on a wonderful dive.

"That was great," she said. "Just great."

Christy agreed. "We wouldn't have seen half that stuff on our own."

Stark bowed his head slightly to acknowledge their gratitude. "My pleasure," he said. "There is much more to see. You'll never forget this week of diving. I'll make sure of that."

At the National Meteorological Center in Belize Chief Meteorologist Fuller prepared to receive the 5:00 p.m. report from the NWS. He and Justin Hulse traded theories about the strength and movement of Hurricane Iris and wanted to test their observations. They both felt the storm was beginning to be influenced by warmer temperatures and should begin strengthening. The wind strength on the north side of the storm would begin pushing it south.

BULLETIN
HURRICANE IRIS ADVISORY NUMBER 13

NATIONAL WEATHER SERVICE, MIAMI, FL
5 P.M. EDT, SUN OCT 07 2001

...IRIS IS MOVING DUE WEST... HAS NOT STRENGTHENED...

A HURRICANE WATCH IS IN EFFECT FOR THE EAST COAST OF YUCATAN FROM CABO CATOCHE SOUTHWARD AND FOR BELIZE FROM BELIZE CITY NORTHWARD. THE HURRICANE WATCH MAY BE UPGRADED TO HURRICANE WARNING TONIGHT.

AT 5 P.M. EDT...2100 UTC...THE GOVERNMENT OF HONDURAS HAS ISSUED A TROPICAL STORM WARNING AND A HURRICANE WATCH FOR THE NORTH COAST OF HONDURAS AND THE ADJACENT ISLANDS FROM LIMON WESTWARD.

AT 5 P.M...2100 UTC...THE GOVERNMENT OF JAMAICA HAS DISCONTINUED THE HURRICANE WARNINGS FOR JAMAICA.
AT 5 P.M. EDT...2100 Z...THE CENTER OF HURRICANE IRIS WAS LOCATED NEAR LATITUDE 17.3 NORTH...LONGITUDE 79.7 WEST OR ABOUT 170 MILES...275 KM SOUTHEAST OF GRAND CAYMAN.

IRIS IS MOVING TOWARD THE WEST NEAR 18 MPH...30 KM/HR... AND THIS MOTION IS EXPECTED TO CONTINUE DURING THE NEXT 24 HOURS. ON THIS TRACK... THE CORE OF IRIS WILL BE PASSING WELL SOUTH OF GRAND CAYMAN TONIGHT AND HEADING TOWARD YUCATAN OR NORTHERN BELIZE.

DATA FROM A NOAA RECONNAISSANCE PLANE INDICATE THAT IRIS HAS NOT STRENGTHENED AND MAXIMUM SUSTAINED WINDS REMAIN NEAR 85 MPH...140 KM/HR...WITH HIGHER GUSTS. HOWEVER... STRENGTHENING IS FORECAST DURING THE NEXT 24 HOURS.

HURRICANE FORCE WINDS EXTEND OUTWARD UP TO 25 MILES... 35 KM... FROM THE CENTER...AND TROPICAL STORM FORCE WINDS EXTEND OUTWARD TO 115 MILES...185 KM.

LATEST CENTRAL PRESSURE REPORTED BY AN NOAA
RECONNAISSANCE PLANE WAS 991 MB...29.26 INCHES.
REPEATING THE 5 P.M. EDT POSITION...17.3 N...79.7 W.
MOVEMENT TOWARD...WEST NEAR 18 MPH EDT FOLLOWED BY
THE NEXT COMPLETE ADVISORY AT 11 P.M. EDT.

AN INTERMEDIATE ADVISORY WILL BE ISSUED BY THE NATIONAL
HURRICANE CENTER AT 8 P.M. EDT FOLLOWED BY THE NEXT COMPLETE
ADVISORY AT 11 P.M. EDT.

FORECASTER AVILA

HURRICANE IRIS ADVISORY NUMBER 13
NATIONAL WEATHER SERVICE, MIAMI, FL
5 P.M. EDT, SUN OCT 07 2001

IRIS IS A TINY HURRICANE WITH THE STRONGEST WINDS LIMITED TO
A VERY SMALL AREA SURROUNDING A 12 N MI EYE. THE ONLY REPORT
RECEIVED SO FAR FROM THE NOAA PLANE IS NORTHWEST OF WIND
OF 75 KNOTS AT FLIGHT LEVEL... SOUTHWEST OF THE CENTER AND A
MINIMUM PRESSURE OF 990 MB AND THEN 991 MB. FOR A WESTWARD
MOVING HURRICANE...WINDS MUST THEN BE STRONGER ON THE
NORTHEAST SIDE...SO THE INITIAL INTENSITY IS KEPT AT 75 KNOTS...
HOWEVER...THIS MAY BE ON THE HIGH SIDE. DURING THE NEXT 24 TO
36 HOURS...IRIS WILL BE MOVING OVER THE NORTHEASTERN CARIBBEAN
WHERE THE UPPER OCEANIC HEAT CONTENT IS VERY HIGH. THIS...
IN COMBINATION WITH LOW SHEAR... WILL PROVIDE A FAVORABLE
ENVIRONMENT FOR STRENGTHENING. HISTORICALLY... A LARGE NUMBER
OF HURRICANES HAVE BECOME MAJOR HURRICANES IN THIS REGION.

IRIS IS TRAPPED SOUTH OF A STRONG AND PERSISTENT MID LEVEL RIDGE.
THEREFORE A WESTWARD TRACK IS FORECAST. IRIS COULD EVEN MOVE
SOUTH OF DUE WEST AS INDICATED BY SOME OF THE TRACK MODELS.

IRIS COULD REACH EASTERN YUCATAN OR NORTHERN BELIZE AS A MAJOR HURRICANE IN ABOUT 36 HOURS OR LESS. IT SHOULD THEN GRADUALLY WEAKEN INLAND OVER LAND. HOWEVER...BECAUSE THERE IS A CHANCE THAT IRIS MAY MOVE SOUTH OF DUE WEST...MORE THAN ANTICIPATED...A TROPICAL STORM WARNING AND A HURRICANE WATCH IS BEING ISSUED FOR THE NORTH COAST OF HONDURAS.

FORECASTER AVILA

After reviewing the report, Fuller called the weather center in Miami. He had called twice in the past twenty-four hours, and now as the storm began to bear down on his country he wanted to talk with the meteorologists there every couple of hours. The written reports they sent were helpful, but their informal observations might prove invaluable if the hurricane became unpredictable.

Chapter Nine

"I don't know why it is that all of us are so committed to the sea...I think it's because we all come from the sea...And it is an interesting biological fact that all of us have in our veins the exact same percentage of salt in our blood that exists in the ocean. And therefore we have salt in our blood, in our sweat, and in our tears. We are tied to the ocean, and when we go back to the sea—whether it is to sail or to watch it—we are going back from whence we came."

John F. Kennedy

Verbal brinkmanship dominated the pre-dinner conversation in the salon. The divers gave epic accounts of what they had seen and done during their dives, topping each other's stories with just a modicum of diplomacy. Sipping a soft drink, Cheryl listened to the stories. Christy, DeBarger, Prillaman, Webb, and Patterson stood around her as she casually mentioned the three six-foot black-tip reef sharks she had seen. Webb said that he and Mars had seen at least four six-to-eight-foot black-tips and one nurse shark. Patterson, not wanting to get in the conversation, knowing how the game would end, listened as Prillaman cleared his throat.

"I saw at least eight nine-footers and two eight-foot nurse sharks," Prillaman told them. "At one point I surfaced to locate the boat," he added with a twinkle in his eye, "and two big sharks were circling me—one with a knife and the other with a fork."

The men laughed. Cheryl rolled her eyes while Christy shot him a playful glare.

"And now, Glenn, let's return to reality," Christy said.

"What makes you think all these stories have anything to do with reality?" Prillaman asked.

As the stories continued, Eloisa signaled to Stark, who rang the dinner bell. Earlier in the afternoon Eloisa had given each guest two options—either grilled Halibut or New York strip—for the main course of their evening meal and had prepared both magnificently. She was considerate of her guests, good to her staff, and thoughtful in her attention to detail. Now it was time for dinner and her chance to shine once again.

After everyone had finished the main course, Angela and Brenda served pineapple upside-down cake with a maraschino cherry in the center of the fruit ring and whipped cream on top. While everyone savored Eloisa's made-from-scratch specialty, Captain Martin calmly walked into the dining area for his evening update. Almost nonchalantly he said he needed to discuss their diving itinerary, changes in the weekly schedule and, oh yes, Hurricane Iris.

"According to my most recent reports and confirmation with the home office, Hurricane Iris has moved south of its original projected direction," he told the group. "The storm is expected to hit the coast of northern Belize sometime Monday evening, which means it is still staying north of our present position. After the night dive I'm going to move the *Wave Dancer* to a night mooring at Lighthouse Reef. In the morning, during breakfast, I'll take you to the mooring at the Blue Hole, do the dive you all came to Belize for, then go south to a safe harbor at Big Creek to ride out Iris."

The group sat in complete silence. Though some had carried the hurricane in the backs of their minds throughout the day's diving, none had thought it was anything serious. The captain, until now, had not seemed at all worried about it.

"From what I understand, Big Creek has been a safe harbor for boats to ride out storms," Captain Martin said. "I am told this is where the *Wave Dancer* tied up during Hurricanes Mitch and Keith. As I said, I think the storm will stay north of us, but I'm going to give you two options. I can take you now to Belize City, where you can get off the boat, and I'll get you rooms in the St. George Radisson Hotel. The crew and I will make the sixty-mile trip south to Big Creek, ride out the storm, and come back to get you after it's over. Or you can stay on board, go to Big Creek with the boat, and we'll all ride out Iris together. The difference is that with option one I'll have to come back to get you and then go out to Lighthouse Reef, which could cost you a day of diving. If we stay together, you'll miss the Monday afternoon and night dives, but we'll be able to dive Tuesday morning at Glover's Reef. The decision is yours. Discuss your options and tell me what you want to do." He left as quickly as he had entered.

The divers looked at each other for a few moments, trying to take in precisely what the captain had just told them. A few mumbled about the prospect of a hurricane coming in their general direction. Prillaman shrugged his shoulders and looked at DeBarger, who in disbelief looked first at Lisa, then at Mary Lou. Webb, Mars, and the Garrisons had been sitting together through the captain's talk. No one spoke, until Kim told Jim that he needed to use the boat's phone and call home to let their family know what was going on, that they were safe, the hurricane was north of them, and they were going to miss some diving, but not to worry. Webb was concerned, but felt that since the captain had assured them they would be okay whichever decision they made, he supported going to Big Creek.

Mars reminded them that he and his wife had been celebrating their thirtieth wedding anniversary in the Turks and Caicos in 1998 when Hurricane Bonnie came close to the islands. The staff of their hotel had slipped updates under their door several times each day. "When they told us about the storm, I found out where the hurricane shelter was, how safe it was, and how Teresa and I could get there if needed," he said. "It wasn't a fancy hotel, no facilities at all, no running water, nothing. But I figured we'd survive even if we took a direct hit."

He told them that the weather channel had also been on in every restaurant and store with up-to-the-minute reports on Bonnie's path. "The preparedness was phenomenal," he said. "They pulled their smaller boats up on shore and put the larger ones in a sheltered area of the water, kind of a cove, and all were evacuated. The boats still in the water were tied up in elaborate patterns. They all seemed to be moored the same way, so it must have been the correct thing to do. The hotel covered the sliding glass doors in every room with plywood, laying it right by the doors, ready to go."

"Sounds like they knew what they were doing," Webb said.

Jim Garrison agreed. "They'd learned from experience."

"All of this took at least three days," Mars said, "so the warning time was at least that long. Teresa and I watched first hand, walking along the dock where the boats were tied up. It was amazing. Everybody on that island was ready, even the tourists, whether they wanted to be or not. I was ready to evacuate to a shelter, no questions asked, if necessary." He took a gulp of his soft drink and gazed at the plate in front of him, memories of that trip still fresh in his mind.

"So what happened?" Kim Garrison said.

"Bonnie didn't hit there," he shrugged. "The rest of our vacation was fine. But I can imagine the people of Belize are doing the same things right now."

Christy, as trip organizer, knew she had to take charge of the situation. Interrupting the conversations, she announced, "If I heard Captain Martin correctly he said he will take us to Belize City and get us hotel rooms. He and the crew will take the *Wave Dancer* to Big Creek, ride out the hurricane, and come back to get us after its over. With that scenario we'll lose two days of diving. If we stay on the *Wave Dancer* and go to the safe harbor at Big Creek we will only lose one day of diving. Is that the way you all understand the options?"

She asked the group if anyone had a comment or question about the options. A few whispers continued, but no one raised a hand to speak. She then asked for a show of hands for those preferring to go to Belize City and leave the boat. They all looked around the room to see how many hands went up. There were none. She then asked for a show of hands for those in favor of going to the safe harbor at Big Creek. Immediately, everyone in the room raised their hands. All the divers wanted to stay together on the boat and only lose a few dives rather than getting off the boat and losing two days of diving.

After the vote, the group stayed seated and discussed the potential effect of the hurricane on their vacation. They were a positive-thinking group of people who had overcome challenges in their lives. Given Martin's assurances of safety, they felt secure in their decision. They came to Belize to dive, and in spite of Hurricane Iris they wanted to dive as much as possible. As they splintered into smaller groups to talk about the news, Christy asked Prillaman and DeBarger to meet her in the far corner of the salon.

"This is a serious situation," she said in a low voice, "and I want to be sure everyone is comfortable with the decision."

"Seems like everyone had a chance to say how they felt," Prillaman said.

Christy nodded. "But I want to be sure each person voted the way they really felt and that they weren't just going along with the group."

Prillaman and DeBarger agreed and asked what she wanted to do.

"I want to get each person or couple alone and ask them if their vote was their final decision," she said. "They'll be more candid one-on-one, don't you think?"

"Yeah, I do," Prillaman said.

DeBarger added, "Good plan."

Christy left to begin her survey. The first person she talked with, Jimmy Topping, told her he was comfortable with his decision as were Bill and Sheila Kelley, her next contacts. No one changed their vote or offered further comments, with the exception of Ray Mars. He agreed to continue to Big Creek, but once there he felt they should get off the boat and find a hurricane shelter. When she completed her survey she told Prillaman and DeBarger that everyone stood by their original decision.

After the vote, Baechtold and Stanley entered the meeting area to announce the slide show would begin in fifteen minutes. Although there was little doubt that everyone in the audience was intensely aware of the choice they'd just made, most, if not all, felt some comfort in the fact that they had acted as a group. Now that the decision was final, they would try to regain the excitement they'd felt about the night dive. With luck, the slide show would help them get back in the mood.

Stanley said that he and Baechtold had reviewed the developed slides and would show four from each group of submissions. As Baechtold dimmed the lights, Stanley flipped on the projector to present the first four slides chosen for the competition—from Bill and Sheila Kelley. The first was a shot of a green moray eel with its head barely sticking out of the coral. Around the eel's mouth two cleaner shrimp picked at leftover morsels from an earlier meal. It was a good clear picture of the critter with a nice colorful coral background. As Stanley clicked to the next slide, he noticed that the divers were surprisingly quiet and respectful, as if replaying the earlier dives in their minds.

They worked their way through the Kelley slides then came to Byron and Shirley Johnston's contributions. From viewer reaction, the best of the four focused on a Pederson shrimp cleaning the cuticle of one of Shirley's fingernails. The shot of the small transparent shrimp on the bright red fingernail made a very interesting contrast in size and color. Charlie and Cindy Pike's collection provided the final four slides. The first showed a spotted scorpion fish against a coral background. The fish's camouflaged body was almost indistinguishable against the background of the reef, but Cindy nudged the tail, causing its pink and black pectoral fins to flare out just long enough for Charlie to click the shutter. Stanley and Baechtold felt this one would be hard to beat. The Pike's next three slides were of a spotted eagle ray, a barracuda, and a lobster. By the end of the show, the group's mood had brightened considerably.

Despite what they had heard about the approach of the storm, it still seemed far away as they gathered on the dive deck for the briefing before the night dive. The sun had set, and the lights of the *Wave Dancer* glowed against the dark blue ocean. Above them, the moonlit, star-filled sky cast a glow of its own.

Stanley began his briefing by telling them it was an excellent night for a dive because there was no wind, the sky was clear, and the full moon would act as an extra beacon for them. "But," he said, "I don't want you to do what I did. A few years ago I was doing a night dive off a boat about a third the size of the *Wave Dancer*. It was well lit and had a flood light on the back of its dive deck for orientation purposes, much like ours. I started the dive at about thirty feet deep and was covering the reef, always keeping the floodlight over my shoulder. After about thirty minutes I'd covered quite a bit of the reef but hadn't checked my position in relation to the boat. I looked and sure enough there was the bright beacon slightly behind me over my right shoulder. I continued my dive for another ten minutes, still checking my bearings with the beacon. Then I got suspicious because even though I'd moved around a lot the beacon was still over my shoulder. I did a slow ascent to see where I was, and when I surfaced I saw the boat a hundred and fifty yards away in the opposite direction of where I thought it should be. The full moon was so bright it came through the water like the boat's beacon, and I'd been using it as my navigational device. The moral of my story is make sure you're using the right light as your navigational device. If you have an orientation problem you can always do a slow ascension."

"Okay, you're going to like this site," he continued. "You'll probably see octopus, turtles, squirrelfish, maybe a nurse shark, and many sleeping fish. You'll see parrotfish that form a clear sack around them at night to shield off predators. And there'll be small group of ten-to-twelve-inch squid attracted by the lights of the boat. A note about the squid—they're a favorite food for tarpon, so don't leave your light on them too long or they'll be an easy meal.

The tarpon are attracted by the lights too, and as we speak they're gathering off of the dive deck looking for a quick meal. Go back and watch them circle on top of the water. Right now there are about twenty of them back there. With their red little eyes and silvery bodies they're a show in themselves."

Baechtold arrived with his video camera running just as Stanley said, "As for the dive itself, do a giant stride to enter the water the way you did all day. As you descend, turn on your lights, wait for your buddy to join you, then follow your dive plan. The *Wave Dancer* has underwater floodlights, so you'll always know where the boat is as long as you don't get too far away from us. Before entering the water, check with your dive buddy to make sure you both understand your signals. One last safety issue—as you prepare to emerge to about the last ten feet look around and above you for jellyfish or fire worms. If you see one, just take your regulator out of your mouth and shoot a blast of air in their direction. That should move them out of your way and keep you from getting stung. The dive masters will be available to lead you if you want. Otherwise we'll watch you from the dive deck. That's all I have. Have a fun and safe dive. The pool is open."

Baechtold moved through the group as they put on their gear. Webb put on his BC and weight belt over his T-shirt and shorts. Lisa looked at him, put her arms around herself and in a cold shivering motion said, "Don't you ever get cold?" Cheryl, brushing back her hair before putting on her mask, smiled at Baechtold and gave him a thumbs-up. Mary Lou looked into the camera while putting on her wet suit and in a nonchalant manner said, "You know there's a hurricane coming." At this moment, however, all she cared about was this dive. Any concern about Hurricane Iris would wait until later.

Although Prillaman loved diving, he did not like night dives, feeling that he couldn't see as well, and so he didn't do them anymore. He went to the dive deck only to support his buddies. He gave Baechtold's camera a big "hi" when it traversed in his direction but stayed on board while, DeBarger, teamed with Webb. Though the night was almost perfect for a dive, the fear of the advancing hurricane began to affect many of the passengers.

---

*   *   *

After the divers entered the water, Stanley begged Wouters to ask Captain Martin about getting the passengers and crew off the *Wave Dancer*. Feeling that he'd pushed the limit with his boss already, Wouters suggested they confront the captain together. Stanley told Wouters that he would do the talking but wanted Wouters to back him up. In the wheelhouse Captain Martin monitored his weather fax machine. When he saw the crewmen coming, he stiffened his back. He bristled with anger as Stanley asked him again to reconsider his position regarding the disposition of the passengers and crew. Despite Martin's chilly reception, Stanley kept talking, reminding Martin that it was always better to be safe than sorry and asking him how he thought a decision about their safety could be made by the home office in Florida when they were in Belize.

Captain Martin's jaw tightened and his neck turned red as he pointed his finger at Stanley and accused both men of second-guessing his decisions and trying to undermine his authority. He told them he had been in contact with Ryan Vernon, who said the hotels in Belize City were being evacuated. Therefore, as he saw it, there was no place to off-load the passengers and crew anyway. He intended to finish the night dive, go into a lagoon at Lighthouse Reef, tie up for the night, and dive the Blue Hole in the morning before going to Big Creek. That was his decision, the main office agreed with him, so "case closed!" Stanley, not giving up yet, insisted that Belize would provide transportation and hurricane shelters for everyone. Captain Martin sharply dismissed them both.

Stanley knew there was nothing he could do. He was beginning to understand how the crew and passengers aboard the *Reef Explorer* must have felt in October 1997 when they physically took over their ship. Stanley had read that Troy Dallman, the skipper of a live-aboard diving vessel out of Port Douglas, Queensland, Australia, had been restrained by crew and passengers during what they referred to as a nightmare trip. After the incident, one of the passengers said, "It was the three-thousand-dollar cruise from hell. The boat left the port seven hours late. The dinghy leaked, the hoist on board broke, and the seals on the winch exploded. The batteries failed, shutting down the navigation system, running lights, toilets, and cabin lights. Added to that, the gas stove broke down, forcing everyone to eat cold food for a week."

After one of the final dives, the passengers returned to the *Reef Explorer* to discover the skipper had tried to abandon them near the Great Barrier Reef in the Coral Sea, almost 250 miles from Thursday Island. Dallman is said to have ordered the crew to cut the anchor chain with a hacksaw and then held a flare gun to the head of Federico Farin, one of the passengers from New York City. The boat finally crashed into a reef. The crew and passengers overpowered Dallman, tied him up hand and foot, and secured him in a cabin. They then used a hand-held compass and a flashlight to safely guide themselves to Thursday Island, where Dallman was put under hospital care.

Stanley felt that while Captain Martin might not be as crazy as the skipper of the *Reef Explorer*, he was nonetheless a bad skipper—belligerent, stubborn, and ready to put his passengers, crew, and boat in harm's way.

DeBarger and Webb climbed from the water giving each other high fives. Just as Stanley had said, with the moon so bright their underwater playground was absolutely stunning. Not only did the coral reef shine with beautiful colors as their flashlights scanned its surface, but the sea life was far different from what they'd seen during the day. As DeBarger and Webb submerged and reemerged, they enjoyed the magnificent feeding frenzy put on by the glistening tarpon under the lights of the dive deck. At least twenty large predators skimmed back and forth on the surface waiting for any edible morsel to leave the safety of the coral darkness. When a fish or squid did surface, the tarpon raced to it, creating quite a stir in the water.

DeBarger and Webb agreed that this was their best night dive ever. They encountered an octopus moving one appendage at a time across the coral surface in about forty feet of water. For ten minutes, they kept their lights from shining directly on it so it wouldn't jet away from them. It finally sensed their presence, changed colors to show its irritation, and oozed its jelly-like body into a small crevasse. They moved on, scanning the surface of the reef, crisscrossing their beams in hopes of locating another nocturnal sea creature.

They saw a number of butterfly fish sleeping in their nighttime territory as well as parrot fish nestled in their protective sacks. As daylight came back to the ocean, they would devour their shield and recycle it for the next night. The divers also saw an abundance of squirrelfish, well-equipped with their big eyes for nocturnal feeding. At a depth of forty feet, they started to head back to the boat when they came to a ten-foot drop in the reef. At the floor of the drop they noticed some movement and as they focused their lights on the subject they discovered two lobsters foraging the surface for their evening meal. They were about ten feet above the lobsters, observing their actions, when a six-foot nurse shark cruised between them and the lobsters, eyed its quarry, made a quick turnaround, and swiftly snatched one in its vice-like mouth. While the nurse shark does not have razor-sharp teeth, it has powerful jaws, which can make quick work of a lobster's shell. DeBarger and Webb realized they had witnessed a once-in-a-lifetime event and could not wait to tell their friends.

Lisa and Mary Lou had intended to do the dive with DeBarger and Webb but ventured off on their own instead. The water was warm and clear, and the full moon lit the glistening surface like a Tiffany jewelry display. They both thought that even if they didn't see anything worth bragging about just being in the water on such a beautiful night was a story in itself. As they moved away from the lights of the other divers and the *Wave Dancer*, Lisa, twenty feet behind Mary Lou, covered her beam with her hand, then shut off the flashlight. She looked back toward the boat and paused for a moment in the darkness, watching the other singular beams traversing in the distance, like a search group looking for a lost victim. It was so dark at fifty feet beneath the surface she could not see her hand in front of her face. It felt eerie to be alone in such a dark place. She thought that this is how it must feel to be lost in a forest at night with no light to find a path or voice to scream for help, wondering what is lurking out there. Will it devour or save me? Which will come first, assistance or disaster? Then, with a flip of the switch, she was back to reality.

Lisa and Mary Lou stayed at about forty feet of depth, enjoying the variety of reds and oranges reflected from the reef exposed by the beams of their flashlights. As Stanley had said, the nighttime colors of the reef were decidedly different from the blues, greens, and blacks prevalent during the day. However, he hadn't told them that their beams would attract large numbers of harmless but pesky worms and small indescribable creatures. At times it was difficult to focus on the intricacies of the reef for all of the confusion created in their beams by the squiggly, squirmy creatures. A couple of times Lisa shut off her flashlight just to see if they would leave, but as soon as she relit the beam they came back as annoying as ever. Mary Lou, in her search for the exotic, discovered a giant basket star leaning into the current with arms spread to create a net, catching and feeding on passing plankton.

It was fun to watch the protracted net curl one of its arms around its prey and the fine spines and tube feet work together to transfer the captured food to its mouth. The feeding motions of the giant basket star attracted Lisa, and she slowly moved her beam close to its extended arms and watched as the squiggly worm population declined. As they made a ninety-degree turn to complete the last leg of their route Lisa spotted a large hawksbill turtle off to her left and slightly behind her. She tugged on Mary Lou's fin to get her attention, and they both watched as the coffee-table-sized turtle, less than thirty feet away, swam into their beams then made a forty-five-degree turn and moved parallel to their position. A five-foot nurse shark followed the turtle, mimicking every twist, turn, and undulating motion. Lisa found the scene amusing. Like a dog chasing a car, the nurse shark would not know what to do with the turtle if he did catch it. After slowly covering the short distance back to the boat, Lisa and Mary Lou emerged among the tarpon. Although the water temperature was still eighty degrees,

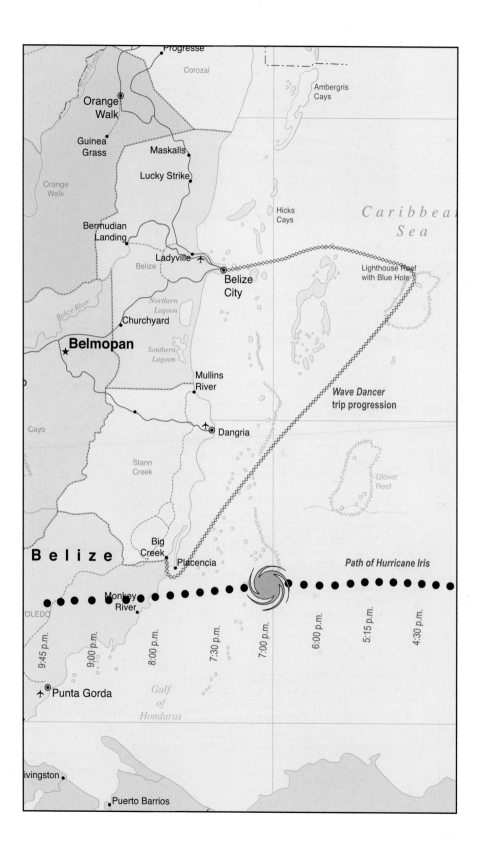

Corozal

Progresse

Ambergris
Cays

Orange
Walk

Guinea
Grass

Maskalls

Orange
Walk

Lucky Strike

*Caribbean
Sea*

Hicks
Cays

Bermudian
Landing

Belize

Ladyville

Belize
City

Lighthouse Reef
with Blue Hole

*Northern
Lagoon*

Churchyard

Belmopan

*Southern
Lagoon*

Mullins
River

Wave Dancer
trip progression

Dangria

Cayo

*Stann
Creek*

*Glover
Reef*

B e l i z e

Big
Creek

Placencia

Path of Hurricane Iris

Monkey
River

OLEDO

9:45 p.m.

9:00 p.m.

8:00 p.m.

7:30 p.m.

7:00 p.m.

6:00 p.m.

5:15 p.m.

4:30 p.m.

Punta Gorda

*Gulf
of
Honduras*

ivingston

Puerto Barrios

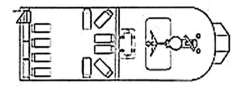

Sky Deck

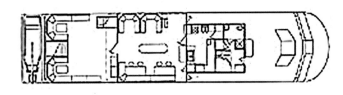

Lido Deck

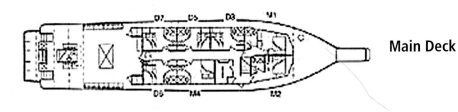

Main Deck

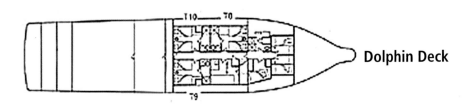

Dolphin Deck

Layout of the *Wave Dancer*'s decks

A view from the skydeck as the *Wave Dancer* cruises to the dock at Big Creek. Doug Cox stands in profile at right. Phyllis stands by the rail at the left. In the distance, the banana warehouse stands far left.

Passengers stand at the rails as the *Wave Dancer* cruises up the channel to the Big Creek dock.

Phyllis Cox

Doug Cox

Dave DeBarger

Jim and Kim Garrison

Mary Lou Hayden

Byron Johnston

Shirley Johnston

Bill and Sheila Kelley

Cheryl Lightbound

Christy McNiel

Ray Mars

Rick Patterson

Charlie and Cindy Pike

Lisa Powell

Glenn Prillaman

Jimmy Topping

Buddy Webb

Doug Cox (left) and Glenn Prillaman smile with their Dr. Bukk teeth.

Dave Mowrer

Chief Meteorologist
Carlos Fuller

Aaron Stark ties the *Wave Dancer* to the dock at Big Creek. On the sky deck Bill Kelley leans at the railing (facing the dock) while Byron Johnson and Kim Garrison look at the camera. On the middle deck, Jim Garrison leans at the railing (facing the dock) while Doug Cox faces the camera. On the lower deck, Chico (in dark shirt) helps tie the boat, while Glenn Prillaman (wearing baseball hat) and Cheryl Lightbound watch.

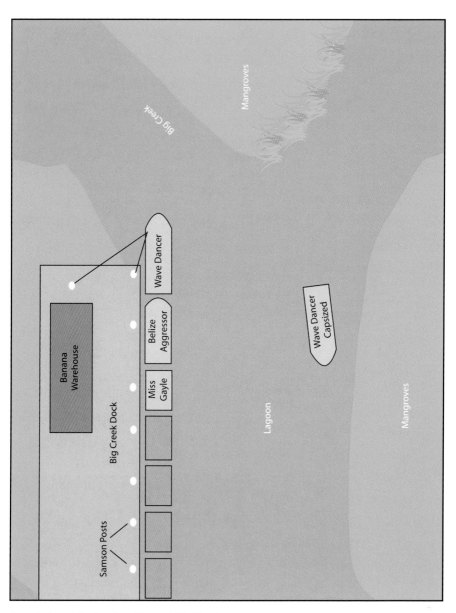

A rendering of the boat positions at Big Creek.

The *Wave Dancer* as it looked the day after Hurricane Iris.

A view of the capsized *Wave Dancer* from the deck of the *Aggressor*.

An aerial view of Big Creek harbor showing how far the *Wave Dancer* was carried by the hurricane.

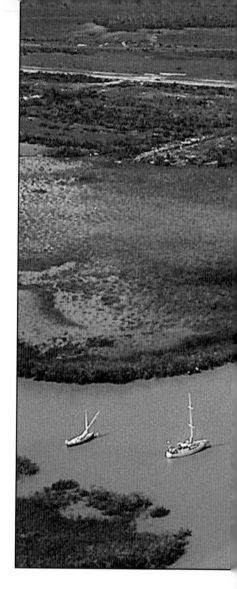

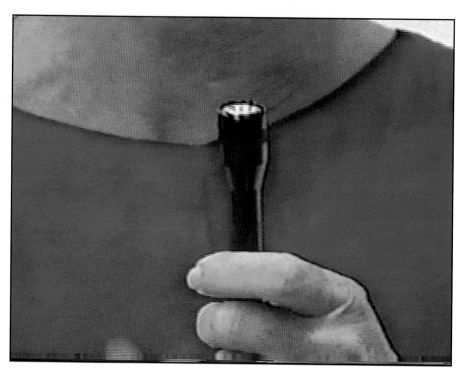

Mary Lou holds the Maglite that saved her.

Reef Ball Memorial for the deceased members of the Richmond Dive Club, a gift from the Virginia Beach Hammerheads Diving Club.

they looked forward to a warm shower on the dive deck, a refreshing end to a beautiful night dive.

As the last diver emerged and boarded the *Wave Dancer*, Stanley untied the line to the mooring ball and Captain Martin started the engines. Stanley's and Wouter's arguments, however sound, had not caused him to alter his plan to move to a cove at Lighthouse Reef and tie up to the night mooring. As the *Wave Dancer* pulled away from Front Porch, the sky deck was filled with divers sharing their many stories and adventures while enjoying a Belikin.

Earlier that evening, while Captain Martin gave his guests their options, Captain Schnabel informed the passengers of the *Belize Aggressor* of the potential threat they faced now that it had been confirmed that Hurricane Iris had moved south of its previously projected path. He told them he wanted everyone doing the night dive to be back on board by nine o'clock because he was pulling up anchor and going to Belize City, where he could get a better report of the exact direction and intensity of Iris. Captain Schnabel said that while he had received several updates he needed more local information about the advancing storm. While in Belize City he would top off with fuel in case he had to take the boat south to Big Creek.

Chief Meteorologist Fuller called the NWS at 7:00 p.m. to ask if there had been any change in Iris's direction or strength. He was told they were in the process of updating their forecast but didn't believe there were many changes from the earlier report. At 8:00 p.m. he received the following report.

BULLETIN

Hurricane Iris intermediate advisory number 13A

National Weather Service, Miami, FL

8 p.m. edt, Sun Oct 07 2001

...Iris continues moving westward...

A HURRICANE WARNING REMAINS IN EFFECT
FOR THE CAYMAN ISLANDS.

A HURRICANE WATCH REMAINS IN EFFECT FOR THE EAST COAST OF THE
YUCATAN PENINSULA OF MEXICO FROM CABO CATOCHE SOUTHWARD.
THE HURRICANE WATCH FOR BELIZE IS EXTENDED SOUTHWARD AT 8 P.M.
AND IS NOW IN EFFECT FOR ALL OF THE COAST OF BELIZE. THESE WATCHES
WILL LIKELY BE UPGRADED TO HURRICANE WARNINGS LATER TONIGHT.

A TROPICAL STORM WARNING AND A HURRICANE WATCH REMAINS IN
EFFECT FOR THE NORTH COAST OF HONDURAS AND THE ADJACENT
ISLANDS FROM LIMON WESTWARD.

AT 8 P.M. EDT...0000Z... THE CENTER OF HURRICANE IRIS WAS LOCATED
NEAR LATITUDE 17.3 NORTH... LONGITUDE 80.5 WEST OR ABOUT 145
MILES...235 KM...SOUTH-SOUTHEAST OF GRAND CAYMAN.

IRIS IS MOVING TOWARD THE WEST NEAR 18 MPH...30KM/HR...

AND THIS MOTION IS EXPECTED TO CONTINUE DURING THE NEXT
24 HOURS. THE SMALL CORE OF THE STRONGEST WINDS IS PASSING
WELL TO THE SOUTH OF GRAND CAYMAN TONIGHT AND IS HEADING
TOWARD THE YUCATAN PENINSULA AND BELIZE AND ALSO THREATENS
HONDURAS. MAXIMUM SUSTAINED WINDS REMAIN NEAR 85 MPH...
140 KM/HR...WITH HIGHER GUSTS. STRENGTHENING IS FORECAST
DURING THE NEXT 24 HOURS.

HURRICANE FORCE WINDS EXTEND OUTWARD UP TO 25 MILES...35
KM...FROM THE CENTER...AND TROPICAL STORM FORCE WINDS EXTEND
OUTWARD UP TO 115 MILES...185 KM.

THE LATEST MINIMUM CENTRAL PRESSURE RECORDED BY AN NOAA
RECONNAISSANCE PLANE WAS 988 MB...29.17 INCHES.

REPEATING THE 8 P.M. EDT POSITION...17.3 N...80.5 W. MOVEMENT

TOWARD... WEST NEAR 18 MPH. MAXIMUM SUSTAINED WINDS...85 MPH.
MINIMUM CENTRAL PRESSURE...988 MB.

THE NEXT ADVISORY WILL BE ISSUED BY THE
NATIONAL HURRICANE CENTER AT 11 P.M. EDT.

FORECASTER LAWRENCE

Fuller read the report with much trepidation. He had been monitoring and comparing the previous NHC reports, which showed the barometric pressure consistently dropping, meaning that Iris, though not indicated in the latest NHC report, was strengthening as it swiftly moved closer to Belize. He would have to compare the previous day's barometric readings with the latest NHC reports to be sure he had an accurate analysis of the situation. Belize and the tropics are a semi-durnal area, which means the barometer rises or falls twice a day, so to get a precise barometric reading, the previous day's measurements have to be compared to the present ones. This was a formality for Fuller, because he already knew the answer to this question, but he made the comparison anyway. It was immediately obvious the actual barometric pressure was dropping, which confirmed there were stronger winds relative to the surrounding pressure.

At 9:00 p.m. Fuller went on national television and announced that the country of Belize was being upgraded to Red 1 Watch, the second phase of the hurricane-monitoring program. This changed the hurricane watch to a hurricane warning. Iris was now centered near 17.3 north longitude and 81.3 degrees west latitude or about 460 miles east of Belize City. The hurricane had picked up speed and strength and was moving to the west at twenty mph with maximum sustained winds of ninety mph.

Fuller characterized Iris as a small hurricane with a thirteen-mile diameter eye and hurricane-force winds extending only twenty-five miles from the center. But, he said, it continued to strengthen. He warned that Iris would become a major hurricane and would hit Belize within twenty-four hours. They should prepare accordingly and stay tuned to local radio and television stations for official hurricane advisories and safety information. "Do not listen to rumors," he said

Earlier in the day, as he became aware of the potential threat of Iris to his country, Fuller purchased hurricane supplies and advised the meteorologist on duty to install hurricane shutters on the National Meteorological Service Center. The aqua-green, two-level, concrete-block building was as gaudy in color and shape as it was secure from invaders and storms. It featured Central America's only weather radar dish extending above its roof. Located at the end of Philip Goldson International Airport's runway, in a passes-only military compound, the operations of the NMS had been moved, following the preliminary phase announcement, to the second level of the building, where the weather-monitoring equipment reported the latest information on the advancing hurricane. Fuller knew the well-being of his country rested on his reporting of the impending crisis, so he had to make sure his associates and headquarters were safe before advising others to do the same.

With Hurricane Iris closing in on the coastline of Belize, gaining in wind speed, moving in a more southerly direction and fluctuating size eye, Fuller and his associates began calling the NHC for hourly updates. The information needed by the Belizean meteorologists changed with every report, so they had to be aware of each shift in order to revise their landfall and storm-severity projections. If their latitude readings were misquoted by a tenth of a degree their projection would be off by ten miles; if it were misquoted by a full degree they would error by sixty miles. Since Iris was such a small hurricane, accuracy was crucial in knowing which locations would be hit hardest.

After receiving the latest update from the NHC and communicating several times during the day and evening with them, Fuller knew the twenty-four hours before Iris hit Belize and the twenty-four hours thereafter would be extremely tense and demanding. He brought some personal necessities and an inflatable mattress from home and prepared to ride out the storm at the NMSC.

* * *

Captain Martin navigated the *Wave Dancer* around the leeward side of Lighthouse Reef to the night mooring site. Nestled between two outcroppings from the island, at this location the boat would be well protected. The soft tropical breezes and gentle waves would rock the boat so delicately that the exhausted members of the RDC would sleep like babes in a cradle. They trusted the crew and the beautiful boat to keep them safe.

The *Wave Dancer* had been refitted in the United States but that did not necessarily mean the work met strict US Coast Guard standards. Since the *Wave Dancer* was going to Belize to be registered as a flag of convenience [FOC] ship, a lesser standard of quality and safety could be met. The flag of convenience is common in the maritime industry as it allows the country of ownership to differ from the flag country. Cheap registration fees, low or no taxes, cheap labor, and less stringent safety and maintenance enforcement inspections are among the many reasons ship owners elect to register their boats in FOC countries. By 'flagging out', the boat owner is not subjected to the rigorous safety and environmental standards imposed by the UN's International Maritime Organization [IMO].

In many cases these registers are not even run from the country concerned. A good example is the Liberian register. A private company in the US can do all of its paperwork. The Cambodian registry is based in Singapore. While perfectly legal, ships with an FOC registration sometimes do not meet the standards other countries require. To spotlight some of these deficiencies, the International Transport Workers' Federation developed a network of inspectors to investigate abuses of seafarers on FOC ships. They reported a pattern of very low wages, long periods of work without proper rest leading to stress and fatigue, little or no shore leave, inadequate safety training, and neglected ship maintenance. Casualties are higher among FOC vessels. In 1997, 46 percent of all loses in absolute terms of tonnage were accounted for by just eight FOC registers. The top ten registers in terms of tonnage lost as a percentage of the fleet includes five FOC registers: Cambodia [first], St. Vincent [fifth], Antigua [eighth], Cyprus [ninth] and Belize [tenth].

However, it's not just the state of the ships that contributes to these high percentages. The maritime industry recognizes that 80 percent of all accidents at sea are caused by human error. Since 9/11 the FOC ships have created another international concern. It is now seen as a danger to allow shipping to operate under the cloak offered by FOCs: no questions asked as long as the ship owner pays registration fees and tonnage taxes. Brass plates (mail-box-only offices) in such places as Liberia, Panama, and the Bahamas, as well as single-ship companies to limit liability and cats' cradles of ownership structures create a wall of secrecy behind which a vessel's real owners can hide. The United States, spooked that terrorists might turn ships into floating bombs and sail them into American ports, demanded that shipping open up its books. The American government presented proposals to make ownership more transparent at a meeting of the International Maritime Organization. A chorus of protest, led by Greek ship owners, responded that America only needs to know who is in day-to-day control.

The ownership of the *Wave Dancer*, however, was no secret. Peter Hughes publicly acknowledged ownership interest in the vessel. Additionally, to satisfy its insurance company, Lloyds of London, the *Wave Dancer* had to pass a stability test. The problem was that, like many international ship owners, Peter Hughes was based in the United States, and his clients mostly were Americans who paid him with American dollars, and so when they boarded his boat they expected it to meet US Coast Guard standards.

Prillaman, DeBarger, Lisa, and Mary Lou were the only holdouts left on the sky deck. The salon and dive decks were deserted as the other members of the RDC had gone to bed. The foursome enjoyed one last Belikin before turning in, chatting about the day behind them and the one ahead.

They fell silent for a short while, taking in the night, before Prillaman began discussing his need to prepare for the Tacky Christmas Light Tour when he got back home. He planned to add more track, a tunnel, a bridge, and a new building to his backyard model train extravaganza. With the publicity the *Richmond Times-Dispatch* gave his display the previous year he expected more visitors than ever. He delighted in having cars, buses, and even limos drive past his home to see his train village. Resplendent in his engineer hat and overalls, with signature red bandanna hanging out of his hip pocket, Prillaman gave tours to all.

Leaning against the rail of the sky deck, a frosty Belikin in one hand and a cigarette in the other, he told them he hoped for snow this year.

"It's hard to think about snow in a place like this," DeBarger said.

"But wouldn't it be great?" Prillaman said. "It'd really add to the Christmas spirit. My village would look awesome in snow."

"You're a couple of holidays ahead of me," Lisa said. "When I get back I've got to start planning for Halloween." She said she hadn't decided on her costume yet, but she and her best friend, Catherine Potter, would come up with something, they always did. "Two years ago I dressed up as Prince. Catherine and I dyed my hair black and even glued some hair on my chest.

"Does Prince have hair on his chest?" Prillaman asked.

"Last year I dressed up as Gene Simmons from Kiss," Lisa said.

Prillaman released a hearty puff of smoke. "Did you put hair on your chest?"

Lisa laughed. "No, but we used a lot of Reynolds Wrap."

They all laughed at the thought then surrendered to the silent night again, feeling a bit homesick even in this beautiful paradise.

Chief Meteorologist Fuller answered a phone call from Prime Minister Musa, who wanted an update on Hurricane Iris. Fuller had fielded several calls since his TV broadcast. The general manager of LOVE 95 had begun calling him every hour on the hour to get the latest updates for the station's listeners. Fuller took each call seriously, conveying the information from the NWS as well as giving them his prediction of the storm's path and strength.

He wanted the people of Belize to be as well prepared as possible.

BULLETIN
Hurricane Iris advisory number 14
National Weather Service, Miami, FL
11 p.m. edt, Sun Oct 07 2001

...Iris continues moving westward...

At 11 p.m. edt...0300z...the government of Belize has issued a hurricane warning for the coast of Belize.

At 11 p.m. edt...0300z...the government of Guatemala has issued a tropical storm warning and a hurricane watch for their caribbean coastline.

A hurricane watch remains in effect for the mexican east coast of the Yucatan peninsula from Cabo Catoche southward to the Belize border. A hurricane watch and tropical storm warning remain in effect for the north coast of Honduras from Limon westward to the Belize border including adjacent islands.

A hurricane warning remains in effect for the Cayman Islands. This warning will likely be lowered early on Monday morning.

At 11 p.m. edt...0300z...the center of Hurricane Iris was located near latitude 17.3 north...longitude 81.3 west or about 135 miles...220 km...south of Grand Cayman. This position is also about 460 miles...745 km...east of Belize City, Belize.

Iris is moving toward the west near 20 mph...32 km/hr...and this motion is expected to move the hurricane inland over northern Central American in the next 24 to 36 hours.

MAXIMUM SUSTAINED WINDS HAVE INCREASED TO NEAR 90 MPH...150 KM/HR...WITH HIGHER GUSTS. ADDITIONAL STRENGTHENING IS FORECAST DURING THE NEXT 24 HOURS.

HURRICANE FORCE WINDS EXTEND OUTWARD UP TO 25 MILES...35 KM...FROM THE CENTER...AND TROPICAL STORM FORCE WINDS EXTEND OUTWARD UP TO 115 MILES...185 KM.

THE ESTIMATED MINIMUM CENTRAL PRESSURE IS 988 MB...29.18 INCHES.

REPEATING THE 11 P.M. EDT POSITION...17.3 N...81.3 W. MOVEMENT TOWARD...WEST NEAR 20 MPH. MINIMUM CENTRAL PRESSURE 988 MB.

AN INTERMEDIATE ADVISORY WILL BE ISSUED BY THE NATIONAL HURRICANE CENTER AT 2 A.M. EDT FOLLOWED BY THE NEXT COMPLETE ADVISORY AT 5 A.M. EDT MONDAY.

FORECASTER LAWRENCE

HURRICANE IRIS DISCUSSION NUMBER 14
NATIONAL WEATHER SERVICE, MIAMI, FL
11 P.M. EDT SUN OCT 07 2001

THE INITIAL MOTION IS 270/17. WITH A STRONG RIDGE HOLDING TO THE NORTH... THE GUIDANCE IS CLUSTERED BETWEEN THE EAST AND WEST-SOUTHWESTWARD. THE GFDL AND AVIATION MODELS ARE THE LEFT-MOST MODELS. THE OFFICIAL TRACK FORECAST IS ADJUSTED SLIGHTLY LEFT OF THE PREVIOUS ADVISORY AND IS STILL A LITTLE TO THE RIGHT OF THE CONSENSUS OF THE MODELS.

AN NOAA AIRCRAFT WAS IN THE HURRICANE TONIGHT. THE HIGHEST FLIGHT LEVEL WIND SPEED WAS 82 KNOTS JUST NORTH OF THE CENTER. THE LATEST CENTRAL SURFACE PRESSURE WAS 909 MB. A CLOSED CIRCULAR EYEWALL HAD A 13 MILE DIAMETER. A GPS DROPSONDE INDICATED RATHER STRONG WINDS IN THE NORTH EYEWALL AND THE

INITIAL WIND SPEED IS INCREASED TO 80 KNOTS. THE DROPSONDE
DATA SUPPORTS A SURFACE WIND OF 90+ KNOTS...BUT THE PRESSURE
IS A LITTLE HIGH TO INCREASE THE WIND THAT MUCH. THE FORECAST
IS FOR STRENGTHENING TO 90 KNOTS BEFORE LANDFALL IN CENTRAL
AMERICA OR MEXICO. THIS IS ABOUT WHAT THE SHIPS AND GFDL
MODEL ARE SHOWING WITH AN ABSENCE OF SIGNIFICANT VERTICAL
SHEAR AND PLENTY OF OCEANIC HEAT CONTENT. THE LATEST INFRARED
IMAGERY LOOKS VERY IMPRESSIVE WITH A SMALL COLD CDO AND A COLD
COLLECTIVE BAND TO THE NORTH AND EAST OF THE CENTER.

BELIZE IS POSTING A HURRICANE WARNING FOR THEIR COAST SINCE
THE FORECAST TRACK IS RIGHT OVER THEM. MEXICO AND HONDURAS
ARE WAITING A LITTLE LONGER. A SLIGHT TURN TOWARD WEST-
SOUTHWEST...AS FORECAST BY THE AVIATION MODEL...AND HONDURAS
OR EVEN GUATEMALA COULD BECOME THE MOST THREATENED AREA.

FORECASTER LAWRENCE

Fuller knew Iris was going to be a bad one. Since the last report the
minimum central pressure had dropped three degrees compared to the
previous twenty-four hours, when it only dropped one degree. Iris was
getting stronger.

At 2:00 a.m. Chico, the night security guard, made his rounds on the *Wave
Dancer*. He checked to be sure the boat stayed at the mooring, that there
were no safety problems, or any unwelcome guests. After 9/11 everyone
in the live-aboard industry became aware that anything could happen
anywhere, even in the peaceful waters of Belize. Chico walked the perimeter
of the *Wave Dancer* every fifteen minutes. As he passed the wheelhouse he
saw Wouters and Stark looking at the fax machine. They had always been
friendly to him. Wouters looked up from the fax, shrugged his shoulders,
and without being asked said, "Chico, it looks like Iris is going to hit land

well north of us. We'll keep tracking her and let you all know if anything changes." Chico nodded and continued on his rounds.

After four hours of tossing and turning, Eloisa padded to the salon for a cup of warm tea, which she hoped would help her relax. While she heated the water, her cabin mate, Brenda, came in and asked if something was wrong. Eloisa told her that she was concerned about Hurricane Iris and Captain Martin's stubborn opposition to their suggestions to go to Belize City and let them off the boat. Her intuition told her something was wrong, and she didn't know what to do. Angela, the other member of the staff, came into the salon. She, too, couldn't sleep. The three sat together talking for a while before Chico interrupted his routine to join them. Except for Chico, they all had the same sense that something was not right. They wondered if Captain Martin was communicating with Peter Hughes and if Hughes was giving orders that were being ignored. Who was making the decisions? Why wouldn't they listen to the crew? And what about Ryan Vernon? He was a Belizean. He should know what was going on with Iris. He should tell Hughes and Martin to get the people off the boat. Why wasn't this happening? Maybe tomorrow morning they would decide to go to Belize City and let everyone off.

Dennis Gonguez awakened Fuller from a catnap and handed him the 2:00 a.m. NWS report, which read:

BULLETIN
Hurricane Iris intermediate advisory number 14a
National Weather Service, Miami, FL
2 a.m. edt, Mon Oct 08 2001

...Iris continues westward...

A hurricane warning remains in effect for the coast of Belize. A tropical storm warning and a hurricane watch

REMAIN IN EFFECT FOR THE CARIBBEAN COAST OF GUATEMALA. A HURRICANE WATCH REMAINS IN EFFECT FOR THE MEXICAN EAST COAST OF THE YUCATAN PENINSULA FROM CABO CATOCHE SOUTHWARD TO THE BELIZE BORDER.
A HURRICANE WATCH AND A TROPICAL STORM WARNING REMAIN IN EFFECT FOR THE NORTH COAST OF HONDURAS FROM LIMON WESTWARD TO THE BELIZE BORDER INCLUDING ADJACENT ISLANDS.

A HURRICANE WARNING REMAINS IN EFFECT FOR THE CAYMAN ISLANS. THIS WARNING WILL LIKELY BE LOWERED LATER THIS MORNING.

AT 2 A.M. EDT...0600Z...THE CENTER OF HURRICANE IRIS WAS LOCATED NEAR LATITUDE 17.3 NORTH...LONGITUDE 82.1 WEST OR ABOUT 145 MILES...235 KM...SOUTH-SOUTHWEST OF GRAND CAYMAN. THIS POSITION IS ALSO ABOUT 410 MILES...660 KM EAST OF BELIZE CITY, BELIZE.

IRIS IS MOVING TOWARD THE WEST NEAR 20 MPH...32 KM/HR...AND THIS MOTION IS EXPECTED TO BRING THE HURRICANE INLAND OVER NORTHERN CENTRAL AMERICA IN 24 HOURS OR SO.

MAXIMUM SUSTAINED WINDS ARE NEAR 90 MPH...150 KM/HR... WITH HIGHER GUSTS...OVER A SMALL AREA NEAR THE CENTER. SOME INCREASE IN STRENGTH IS FORECAST DURING THE NEXT 24 HOURS.

AN AIR FORCE HURRICANE HUNTER AIRCRAFT IS APPROACHING THE CENTER OF IRIS.

HURRICANE FORCE WINDS EXTEND OUTWARD UP TO 25 MILES... 35 KM...FROM THE CENTER...AND TROPICAL STORM FORCE WINDS EXTEND OUTWARD UP TO 115 MILES...185 KM.

THE ESTIMATED CENTRAL PRESSURE IS 988 MB...29.18 INCHES.

REPEATING THE 2 A.M. EDT POSITION...17.3 N...82.1 W. MOVEMENT TOWARD...WEST NEAR 20 MPH. MAXIMUM SUSTAINED WINDS...90 MPH.

MINIMUM CENTRAL PRESSURE...988 MB.

THE NEXT ADVISORY WILL BE ISSUED BY THE NATIONAL HURRICANE CENTER AT 5 A.M. EDT.

FORECASTER PASCH

The forecast caught Fuller a little by surprise. It stated pretty much the same conditions as the 11:00 p.m. report. With the drop in the minimum central pressure, he thought Iris would intensify. Maybe the storm was taking a rest, too. He handed the report to Hulse and went back to bed.

Chapter Ten

"The sea cries with its meaningless voice,
Treating alike its dead and its living."

Ted Hughes

At 5:00 a.m. Hulse woke Fuller to give him the formal report just received from the NWS. The short nap gave Fuller enough energy to sustain him through what would prove to be a very long day. As he sipped black coffee and munched on a health bar he listened as Hulse read him the report.

BULLETIN
Hurricane Iris advisory number 15
National Weather Service, Miami, FL
5 a.m. edt, Mon Oct 08 2001

...Iris strengthening rapidly. Becoming a dangerous
hurricane...expected to make landfall tonight...

At 5 a.m. edt...0900 utc...the government of Honduras has issued a hurricane warning for Honduras from Limon westward to the Guatemala border. Also at 5 a.m. edt...0900 utc. A hurricane warning is recommended for the caribbean coast of Guatemala. A hurricane warning remains in effect for the coast of Belize.

A hurricane watch remains in effect for the mexican east coast of the Yucatan peninsula from Cabo Catoche southward to the Belize border.

At 5 a.m. edt...0900 utc...the hurricane warning for the Cayman Islands is discontinued.

At 5 a.m. edt...0900z...the center of Hurricane Iris was located near latitude 17.1 north...longitude 83.1 west or about 345 miles...555 km...east of Belize City, Belize.

Reports from an air force reserve unit hurricane hunter plane indicate that the maximum sustained winds have increased to near 110 mph...175 km/hr...with higher gusts. Although some fluctuations in strength may occur today... Iris is likely to become a major hurricane before landfall. Hurricane force winds extend outward up to 25 miles...35 km... from the center...and tropical force winds extend outward up to 115 miles...185 km.

The hurricane hunter plane recently measured a minimum central pressure of 963 mb...28.44 inches.

Storm surge flooding of more than 10 feet above normal tide levels...along with large battering waves...are likely near and to the right of where the center of the hurricane crosses the coast.

REPEATING THE 5 A.M. POSITION...17.1 N...83.1 W. MOVEMENT TOWARD...WEST NEAR 20 MPH. MAXIMUM SUSTAINED WINDS...110 MPH. MINIMUM CENTRAL PRESSURE 963 MB.

AN INTERMEDIATE ADVISORY WILL BE ISSUED BY THE NATIONAL HURRICANE CENTER AT 8 A.M. EDT FOLLOWED BY THE NEXT COMPLETE ADVISORY AT 11 A.M. EDT.

FORECASTER PASCH

HURRICANE IRIS DISCUSSION NUMBER 15
NATIONAL WEATHER SERVICE, MIAMI, FL
5 A.M. EDT, MON OCT 08 2001

IRIS IS BECOMING A DANGEROUS HURRICANE. LATEST INFORMATION FROM THE HURRICANE HUNTER AIRCRAFT SHOW THAT THE SYSTEM HAS STRENGTHENED RAPIDLY OVER THE PAST SEVERAL HOURS. THE INNER CORE IS VERY TIGHT AND RECON REPORTED CONCENTRIC EYE WALLS...WITH AN INNER WALL DIAMETER OF AROUND 8 N MI...OR LESS. THE CENTRAL PRESSURE HAS FALLEN PRECIPITOUSLY...AT A RATE OF MORE THAN 3 MB/HR SINCE 00Z...WITH THE LATEST DROPSONDE MEASURING 963 MB. IRIS IS APPROACHING MAJOR HURRICANE STATUS...INDEED IT MAY BE ONE ALREADY. HOWEVER IT IS POSSIBLE THAT AN EYE WALL REPLACEMENT CYCLE IS UNDERWAY...SO THERE MAY BE UPWARD/DOWNWARD FLUCTUATIONS IN INTENSITY TODAY. NOTWITHSTANDING...THE CYCLONE IS OVER A REGION OF HIGH UPPER-OCEANIC HEAT CONTENT AND THE UPPER-LEVEL OUTFLOW IS BECOMING BETTER-DEFINED. THEREFORE A NET INCREASE IN STRENGTH IS LIKELY BEFORE LANDFALL. THE OFFICIAL INTENSITY FORECAST MAY BE CONSERVATIVE...BUT WE HAVE LITTLE GUIDANCE FOR SUCH RAPIDLY INTENSIFYING HURRICANES.

THE MOTION IS WEST...OR SLIGHTLY SOUTH OF DUE WEST...260/17. THERE IS A PRONOUNCED DEEP-LAYER ANTICYCLONE TO THE NORTH

OF IRIS...AND GLOBAL MODELS INDICATE A CONTINUATION OF THIS
REGIME OVER THE NEXT FEW DAYS. NUMERICAL TRACK GUIDANCE
SHOWS A WEST TO WEST-SOUTHWESTWARD MOTION...AND SO DOES THE
OFFICIAL FORECAST.

SINCE THERE IS THE POSSIBILITY OF A MORE SOUTHWARD EXCURSION
OF THE HURRICANE THAN SHOWN HERE...A HURRICANE WARNING IS
ISSUED FOR THE COAST OF HONDURAS...AND A HURRICANE WARNING IS
ISSUED FOR THE CARIBBEAN COAST OF GUATEMALA.

FORECASTER PASCH

As he and the NWS had predicted, Iris had strengthened overnight.
With the minimum central pressure dropping to 963 MB from 992 on
Saturday and 988 MB just three hours earlier, Iris posed an increasing
threat to Belize. NWS Discussion 15 stated that Iris was approaching
major hurricane status. The question was just how strong and dangerous
she would become.

Chico ran to Stanley's cabin at six in the morning and banged on the door.
"Come quick!" Chico shouted. "There's a helicopter next to the boat."
Throwing on a pair of shorts, Stanley said, "Where's Captain Martin?"
"Upstairs in the wheelhouse," Chico said. "And he won't come out."
Stanley jammed his feet into a pair of thongs, and ran to the sky deck,
where he saw a Royal Air Force helicopter hovering less than 150 feet from
him. The pilot maneuvered the aircraft to be parallel with the wheelhouse.
Looking over his left shoulder, he maintained his position, the whirring
propeller stirring the water below into a frothy chop.
Prillaman, Cox, Webb, and Garrison drank their morning coffee as they
watched the spectacle, unsure what was happening. A crewman wearing a
radio-monitoring helmet and a military-looking uniform, slid open the side
door and held out a sign identifying the helicopter and its crew. He then

held up a second sign that read "Hurricane—Go in!" and waved his arm aggressively to the crew of the *Wave Dancer*.

Prillaman, Cox, and Webb jumped to their feet, spilling coffee everywhere. Garrison ran downstairs to his cabin to get his camera. He wanted a photo of this dramatic moment to show his friends back in Richmond. They wouldn't believe the helicopter warning sign "Hurricane—Go In!" unless they saw it. By the time he grabbed his camera and raced back to the sky deck, however, the tail of the helicopter had skimmed off into the horizon.

Eloisa, Angela, and Brenda joined Stanley on deck, staring in disbelief at the ominous warning. Stanley acknowledged the helicopter crew's signal and as they flew away he raced to the wheelhouse just in time to hear Captain Martin order Chico, "Start the engines. We're going to Belize City."

Stanley said, "Let me get some clothes on, and I'll start clearing the deck. I'll find some ropes to tie up the equipment and dive gear and clean off the dive deck."

Mary Lou and Lisa were still in bed when they heard the engines start. Mary Lou sat up and said, "Sounds like we're heading to the Blue Hole."

Lisa sleepily replied, "Good. I want to dive it before we go to Big Creek."

Mary Lou threw back her covers and stood to stretch. "Let's get some breakfast and see what our schedule is."

After clearing the dive deck Stanley went to the salon for coffee and toast. Then he felt the *Wave Dancer* change directions. He ran back to the wheelhouse.

"What's going on?" he asked Captain Martin.

"Ryan Vernon says there's no place to go in Belize City," the captain answered, his eyes on the water in front of the boat. "The hotels are closed, and there's no way to transport people there. I have orders to ride out the storm at Big Creek."

Stanley knew it was a nine-hour trip, at least a hundred miles. More upset than ever, he rushed to the back of the dive deck to huddle with Eloisa, Brenda, Angela, and Chico. They, too, wondered about the change of plans. There were safety shelters in Belmopan and transportation for everyone to get there. Was Martin lying to them? They decided that Stanley would be their spokesman, and he would ask Wouters if he knew anything about this change of plans.

"Captain Martin is the captain of the *Wave Dancer*," Wouters barked in response to Stanley's question. "His orders will be followed."

"But it doesn't make sense."

Wouters glared at Stanley. "He's the captain," Wouters said. "His orders will be followed."

The visit by the Royal Air Force helicopter fueled the conversation about the advancing hurricane as the guests sat down for breakfast. Since the helicopter had arrived so early, most of them had still been in bed. It was up to Prillaman, Cox, Webb, and Garrison to convey the story of the helicopter with the "Hurricane—Go In!" sign to the rest of the group. They seated themselves at separate tables. Garrison sat with Kim, Christy, and Cheryl, giving his account along with his disappointment at not getting a photograph of the aircraft and the sign. Cheryl, a little nervous about the warning, wondered out loud if Hurricane Iris was closer than they were being told.

"The storm must be a threat to us," she said. "Why else would the government go to so much trouble to warn us? This is beginning to make me uncomfortable."

"Maybe Captain Martin is going to tell us what's going on," Kim said.

Cheryl, looking at Christy, said, "Someone needs to ask him." Then she turned to Garrison and added, "I have to admit, it would've been cool to have a picture of the helicopter with that sign."

Before long, anxiety filled the salon. Like Cheryl, each member of the RDC speculated about the helicopter's warning. They asked each other what this visit by the helicopter meant. Was Iris closer than they thought? Why had plans changed? Where were they going? Did this mean they wouldn't be diving at the Blue Hole this morning? Prillaman, who had refilled his coffee cup, munched a piece of jelly-topped toast as the conversations buzzed through the room. Then he stood up next to his table.

"I talked with Captain Martin a few minutes ago," he yelled above the din. The conversations around him stopped. "He said the morning plans were changing, and he would explain what's going on after breakfast. There's no need to worry."

A few minutes later Captain Martin entered the salon. Although he had not shaved yet, his pressed "Eat, Sleep and Dive" polo shirt, khaki shorts, and canvas deck shoes gave him an air of authority. His natural smile had faded to a slight look of disappointment, but otherwise, he appeared calm and collected. With all eyes and ears focused on his every word he maintained his Joe Friday "just the facts, ma'am" approach.

"During the night, Hurricane Iris moved farther south than I had projected, causing us to abandon my morning plans to dive the Blue Hole."

"The hurricane also has picked up intensity and is now classified as a category two hurricane."

Murmurs and whispers scattered through the room.

"Earlier this morning, I was in contact with my home office, and they ordered me to go to Big Creek. It will take us about seven hours to get there, which means we should arrive around three o'clock this afternoon. According to our calculations, Hurricane Iris is still well north of us and will make landfall in the Belize City area about eight or nine o' clock tonight. This will give us plenty of time to get to Big Creek and prepare for the storm's arrival. I expect the storm to pass quickly, and we will be diving again tomorrow."

He paused. Despite the dark stubble of beard and bleary eyes, he projected an air of control and confidence, as if this delay was more of an annoyance than a threat. "Any questions?" he asked.

Prillaman spoke first: "Is there was any way we can keep track of the storm's progress?"

"I'm receiving weather faxes every other hour and will be happy to show you our location on them so you can see where we are in relation to Hurricane Iris," Martin said.

A few of the divers who kept in-depth diving records liked that idea and asked if they could make copies of the faxes for their logbooks. After all, it was one thing to be in one of the best diving locations in the world and to brag about your underwater adventures, but to have a record of your boat plotted on a weather fax with a hurricane was off the charts!

Ray Mars asked, "Is there a way I can call my wife? I know she's watching the weather reports. She'll be worried."

"No problem," Captain Martin said. "There's a satellite telephone available to anyone who wants to use it." When no other questions arose, the captain headed back to the wheelhouse.

After he left, the salon erupted with discussion about the change in plans and the intensity and direction of the hurricane but no one seemed truly frightened. They knew they could come back and dive the Blue Hole later in the week, and though the storm caused some anxiety, they had already voted to stay on the boat, so there was no reason to belabor the point. The Peter Hughes Company had experience with hurricanes and knew how to handle the situation. They just needed to relax and make the best of the situation.

Fuller called the NWS every hour to get the latest update on Hurricane Iris. Though no formal report would be released until eight that morning, he hoped to pick up information relayed to the NWS by ships at sea and other island weather stations. Concern for the safety of the residents of Belize grew with every hour, and Fuller knew he must be aware of even the smallest change in the weather.

BULLETIN
Hurricane Iris intermediate advisory number 15A
National Weather Service, Miami, FL
8 a.m. edt, Mon Oct 08 2001

IRIS IS NOW AN EXTREMELY DANGEROUS CATEGORY FOUR HURRICANE... THE STRONGEST OF THE SEARON...AND EXPECTED TO

MAKE LANDFALL TONIGHT...

AT 8 A.M. EDT...1200Z...THE GOVERNMENT OF GUATEMALA HAS ISSUED A HURRICANE WARNING FOR THE CARIBBEAN COAST OF GUATEMALA. A HURRICANE WARNING REMAINS IN EFFECT FOR THE COAST OF BELIZE... AND FOR THE COAST OF HONDURAS FROM LIMON WESTWARD... INCLUDING THE ADJACENT ISLANDS.

A HURRICANE WATCH REMAINS IN EFFECT FOR THE MEXICAN EAST COAST OF THE YUCATAN PENINSULA FROM CABO CATOCHE SOUTHWARD TO THE BELIZE BORDER.

AT 8 A.M. EDT...1200Z...THE CENTER OF HURRICANE IRIS WAS LOCATED NEAR LATITUDE 17.1 NORTH...LONGITUDE 84.0 WEST OR ABOUT 285 MILES...460 KM...EAST OF BELIZE CITY, BELIZE.

IRIS IS MOVING TOWARD THE WEST NEAR 20 MPH...32 KM/HR...AND THIS MOTION IS EXPECTED TO BRING THE CENTER OF THE HURRICANE INLAND OVER NORTHERN CENTRAL AMERICA TONIGHT.

REPORTS FROM AN AIR FORCE RESERVE UNIT HURRICANE HUNTER PLANE INDICATE THAT THE MAXIMUM SUSTAINED WINDS HAVE RAPIDLY INCREASED AND ARE NOW NEAR 140 MPH...220 KM/HR... WITH HIGHER GUSTS. SOME FLUCTUATIONS IN STRENGTH ARE LIKELY BEFORE LANDFALL.

HURRICANE FORCE WINDS EXTEND OUTWARD UP TO 25 MILES...35 KM...FROM THE CENTER...AND TROPICAL STORM FORCE WINDS EXTEND OUTWARD UP TO 115 MILES...185 KM.

THE ESTIMATED MINIMUM CENTRAL PRESSURE IS 950 MB...28.05 INCHES.

STORM SURGE FLOODING OF 13-18 FEET ABOVE NORMAL TIDE LEVELS... ALONG WITH DANGEROUS LARGE BATTERING WAVES...ARE LIKELY NEAR AND TO THE RIGHT OF WHERE THE CENTER OF THE HURRICANE

CROSSES THE COAST.

RAINFALL TOTAL OF 5 TO 8 INCHES...LOCALLY HIGHER...ARE LIKELY ALONG THE PATH OF IRIS. THESE RAINS COULD CAUSE LIFE-THREATENING FLASH FLOODS AND MUD SLIDES OVER MOUNTAINOUS TERRAIN.

REPEATING THE 8 A.M. EDT POSITION...17.1 N...84.0 W. MOVEMENT TOWARD...WEST NEAR 20 MPH. MAXIMUM SUSTAINED WINDS...140 MPH. MINIMUM CENTRAL PRESSURE...950 MB.

THE NEXT ADVISORY WILL BE ISSUED BY THE NATIONAL HURRICANE CENTER AT 11 A.M. EDT.

FORECASTER PASCH/FRANKLIN

Fuller read the report twice. Iris was now an extremely dangerous category four hurricane, the strongest of the season. The minimum central pressure had fallen another thirteen degrees and now was at 950 MB.

The Belize government declared Phase III or Red II of the Hurricane Emergency Plan. The rating change prompted all government agencies to issue their highest warning alert and add a second red warning flag with a black square in its center to the one already posted. Fuller prepared to leave for Belmopan, where he would brief NEMO on the potential danger Hurricane Iris would pose to Belize. According to his present calculations, the storm's slightly south or west motion would continue until it hit land.

At nine o'clock Prillaman and DeBarger headed to the wheelhouse to get their first weather fax update. True to his word, Captain Martin gave them the *Wave Dancer's* location on the fax, which showed it well south of the center of Iris. In addition to his many other talents, Prillaman had some navigation experience and was able to distinguish the general location of Iris and the *Wave Dancer* depicted on the weather fax. He was satisfied with Martin's report. With each update, he charted the position of Iris and the

Wave Dancer and taped it on the front of the television screen in the salon for everyone to see.

In disbelief, Stanley scanned the posted weather fax for a few moments. He recognized that Iris had shifted farther south than the previous report Wouters had shown him. He knew that the report Captain Martin gave the passengers about being out of harm's way at Big Creek was wrong. According to the weather fax, Iris was heading directly for Big Creek, and Stanley felt sure Captain Martin knew it, too. Generally a soft-spoken person, he knew he must confront the captain. It was his responsibility to enlighten the captain, a hurricane rookie, and remind him of his responsibility for the safety of the passengers and crew.

When he entered the wheelhouse, Stanley saw Martin stiffen his back and neck then turn to give him a dark glare. Nevertheless, Stanley said it was his opinion that Hurricane Iris was moving directly toward Big Creek and that the *Wave Dancer* should go, instead, to Belize City to seek safety.

Looking down at the much shorter Belizean, the captain said that he had received his orders and intended to follow them. He told Stanley that they both had jobs to do and ordered him out of the wheelhouse. Stanley went to Wouters to ask for help in dealing with Martin. Wouters once again told Stanley that Captain Martin had made his decision, he was the captain of the ship, and his orders would be followed.

Outraged by the captain's failure to grasp the severity of the situation, Stanley huddled with Eloisa, Brenda, and Angela to explain what had happened with Martin and Wouters. By this time Stanley was sure they were all looking down the barrel of a gun with a crazy man ready to pull the trigger. He told the women he didn't know what to do but was sure they were headed for disaster. Clearly upset, Eloisa said she had tried to call home on her cell phone to see if everything was all right but was unable to get a signal. Angela said she had tried her cell phone too, but they were still too far from land. She said that as soon as the passengers finished with the satellite phone she was going to call her boyfriend.

After receiving instructions on how to use the satellite phone, Ray Mars called his wife, Teresa, at their home in Scaggsville, Maryland. Teresa had been watching the weather reports all day Sunday and already knew that Hurricane Iris was heading for the coast of Belize. She had begun to worry about Ray's safety and said prayers for him. His call startled her because he had said he wouldn't call home unless something was wrong. At first, she thought something happened on a dive, like maybe he'd gotten the bends or was injured. When he told her about the approaching storm, however, she said she knew about it. He told her they were heading to a safe harbor where the boat had ridden out storms before. He tried to hide his nervousness, but after thirty-three years of marriage, Teresa could see through his attempts. She begged him to get off the boat and come home. He told her there was no way he could get off the boat, but everything would be all right. More than once he told her he loved her.

When the passengers finished making their calls home, the crew lined up for their turn. Captain Martin, suspecting the worst from his disgruntled crew, hung around the area to eavesdrop on their conversations. Stanley, first in line, tried to call his wife but couldn't reach her. He worried about her and their two children's safety. His wife was a Honduran who had come to Belize two years earlier when she and Stanley were married. Though familiar with Belize City, she had never been through a weather-related disaster before. He felt sure she was okay but wanted to hear it from her.

Next, Angela tried without success to reach her boyfriend in Belize City. She then called her brother, who lived in Belmopan. She had decided to get off the *Wave Dancer* at Big Creek, believing that Captain Martin was ignorant about hurricanes and too stubborn or arrogant to admit it. She was not going to jeopardize her life for a part-time job and needed someone to meet her at Big Creek to take her off the boat. Speaking in Cantonese so her conversation could not be understood by anyone but her Chinese brother, she told him to contact her boyfriend and have him meet her when she arrived at Big Creek. He should be prepared to take three or four extra people with them.

By the time Eloisa called her sister, Captain Martin had gone back to the wheelhouse. She told her sister, "I don't know if I am ever going to see you guys again." Tears rolled down her cheeks. "We have a new captain, and he doesn't want to listen to us. I've told him, 'Please bring us to Belize City.'" She needed a moment to collect herself before calling her boyfriend.

The first of several meetings with NEMO convened at 9:00 a.m. and Fuller briefed the prime minister and other officials on the overnight progress of Hurricane Iris. He advised that on its present track Iris would make landfall between Placencia and Monkey River Town that night. He recommended that all coastal locations be immediately evacuated.

Upon hearing Fuller's latest update, the 750 permanent residents of Placencia Village, feeling like they wore a huge bull's eye, began preparing for the worst. While some members of each family nailed sheets of plywood to their windows and doors, others hurried to the local service station to top off the family vehicle with gas. All who owned motorized vehicles, which was about half the population, knew it was crucial to get gas before the service station either ran out or, because of the alert, was forced to close, leaving them stranded in Placencia. People everywhere moved swiftly and with purpose.

Percy Neal, a native Belizean, the owner of BJ's restaurant, and former Placencia town manager, was being prodded by his wife, Betty, to make a decision about their evacuation plans. In 1998, Percy and his family chose to ride out Hurricane Mitch in their two-story, concrete-block home and restaurant located one hundred yards west of the beach. Then, as now, they had received NEMO evacuation warnings projecting Mitch to make landfall in Placencia. Now facing the major threat of Hurricane Iris, the Neals had to make another possibly life-altering decision.

During preparations for Hurricane Mitch, Percy, a very religious man, met his fellow parishioners at their church three times a day and prayed that they be spared as the category five hurricane hovered less than a hundred miles from them. Each day, Mitch, one of the deadliest hurricanes ever, stalled over neighboring Honduras but still was projected to hit Placencia. And each day Neal and his friends prayed for deliverance. After pounding them for three days with relentless winds and rain, Mitch made a U-turn and headed inland, sparing their peninsula and town from major damage. Without abandoning Placencia, they were saved. They had made the right decision. During the morning family devotional time, Percy asked God for guidance and with no revelation save clear thinking, they decided to leave Placencia. They loaded seventy-four people into their school bus and family van and headed for Belmopan to seek shelter.

Across the street and just a good stone's throw from the beach, Wende Bryan, a thirty-five-year-old Canadian who had emigrated to Placencia eight years earlier to escape Canada's cold winters, began to stack the furniture and protect, as best she could, her open-air thatched hut bar and restaurant, the Pickled Parrott. A local favorite, due largely to Wende's magnetic personality, the Pickled Parrott would not withstand much wind. Deep down Wende knew her business would not be standing when she returned. Satisfied she had done her best, she called her staff, told them to seek shelter, and then phoned her sister, Denise. She told her to get her family together, gas up the car, pack a few personal necessities, and come get her. They were going to San Ignacio, a small city two and a half hours west of Placencia to seek shelter in a friend's motel.

Like Percy and Barbara Neal, Wende had stayed in Placencia during Mitch and did not want to endure the wrath of another hurricane. When Mitch threatened the area, her former husband, Martin Westby, a boat captain, was asked by the novice skipper of the *Belize Aggressor* to assist him in negotiating the shallow unmarked channel to the dock at Big Creek. Wende went along with her husband and having successfully docked the boat, stayed, along with eight passengers and crew, on the *Aggressor* for four days and three nights, trapped by the relentless storm. The pummeling she received from Mitch at Big Creek convinced her she never wanted to go through another one, so after protecting as much as she could, Wende, along with Denise, her husband John B., his son Bubba, and Bubba's girlfriend, Shannon, set out for San Ignacio.

While the majority of the population prepared to leave Palcencia, Captain Schnabel piloted the *Belize Aggressor* past the town's beaches, heading a mile south toward the channel connecting the open sea to Big Creek. Like most of the coastal area of Belize, the entrance to the dock at Big Creek was shallow, so Captain Schnabel swung the *Aggressor* wide of the point of the peninsula to align the boat with the buoy markers dotting the path to the safe harbor. Two buoys, one green and one red, marked the entry to the half-mile channel and indicated where the boat could safely enter without running aground. Sixteen buoy markers funneled the *Aggressor* into the fifty-yard mouth of the channel, through the shallows, and into the mangroves, which engulfed the boat as it entered the small port. As the *Aggressor* emerged through the opening in the mangroves safety appeared in the form of a large, well-built concrete dock with an adjoining pre-engineered metal warehouse building.

The six-hundred-foot dock featured six equally spaced Samson posts as the main tie-up points to secure stationary boats. Rubber bumpers spaced ten to fourteen feet apart ran along the face of the dock. The dock itself sat six feet above water level and included a concrete apron that extended fifty feet, connecting it to the warehouse. The massive metal structure, large enough to house four boats the size of the *Aggressor*, was substantially affixed to a five-foot block wall, which was then anchored to its foundation. The two structures, the largest of their kind south of Belize City, were owned by local merchant Tony Zabaneh, who used them to store and ship bananas and other produce grown on the surrounding farms.

Although it was only nine o'clock in the morning, several boats had already arrived at the dock and were adequately secured. Fortunately, there was still two hundred feet of space available at the south end of the dock, and Captain Schnabel, traveling north, prepared to maneuver the *Aggressor* into position so he could tie up. The small area of navigational water between the dock and mangroves was only 150 yards wide, necessitating that Captain Schnabel go forward, then reverse his engines several times while making small turns each time to maneuver the *Aggressor* 150 degrees and parallel to the dock. Once close enough to the dock but leaving a twenty-five-foot distance between the *Aggressor* and *Miss Gayle*, a tug boat at his stern, he shut off his engines and ordered his first-mate and senior dive master to prepare the ropes to secure the boat. The *Aggressor's* bow faced south with its portside next to the dock and the stern twenty-five feet from *Miss Gayle's* bow.

Captain Schnabel had ample ropes to secure the bow and stern lines of the *Aggressor* to the Samson posts with enough slack to allow the boat to rise with the surge during the storm. He also set up spring lines between the bow and stern to keep the boat from moving fore and aft and avoid hitting the *Miss Gayle* during the storm. Satisfied the *Aggressor* was adequately moored, Captain Schnabel held a meeting with his passengers to bring them up to date on the location of Hurricane Iris. He explained that the storm was now projected to hit Belize City.

"As a precaution I'm going to call to see if there are any hotels or other accommodations available in the area for you," he said. A man with many years of navigational experience, he felt if his boat were secure then his passengers would be safe as well, but he wanted a back-up plan, just in case.

Chapter Eleven

"When beholding the tranquil beauty and brilliancy of the ocean's skin, one forgets the tiger heart that pants beneath it; and would not willingly remember that this velvet paw but conceals a remorseless fang."

Herman Melville, *Moby Dick*

Doncho Donchev, the general manager of the Princess Hotel and Casino, listened to LOVE 95 radio while he shaved and dressed for the day. Hearing the latest news update, he knew he needed to implement the final evacuation and preservation plans for his establishment. He met with his staff, informed them of his plan, and gave each their orders, which included evacuating the hotel guests and nonessential staff. Donchev, along with the maintenance staff, would stay behind, moving everything not anchored down on the first floor to the second floor and putting hurricane shutters on the large first floor windows that overlooked the waterfront. Then they each would take one of the remaining floors between two and six and duct tape a large X on every window to protect it during the fierce wind. The speed and efficiency of his staff impressed him as they went through their preparations.

While the staff prepared the hotel, Donchev gazed out the front window overlooking the main thoroughfare connecting the harbor area with the main part of the city. He watched the hub of activity as people everywhere carried objects from one place to another. Forklifts moved large pallets of supplies and equipment from the pier to the parking lot across the street from the hotel, where it would have better protection from the expected surge. Every automobile, van, or truck that passed was loaded with people, sacks, and boxes and many even had mattresses strapped to the top. The people in the vehicles knew they were leaving their homes behind. Donchev thought it might look like panic to an outside observer, but he admired the sense of purpose and organization beneath the chaos. Everyone in Belize City seemed unified in their preparation for Iris.

When he finished his own preparations, Donchev knew he had no place to go. Like a captain of a ship, he was compelled, along with a few key maintenance people, to stay at the hotel during the hurricane.

Prior to leaving his office at the meteorological center, Carlos Fuller called the television and radio stations, asking them to run continuous alerts about the advancing hurricane. During his one-hour drive to Belmopan he heard the radio coverage given to the storm. Between each song an announcement alerted residents of imminent danger. When he arrived at the NEMO headquarters in Belmopan he flicked on the television and saw a continuous scroll of the weather alert. At a little after eleven he received the latest NWS report from Justin Hulse.

BULLETIN
Hurricane Iris advisory number 16
National Weather Service, Miami, FL
11 a.m. edt, Mon Oct 08 2001

...Small but extremely dangerous Iris continues westward...

At 8 a.m. EDT...1200 UTC...the government of Mexico has issued a tropical storm warning for the east coast of the Yucatan from Felipe Carrillo Puerto southward to the border with Belize.

A hurricane warning remains in effect for the caribbean coasts of Belize...Guatemala...and Honduras from the border with Guatemala eastward to Limon.

A hurricane watch remains in effect for the Mexican east coast of the Yucatan peninsula from Cabo Catoche southward to the Belize border.

At 11 a.m. EDT...1500Z...the center of Hurricane Iris was located near latitude 17.0 north...longitude 84.9 west or about 225 miles...365 km...east of Belize City, Belize.

Iris is moving toward the west near 20 mph...32 km/hr. A general west or slightly south of west motion is expected prior to landfall...bringing hurricane conditions to portions of Belize...Guatemala...northern Honduras and the adjacent islands later today and tonight. On the projected track... the center is expected to make landfall late tonight or early Tuesday morning.

Maximum sustained winds are near 140 mph...220 km/hr... with higher gusts. Iris is an extremely dangerous category four hurricane. Some fluctuations in intensity are possible prior to landfall.

Iris is an extremely small hurricane...with hurricane force winds extending outward up to 15 miles...30 km...from the center. Tropical storm force winds extend outward up to 115 miles...185 km.

ESTIMATED MINIMUM CENTRAL PRESSURE IS 950 MB...28.05 INCHES.
STORM SURGE FLOODING OF 13-18 FEET ABOVE NORMAL TIDE
LEVELS...ALONG WITH DANGEROUS LARGE BATTERING WAVES...ARE
LIKELY NEAR AND TO THE NORTH OF WHERE THE THE CENTER OF THE
HURRICANE CROSSES THE COAST.
RAINFALL TOTALS OF 5-8 INCHES... LOCALLY HIGHER...
ARE LIKELY ALONG THE PATH OF IRIS. THESE RAINS COULD
CAUSE LIFE-THREATENING FLASH FLOODS AND MUD SLIDES OVER
MOUNTAINOUS TERRAIN.

REPEATING THE 11 A.M. EDT POSITION...17.0 N...84.9 W. MOVEMENT
TOWARD...WEST NEAR 20 MPH. MAXIMUM SUSTAINED WINDS..140 MPH.
MINIMUM CENTRAL PRESSURE...950 MB.

AN INTERMEDIATE ADVISORY WILL BE ISSUED BY THE NATIONAL
HURRICANE CENTER AT 2 P.M. EDT FOLLOWED BY THE NEXT COMPLETE
ADVISORY AT 5 P.M. EDT.

FORECASTER FRANKLIN

HURRICANE IRIS DISCUSSION NUMBER 16
NATIONAL WEATHER SERVICE, MIAMI, FL
11 A.M. EDT, MON OCT 08 2001

RECON REPORTS JUST BEFORE 12Z INDICATED THAT IRIS
STRENGTHENED TO A CATEGORY FOUR HURRICANE...WITH A FLIGHT
LEVEL WIND OF 134 KT ONLY 4 NM NORTHWEST OF THE CENTER. WITH
SUCH A TIGHT CORE...IT WAS IMPOSSIBLE TO GET A DROPSONDE IN
THE CENTER OF THE EYE...SO THE CENTRAL PRESSURE IS ESTIMATED.
THE FLIGHT-LEVEL WIND CORRESPONDS TO 120 KT AT THE SURFACE
USING THE STANDARD 90 PERCENT REDUCTION. THE AIRCRAFT ALSO
REPORTED TRIPLE CONCENTRIC EYEWALLS WITH RADAII OF 3/9/18
NM. SATELLITE IMAGERY SINCE 12Z SUGGESTS THAT THE INNERMOST

EYEWALL HAS PROBABLY COLLAPSED...AND THE WINDS MAY HAVE COME DOWN A BIT. WITH TWO MORE EYEWALLS SO CLOSE...I DO NOT EXPECT ANY RAPID DECREASE IN STRENGTH PRIOR TO LANDFALL.

THE INITIAL MOTION IS 260/17...THE SAME AS BEFORE. MOST OF THE GUIDANCE SUGGESTS A TRACK JUST SOUTH OF WEST. THE AVN IS FURTHEST SOUTH...TAKING THE CENTER INLAND OVER GUATEMALA. RECENT AVN FORECASTS SHOWING A MORE SOUTHERNLY TRACK HAVE BEEN DOING QUITE WELL...AND THE OFFICIAL FORECAST IS NUDGED ALITTLE SOUTH OF THE PREVIOUS ADVISORY.

THE OFFICIAL FORECAST HAS IRIS RE-EMERGING INTO THE PACIFIC... WHERE IT WOULD RETAIN THE NAME IRIS IF IT SURVIVES THE TERRAIN OF CENTRAL AMERICA. HOWEVER...GIVEN THAT THE CIRCULATION IS SO SMALL...IT MAY WELL NOT MAKE IT.

FORECASTER FRANKLIN

Fuller made a mental note that the minimum central pressure had not changed in the last three hours, suggesting Iris would not increase to a category five. He also noted that he and Hulse had been correct in projecting the hurricane would hit the coast of Belize south of Belize City somewhere near Placencia and Monkey River Town. The worst storm of the year would miss the largest populated area of his country. He knew that despite evacuation warnings not everyone would go to hurricane shelters, and the government couldn't force them to do it. Many people would stay in Belize City and face the danger of drowning in the storm surge rather than leave their property behind. Still, at the noon NEMO meeting he would recommend an intensified effort to evacuate the Placencia and Monkey River Town areas.

After talking to her brother, Angela hurried to her cabin and packed her bags so she would be ready to leave the *Wave Dancer* as soon as it docked at Big

Creek. She gathered the Belizean crew and told them her plan. Stanley told her he was worried about his wife and children, was unable to contact them, and he would go with her to make sure his family was safe. Like Stanley, Eloisa decided to go with Angela. Brenda, a shy person who seemed to them oddly indifferent about their situation, elected to stay with the *Wave Dancer* and not risk losing her job. Stanley went to his cabin to pack his bags. With a young family, he desperately needed his job, but he had to make sure they were safe. To him, parental commitment came before his job, and given his considerable skills, maybe Peter Hughes wouldn't fire him.

Eloisa felt she would have time to pack later, so she returned to the galley to prepare lunch while Angela and Brenda went to the guests' cabins to make the beds. As soon as they finished, Brenda went back to the galley. Eloisa tried again to call home and this time got through to Alberto Hall, her boyfriend. When she heard his voice, she burst into tears. Alberto updated her on the continuous announcements about the hurricane, including the evacuation warnings.

"This captain's crazy," she sobbed. "He's not listening to us. He's going to kill us." After a few minutes she told Alberto she had decided to stay on the *Wave Dancer*. They had just bought a house together and planned to get married around Christmas, so she did not want to take the chance of losing her job. "Right now it is too important," she said, added, "I love you," and hung up.

Prillaman went to the wheelhouse at eleven o'clock to get the latest weather fax and chart the new position of the *Wave Dancer* and the storm. Satisfied with their safety, he posted the fax on the TV screen and went to find Webb and Doug Cox. Now that things seemed to be under control, he began concocting plans for the rendezvous at Big Creek with his friends on the *Aggressor*. When he found Cox and Garrison, he explained how Dave Mowrer had bragged about the *Aggressor* having a large hot tub on its deck. He wanted to create a West Virginia Hot Tub to show their friends on the *Aggressor* that the *Wave Dancer* had modern conveniences, too.

He asked Garrison to get his video camera and meet him and Cox on the back of the dive deck. Of course, they would need a supporting crowd, so Prillaman went through the salon and up to the sky deck to get the others involved in his charade. He gathered them around the recently filled rinse tank on the back of the dive deck, and then he and Cox—wearing swim suits, hats, and sunglasses and holding a Belikin in one hand and a cigar in the other—put in their Dr. Bukk teeth and climbed into the sixty-gallon barrel. Cox grabbed a scuba tank, slightly opened the valve to create a stream of air and put it upside down in the rinse tank. The water bubbled into frothy foam. First Prillaman then Cox flailed about acting like they were having the time of their lives while Garrison shot the video. Satisfied he had done his best work, Prillaman told his co-conspirators that when they arrived at Big Creek they needed to board the *Aggressor*, tell them they had done the "Blue Hole" before leaving Lighthouse Reef, and they had partied so much the past two days they were out of beer. He then asked Mary Lou to change the menu board in the galley to read: prime rib, baked potatoes with sour cream, and chocolate mousse. When their friends came on the *Wave Dancer* to check out its accommodations, Prillaman wanted them to think that everything about the *Wave Dancer* was superior to the *Aggressor*.

After the taping, Cindy Pike and several other guests went to the salon where they found Stark asleep on the sofa. Exhausted from being in the wheelhouse most of the night, he did not wake up. Cindy seized the opportunity to paint the toenails on his right foot red. When Stark shifted his position she painted the toenails on his left foot. She then used white polish to paint a diagonal stripe on each toenail, depicting a scuba dive flag.

Stark awoke to laughter. He didn't know what was so funny but sensed everyone was having a good time. Webb rolled up a piece of paper and threw it at his feet. He bent down and picked it up. No recognition, no reaction. Webb threw a second piece of paper at his feet, and this time Stark saw the ten little scuba dive flags looking back at him. He laughed, then left to show his feet to the rest of the crew.

The misgivings about the captain's decision to delay returning to land dissipated among the guests. Prillaman obviously wasn't worried about the impending storm. They relaxed, figuring if they couldn't be diving, at least they'd enjoy the boat ride.

Mary Lou talked with Sheila Kelley about their families. Mary Lou spoke about hiking trails in Guatemala and exploring some recently discovered Mayan ruins in the upper peninsula of the Yucatan with her son Geoffrey. They both liked the adventure of going to hard-to-get-to areas. Sheila told Mary Lou about her daughter, Holly. She had just announced her engagement to a young man and had turned her life around.

"Holly was an academic scholarship student in high school but dropped out of college," Sheila said. "Now she's back in school and going to get married. I'm so proud of her." She then talked about her passion for law and her work with the Petersburg Symphony Orchestra.

Mary Lou excused herself to get some lemonade, and while up lost her seat to Sheila's husband, Bill. As she was pouring her lemonade, however, Mary Lou noticed Eloisa, Brenda, Angela, and Bart having an animated discussion in the corner of the salon. They were making numerous cell phone calls and wore nervous expressions on their faces.

She sat down with Shirley and Byron Johnston. Shirley shared several stories of her passion for artwork and gardening. They discussed the fact that Shirley's favorite subject to paint was the iris. She talked about the vibrant colors and texture of the flower, which was the favorite in her garden. How ironic, they all observed, that a hurricane named Iris threatened their vacation. Byron displayed some of his above-water photos on his laptop—shots of the dive briefings and of people suiting up for dives. He talked about his decision to retire at age sixty and about his earlier life as a "fire jumper."

A short time later Lisa woke from a nap and joined the group in the salon. To prevent seasickness, she had taken medication that always made her sleepy. Rested and relaxed, she got an iced tea and sat down with Cheryl. They both loved outdoor activities, such as hiking, canoeing, and rock climbing, so their mutual interests gave them plenty to discuss. Cheryl recently had gone rock climbing with friends, and she talked about the difficult climbs she had made. Lisa, not as accomplished, said that she was trying to get her friend Catherine interested in rock climbing. They had tried a couple of walls together but not the real thing.

After the West Virginia Hot Tub Show, DeBarger went to the sky deck to rest in the hammock and read a book. He was about half way through Melle Shipwash Starsen's first novel, *I Want to Marry Godzilla and Have His Children*. Melle was a friend, and he hoped to finish the book before arriving at Big Creek.

On Whipray Caye, Julian Cabral was in the process of boarding up the last lodge when he received a call from his fiancée, Beverly. She was still in Pennsylvania, finalizing the sale of her home. She planned to move to Belize by the end of the month. Beverly had been tracking Iris for three days and with the hurricane a few hours from making landfall she wanted to make sure Cabral was safely off the island. He assured her he was less than thirty minutes from leaving Whipray Caye and would take his boat to Belize City, where he would catch a ride to Belmopan and stay with a cousin. Beverly made him promise to call her when he arrived in Belmopan so she would know he was safe. They each said "I love you" and rang off.

At the Turtle Inn, Jan Neel told her maintenance staff to seal off the cabanas and protect as much of the property as possible. She had been watching the weather updates on TV and knew Iris had shifted south, putting Placencia right in the storm's path. Even with her limited knowledge of hurricanes she knew the chances of Francis Ford Coppola's thatched roof resort withstanding the storm were not good. At noon, she told her staff of NEMO's evacuation orders and sent everyone home. She drove to her home, gathered her family, and prepared to ride out Hurricane Iris in her new "hurricane proof" home.

*   *   *

The Mariposa Beach Suites, a small luxury three-unit hotel with owner's quarters above the rental units, stood a half-mile north of the Turtle Inn. The Mariposa, meaning "butterfly" in Spanish, was owned by Peter Fox, a retired engineer from California, and his wife, Marcia, who like most other residents of Placencia, had been monitoring the hurricane's progress for three days. On Sunday, when it appeared inevitable that Iris was heading for Placencia and would hit the following day, the Foxes met Frank Gagliano and over brunch at Rum Point, prepared by their favorite chef, Miles, made their plans for the following day. On Monday morning along with their housekeeper, Ellye, the Foxes prepared the Mariposa as best they could, and around noon boarded their twenty-five-foot boat, also named the *Mariposa*, and met Gagliano on his boat, the *Talisman*, in the harbor area at Placencia. Two other boats, the *Miss Lou* and the *Nancy*, an ocean-going skiff slightly smaller than the *Mariposa*, joined them, and the four boats headed to Big Creek.

As they arrived at the main opening to the lagoon they noticed the *Aggressor* and a few other boats already tied to the banana dock, and so they found a narrow channel cut between the mangroves that meandered south a few hundred yards. This area, they agreed, made a perfect mooring location because the flexible mangroves would move with the waves and storm surge. The horseshoe channel was about fifty yards wide—long enough for thirty boats—and was visually and physically separated from the banana dock by a large area of mangroves. The mangrove area between the smaller spring-lined boats and those at the banana dock was approximately a quarter-mile wide with a thicket height of six to eight feet. The extensive root and tree system of the mangrove area between the two groups was so soggy and thick a person would need boots and a machete to get through it. Normally a sanctuary for juvenile fish, today it would provide a safe haven for many boats.

After setting up in their assigned spot, the Foxes assisted in springing the *Toucan* and the *Carlin*, two sixty-foot sailboats from South Africa. Since the main force of Iris was not expected until later that evening they took the

Mariposa back to Placencia to check on two boats owned by friends and to take a second shot at convincing Elleye that she should go back to Big Creek with them. As much as they pleaded with her, however, she wouldn't budge and insisted on staying on the *Mariposa*.

At 2:00 p.m. the center of Iris appeared on Belize radar and the meteorological office could track her on its own from that point. Fuller read the radar charts and the eye fixes then sent them by fax to the NHC. From now until Hurricane Iris left the range of his radar, Fuller's analysis would become a part of the NWS bulletin. The 2:00 p.m. report from the NWS read:

BULLETIN

Hurricane Iris intermediate advisory number 16a

National Weather Service, Miami, FL

2 p.m. edt, Mon Oct 08 2001

...Small but extremely dangerous Iris heading toward southern Belize...

Preparations to protect life and property in the hurricane warning area should be rushed to completion.

A hurricane warning remains in effect for the caribbean coasts of Belize...Guatemala and Honduras from the border wth Guatemala eastward to Limon.

A tropical storm warning is in effect for the east coast of the Yucatan from Felipe Carrillo Puerto southward to the border with Belize.

A hurricane watch remains in effect for the Mexican east coast of the Yucatan peninsula from Cabo Catoche southward to the Belize border. The hurricane watch for the Mexican coast may be discontinued later this afternoon.

At 2 p.m. edt...1800z...the center of Hurricane Iris was located near latitude 16.9 north...longitude 85.9 west or about 165 miles...265 km...east-southeast of Belize City, Belize. Iris is moving just south of due west near 21 mph...33 km/hr.

A general west or slightly south of west motion is expected prior to landfall...bringing hurricane conditions to portions of Belize...Guatemala...northern Honduras and the adjacent islands later today and tonight. On the projected track...the center is expected to make landfall late tonight or early Tuesday morning.

Maximum sustained winds are near 140 mph...220 km/hr... with higher gusts. Iris is an extremely dangerous category four hurricane. Some fluctuations in intensity are possible prior to landfall.

Iris is an extremely small hurricane...with hurricane force winds extending outward up to 15 miles...30 km... from the center. Tropical storm force winds extend outward up to 115 miles...185 km.

Estimated minimum central pressure is 950 mb...28.05 inches.

Storm surge flooding of 13-18 feet above normal tide levels... along with dangerous large battering waves...are likely near the to the north of where the center of the hurricane crosses the coast.

Rainfall totals of 5 to 8 inches...locally higher... are likely along the path of Iris. These rains could cause life-threatening flash floods and mud slides over mountainous terrain.

Repeating the 2 p.m. edt position...16.9 n...85.9 w. Movement

TOWARD...JUST SOUTH OF DUE WEST NEAR 21 MPH. MAXIMUM
SUSTAINED WINDS...140 MPH. MINIMUM CENTRAL PRESSURE...950 MB.

THE NEXT ADVISORY WILL BE ISSUED BY THE NATIONAL HURRICANE

CENTER AT 5 P.M. EDT.

FORECASTER FRANKLIN

Fuller hoped and prayed that the people of southern Belize took his warning seriously. Preparation time was running out. By now they should be headed to the shelters. He had recorded a public service announcement for Channel 5 and LOVE 95, telling residents to take bedding, folding chairs, water, a radio, and a flashlight with them to the shelter. He added that they should be prepared to spend the night in the shelter, but that the hurricane should be clear of Belize by morning.

Trying to find his best option, Captain Schnabel called the village of Independence, a town of two thousand people and the closest by land to Big Creek, looking for hotel rooms for his passengers and crew. He asked Mrs. Zabaneh about a particular hotel and was told it had been destroyed by fire five years earlier. However, she told him to call back and she would check the area for other possible accommodations. Mrs. Zabaneh then called every area facility only to find they were full or had been evacuated. So, when Captain Schnabel called again, he found that community storm shelters provided the only option. He convened a meeting in the salon of the *Aggressor* with several of his passengers to update them.

With sun still streaming in the windows and air-conditioning wafting over them, Captain Schnabel told the group, "You can stay or leave. But if you leave I can't guarantee the quality of your accommodations or how long you'll be there. You'll also have to take your own provisions. Nothing other than shelter is available. Personally, I think you'll be safer on the boat, but that's up to you."

Dave Mowrer, one of the more experienced and well-traveled divers on the *Aggressor*, observed that outside it was hot and muggy. "All you can see is tin roofs and shacks." By contrast, the *Aggressor* was cool, packed with good food and drink, not to mention medical supplies. Mowrer thought, should we go into a Third World country or stay here? He felt they would be safer and more comfortable where they were. The passengers voted: they'd weather the storm on the ship.

Captain Schnabel called Mrs. Zabaneh to tell her of their decision. She told him her husband, Tony, wanted to speak with him. Mr. Zabaneh, Chairman of Independence Village and area representative of NEMO, apologized that he had been unavailable earlier but that he had been checking shelters and securing transportation for the residents of the Independence area. He understood Captain Schnabel's position, but the inconvenience would last just a few hours. The only shelter available exclusively for the *Aggressor* passengers and crew was the Belize Bank building, a half mile from the Big Creek dock. Mr. Zabaneh assured Captain Schnabel that while it was not used as a bank any longer, it was in good repair and would accommodate everyone on the boat.

Sensing the captain's reluctance, Zabaneh and his son drove their small bus and van to the Big Creek pier and offered travel to the shelter. He pleaded with Captain Schnabel to leave the *Aggressor*. The captain reiterated that they would rather ride out Iris where they were anchored. Feeling uneasy about their situation, Mary Tillet, the long-time Belizean cook on the *Aggressor*, told Zabaneh that some of the passengers wanted to buy phone cards, and she wanted to check again for hotel rooms or other accommodations. Mary went to Independence with Zabaneh to seek the information and cards. While at Zabaneh's grocery and general store Mary watched The Weather Channel, which showed the path and position of Hurricane Iris. It frightened her. She asked Mrs. Zabaneh to write down the storm information so she could give it to her captain. She was sure he was not aware that Iris was coming right at them. Zabaneh told Mary that either

Independence or the bank building was safer than the harbor at Big Creek, and if her captain changed his mind there would be room for everyone. Mary said she was anxious to get back because another boat, the *Wave Dancer*, was coming to Big Creek and she had friends among the boat's staff.

It had been a few hours since anyone had heard from the *Wave Dancer*. Both Ryan Vernon in Belize City and Peter Hughes in Miami tried to make radio contact with Captain Martin but to no avail. The *Wave Dancer's* side-band radio, used for long-range communication, had been broken for months, and the three-meter radio was out of range of mainland contact. The satellite phone, which had been used earlier by passengers and staff, now appeared to be broken. No one had heard from or seen the *Wave Dancer*, and Peter Hughes grew concerned. He called Wayne Hasson, owner of the *Aggressor*, to ask if anyone from his boat knew about the *Wave Dancer*. Hasson, who was on the satellite phone with Captain Schnabel at the time, put Hughes on hold and asked for news of the *Wave Dancer*. Captain Schnabel said he had not communicated for hours with Captain Martin but expected him to seek shelter at Big Creek. Hasson gave Hughes the information he did not want to hear.

When the *Wave Dancer* began to negotiate the buoys into Big Creek, Baechtold, not wanting to miss an opportunity to expand his week's video sales, asked Captain Martin to stop the *Wave Dancer* and off-load him and the dinghy, so he could videotape the boat pulling into Big Creek. Riding the wake of the *Wave Dancer*, Baechtold could be heard saying, "All-Right! Yah, Baby, Yah!" as he shot footage of the boat cruising up Big Creek with the *Belize Aggressor* and the banana warehouse coming into his viewfinder.

The boat maneuvered into position at the dock in front of the *Aggressor* and tossed bow and stern lines to Zabaneh and a warehouse security guard for the initial tie-up. Since dropping off Mary, Zabaneah had been securing the area around the warehouse, supervising the removal of forty stacks of banana pallets and an empty storage container. These items, thought

Zabaneh, could become missiles during a strong windstorm and seriously damage the boats at the dock. After the clean up, Zabaneh checked with Earl Young, his captain on the *Miss Gayle*, and left Big Creek to seek shelter with his family.

Captain Martin seemed considerably relieved to arrive at Big Creek but did not like the amount of room available for his boat. He needed to put a 120-foot boat in only sixty-five feet of dock space. With fifteen feet separating it from the *Aggressor*, the *Wave Dancer* extended approximately seventy feet into the channel with no dock or stable post with which to secure the bow. Martin boarded the *Aggressor* and asked Schnabel for his advice. They walked the full length of the dock, past the *Aggressor* and *Miss Gayle*, reviewing the situation. They studied each boat and the space between them. All were secured with approximately fifteen feet between them, which would allow the boats room to move fore and aft during the storm without bumping into each other.

The only option they could see that would help Martin was a twenty-five-foot space between the *Aggressor* and the *Miss Gayle*. Martin asked Schnabel to move the *Aggressor* and change places on the dock with the *Wave Dancer*. Schnabel paused. He couldn't believe his ears. The brash young captain who, in his opinion, had procrastinated until the last minute before coming to Big Creek, astounded him. Give up his spot on the dock because the *Wave Dancer* arrived late? Schnabel shook his head and told Martin that he should call Hughes and let him know his location. Schnabel, while concerned for the safety of the *Wave Dancer*, knew well that his first responsibility was to the passengers and crew of the *Aggressor*. It would be up to Peter Hughes to deal with Martin. Schnabel was helpless to do more for his foolish fellow captain.

Martin, realizing the seriousness of the situation, immediately called Hughes, explaining that he did not have enough room on the dock to ensure the *Wave Dancer's* safety. Martin also admitted he was short of tie-up ropes. Hughes told him to borrow ropes from Schnabel. Otherwise, he should do the best he could and everything would be okay.

Martin asked Schnabel if he had extra ropes and Schnabel, now exasperated by Martin's incompetence, said he would have to get approval from Hasson before he could give him anything. Schnabel called Hasson and explained the *Wave Dancer's* predicament and asked if he could loan some of his excess rope to the *Wave Dancer*. Hasson said no.

"Tell Captain Martin he needs to run the *Wave Dancer* into the mangroves," Hasson told Schnabel. "The thicket will support the boat and tomorrow the *Miss Gayle* can pull the *Wave Dancer* out."

Captain Martin, although inexperienced when it came to riding out a hurricane, didn't like the idea of running the *Wave Dancer* into the mangrove area. Boats were meant to float, not to be grounded. He had no idea what would happen if the storm pounded the *Wave Dancer* against the mangroves. By contrast, the dock was solid concrete, which seemed like it could withstand any storm. He elected to tie-up and hope for the best.

Captain Schnabel put the *Aggressor's* dinghy on the dive deck platform, creating an extra ten feet for the *Wave Dancer*. Captain Martin backed the *Wave Dancer* to within fifteen feet of the *Aggressor's* bow and tied up his boat. The best tie-up position he could manage was at the stern of the *Wave Dancer*, where he ran two lines from his stern cleat to a Samson post. Another small line ran from the *Wave Dancer's* port ladder to a stationary ladder built into the dock. At the bow, three lines were run, the first two inland one hundred feet to a Samson post and the third line back fifty feet to the Samson post on the dock. One bowline was spliced and tied to make it appear to be a spring line. But the line was tied only to the Samson post, which did not allow much, if any, forward and back action, thus making it basically ineffective for that purpose. The three lines were not equalized, which forced the stress load to be carried by the taut line while the other two lay limp.

With their tie-ups complete the captains reviewed each other's lines. Captain Schnabel had in place four to six bow and stern lines and four mid lines with crossing spring lines to prevent the *Aggressor* from moving forward or aft. All twelve to sixteen lines of the vessel were secured with enough slack to allow for the rise and fall of the storm surge. Captain Martin's two stern lines, while secured directly to a Samson post adjacent to the rear of the *Wave Dancer*, were too taut and thus would not allow for any rise and fall. At the bow, the *Wave Dancer's* tie-up was odd in its placement and definition of a spring line, but it was as good as could be done with the boat's poor position on the dock and the few ropes Captain Martin possessed. Captain Schnabel advised Captain Martin to leave enough slack in his lines for the rise and fall of the storm surge and the two went to their separate boats.

Captain Schnabel was acutely aware of the sometimes overlooked danger of the hurricane storm surge. Historically, novice weather watchers have focused on the wind speed of a hurricane, but Captain Schnabel had read enough to know that the flooding from storm surge causes nine out of ten deaths attributed to a hurricane. He also knew that Captain Martin did not have a clue about the intensity and destructive power of a hurricane's storm surge. He had cautioned him as best he could. And yet, at its location, the *Wave Dancer's* bow faced south extending approximately sixty feet beyond the end of the dock and at a thirty degree angle to the channel connecting the Big Creek Dock with the open Caribbean Sea.

Chapter Twelve

"*If there is magic on this planet, it is contained in the water....Its substance reaches everywhere; it touches the past and prepares the future; it moves under the poles and wanders thinly in the heights of air. It can assume forms of exquisite perfection in a snowflake, or strip the living to a single shining bone cast upon the sea.*"

Loren Eisley, *The Immense Journey*

"Don't come over here without a beer and a blonde!" Prillaman yelled to his friends on the *Aggressor*. Webb and Cox wasted little time boarding the *Aggressor*, asking for directions to the bar and telling all within ear shot that they had partied so hard they were out of beer. The good-natured ribbing and storytelling moved from boat to boat with little interruption. Prillaman, Cox, and Webb corralled a few of their *Aggressor* friends to show them that they, too, had a hot tub. Soon guests from both boats mingled freely, moving from one boat to the next or walking in small groups along the dock. And all enjoyed the merriment that only Prillaman could orchestrate.

After the initial greetings and a Belikin or two, the talk turned more serious. Ray Mars and Dave Mowrer stood on the dock discussing the impending storm. Mowrer told Mars about their decision to stay on their boat rather than go to a shelter. Captain Schnabel assured them they were well prepared.

"Schnabel hasn't planned anything for tomorrow," Mowrer said. "We'll wait and see what the storm brings. It may churn up the water so much we couldn't see anything down there anyway."

"Martin told us everything was okay," Mars said. "He showed us some weather faxes, including the three o'clock report, which came up blank. Glenn posted them, and they show the eye is north of us."

A loud scene erupted a few feet away on the dock. Angela squared off with Martin, yelling that she was leaving. Martin, towering over her, glared down.

"Who's going to clean the cabins and cook?" he snapped.

Angela said, "I don't know, and I don't care."

Martin kept his dark eyes on her, though he clearly felt the stares from the guests on both boats, where the socializing had come to an abrupt halt. Things had spun beyond his control already with the lack of space for his boat, the lack of enough ropes to secure it, and now what appeared to be a public mutiny.

"Well, just so you know," Martin said firmly, "if you leave now you can't come back."

Angela's determined look softened for a brief moment. Then she tightened her jaw and said, "I'm not going to risk my life for you." She spun from him, gave tearful hugs to Eloisa and Brenda, and sped away with her boyfriend.

Martin stood still on the dock, as if waiting for her to change her mind, and then stalked off. Guests on both boats drifted back to what they were doing.

DeBarger inspected the tie-up of the *Wave Dancer* and did not like the way the lines were run or the position of the boat at the dock. He felt there weren't enough lines securing the boat. In fact, it looked to him like the

Aggressor had at least two times as many direct lines and spring lines. And half the *Wave Dancer* extended away from the dock—counter to everything he knew about boating. He found Wouters and mentioned his concerns.

"Captain Martin knows what he's doing," Wouters said. A former Navy seaman, DeBarger considered the captain of a ship as the "Master next to God."

"Okay," he said. "He knows best. It just doesn't look right."

Several other passengers thought the tie-up and position seemed odd but did not challenge Captain Martin, who, after the incident with Angela, did his best to keep his guests upbeat.

On the *Wave Dancer* a few guests stood in the dive deck area when Baechtold came through with his video camera. He said, "Give us a big one, smile. Yeah, baby," as he panned the group. His camera lingered a moment on the erasable board next to them that listed the week's dive sites. Next to Monday someone had crossed out "Blue Hole" and inserted "Hurricane Iris."

Dark clouds rolled in as Bill and Sheila Kelley walked hand-in-hand along the pier. They saw the *Emerald Isle*, an approximately sixty-foot luxury yacht, cruise up the channel, pause for a moment, then slice into the mangroves where Fox, Gagliano, and the other smaller boats had tied up. The Kelleys followed the line from the bow of the *Wave Dancer* out into the ankle-high grass to the Samson post, viewed it for a moment, and strolled toward the receding wake created by the *Emerald Isle* to an abandoned beached tugboat, the *Miss Pamela*. The rusted hulk of the tugboat seemed to wait patiently for a tow to the scrap heap. Its black hull exuded an eerie sense of doom. A slight breeze rose, and the air carried a chill.

After he finished helping Captain Martin tie up the *Wave Dancer*, Stanley went to the engine room and replaced one generator with another, which had to be done daily to keep one charged and one in reserve at all times. He began installing a pump for the water maker, but Wouters told him they were out of ice and that he and Chico needed to hitch a ride into Independence to get two large bags for dinner.

Stanley nodded and put down his tools.

"When you get back," Wouters told him, "we need you to fill in for Angela in the galley."

At 2:00 pm the center of Iris appeared on the Belize radar and the meteorological office now could track the hurricane on its own. An hour later Fuller reported that the intensity of Iris had begun to fluctuate—a common feature of powerful hurricanes. The innermost of the three concentric eyewalls had collapsed, leaving it with a twelve-mile-wide eye. The minimum pressure fell again to 954 mb after a brief rise to 959. The center was estimated to be near latitude 16.8 degrees north and longitude 86.9 degrees west or about one hundred miles east-southeast of Belize City. It moved west at twenty-two mph with maximum sustained winds of 140 mph. He sent this information to the NWS, which sent the following report.

BULLETIN

HURRICANE IRIS ADVISORY NUMBER 17

NATIONAL WEATHER SERVICE, MIAMI, FL

5 P.M. EDT, MON OCT 08 2001

LANDFALL OF EXTREMELY DANGEROUS
HURRICANE IRIS ONLY HOURS AWAY...

PREPARATIONS TO PROTECT LIFE AND PROPERTY IN THE HURRICANE
WARNING AREA SHOULD HAVE BEEN COMPLETED.

AT 5 P.M. EDT...2100Z...THE GOVERNMENT OF MEXICO HAS
DISCONTINUED THE HURRICANE WATCH FOR THE EAST COAST OF THE
YUCATAN PENINSULA FROM CABO CATOCHE SOUTHWARD TO THE
BELIZE BORDER.

A HURRICANE WARNING REMAINS IN EFFECT FOR THE CARIBBEAN
COASTS OF BELIZE...GUATEMALA...AND HONDURAS FROM THE BORDER
WITH GUATEMALA EASTWARD TO LIMON.

A TROPICAL STORM WARNING IS IN EFFECT FOR THE EAST COAST OF THE YUCATAN FROM FELIPE CARRILLO PUERTO SOUTHWARD TO THE BORDER WITH BELIZE.

AT 5 P.M. EDT...2100Z...THE CENTER OF HURRICANE IRIS WAS LOCATED NEAR LATITUDE 16.8 NORTH...LONGITUDE 86.9 WEST OR ABOUT 105 MILES...170 KM...EAST-SOUTHEAST OF BELIZE CITY, BELIZE.

IRIS IS MOVING TOWARD THE WEST NEAR 22 MPH...35 KM/HR...AND A MOTION JUST SOUTH OF DUE WEST IS EXPECTED PRIOR TO LANDFALL. ON THE PROJECTED TRACK...THE CENTER IS EXPECTED TO MAKE LANDFALL ON THE COAST OF BELIZE LATE TONIGHT OR EARLY TUESDAY MORNING.

MAXIMUM SUSTAINED WINDS ARE NEAR 140 MPH..220 KM/HR...WITH HIGHER GUSTS. SOME FLUCTUATIONS IN INTENSITY ARE POSSIBLE PRIOR TO LANDFALL...BUT IRIS IS LIKELY TO MAKE LANDFALL AS A CATEGORY FOUR HURRICANE.

IRIS REMAINS A VERY SMALL HURRICANE. HURRICANE FORCE WINDS EXTEND OUTWARD UP TO 15 MILES...30 KM..FROM THE CENTER...A TROPICAL STORM FORCE WINDS EXTEND OUTWARD UP TO 145 MILES...230 KM.

ESTIMATED CENTRAL PRESSURE IS 954 MB...28.17 INCHES.

STORM SURGE FLOODING OF 13 TO 18 FEET ABOVE NORMAL TIDE LEVEL..ALONG WITH DANGEROUS LARGE BATTERING WAVES...ARE LIKELY NEAR AND TO THE NORTH OF WHERE THE CENTER OF THE HURRICANE CROSSES THE COAST.

HURRICANE IRIS DISCUSSION NUMBER 17
NATIONAL WEATHER SERVICE, MIAMI, FL
5 P.M. EDT, MON OCT 08 2001

RECONAISSANCE REPORTS AND SATELLITE IMAGERY INDICATE THAT
THE INNERMOST OF THE THREE CONCENTRIC EYEWALLS COLLAPSED
LATE THIS MORNING. INITIAL RECON THIS AFTERNOON SHOWED THAT
IRIS HAD WEAKENED A BIT WITH THE COLLAPSE OF THE EYEWALL...
BUT IT IS ALREADY STARTING TO MAKE A RECOVERY. FLUCTUATIONS IN
INTENSITY ARE COMMON WITH INTENSE HURRICANES AS THEIR CORE
STRUCTURE EVOLVES. LATEST RECON REPORTED A 10 NM EYE...UP FROM
3 NM THIS MORNING. CENTRAL PRESSURES ARE HARD TO NAIL DOWN
EXACTLY BECAUSE OF THE VERY SMALL EYE AND STRONG PRESSURE
GRADIENTS...BUT IT APPEARS THAT THE PRESSURE IS BACK DOWN TO
ABOUT 954 MB AFTER RISING TO 959 EARLIER IN THE AFTERNOON.
THE PEAK WIND REPORTED RECENTLY FROM FLIGHT-LEVEL WAS 112
KIT...BUT A GPS DROPSONDE AT 19Z WAS REPORTING 132 KT WHEN IT
FAILED AT 46 METERS ABOVE THE SEA SURFACE. SURFACE-EQUIVALENT
ESTIMATES FROM THIS DROP RANGE FROM 105 TO 120 KT. WHILE THE
CURRENT INTENSITY IS PROBABLY A LITTLE LESS THAN 120 KT RIGHT
NOW...I WILL KEEP THE ADVISORY INTENSITY AT 120KT BECAUSE IRIS
APPEARS TO BE STRENGTHENING AGAIN.

THE MOTION AVERAGED OVER THE LAST 6 TO 9 HOURS IS 265/19. PRETTY
MUCH ON THE PREVIOUS TRACK. THE CENTER SHOULD BE MAKING
LANDFALL WITHIN 12 HOURS. THERE HAS BEEN NO SIGNIFICANT CHANGE
TO THE FORECAST PRIOR TO LANDFALL...BUT THE FEELING IS NOW THAT
THE SMALL CIRCULATION OF IRIS WILL NOT SURVIVE THE PASSAGE
ACROSS THE RUGGED TERRAIN OF CENTRAL AMERICA.

FORECASTER FRANKLIN

After reviewing the report, which combined information gathered by
radar and the hurricane hunters, Fuller and Hulse discussed the need for
extra efforts in alerting the coastal areas of southern Belize. They knew
Percy Neal, Tony Zabaneh, and the other community leaders would prepare

the people and property, but they wondered if more needed to be done. According to their latest calculations, Iris would reach landfall in three to five hours, most likely around Placencia. The area was at sea level, so the battering waves and thirteen- to eighteen-foot storm surge would destroy most, if not all, of the wood-frame buildings within a quarter-of-a-mile of the beaches. People afraid of leaving their homes could be washed away.

Dark clouds packed the sky as Prillaman drifted back to the *Wave Dancer* after the reunion with his friends on the *Aggressor*. They surely would be diving again tomorrow after the storm passed, he thought, but for now, as leader of the group, he needed to make sure everyone had a good time.

In the salon, he saw that the group had returned from the *Aggressor*, and the pre-dinner activity seemed normal. The Coxes and Johnstons huddled at the light table, looking at slides from the previous day's dives. Mary Lou and Lisa painted their fingernails and chatted. Webb, Topping, Christy, and Cheryl played cards, and DeBarger and Patterson, having taken down the weather faxes, watched a James Bond movie. The rest of his group, he thought, must be in their cabins resting or preparing for their later-than-normal dinner. With the abrupt departure of Angela and the need for ice, Eloisa's dinner had been moved back to seven o'clock.

By 6:45 p.m. Stanley and Chico returned with ice, the wind and rain whipping them as they boarded the boat. Stanley headed to the galley, where Eloisa asked him to serve the evening meal. The main course was curried shrimp, and everyone enjoyed Eloisa's fine cooking. During dessert, Captain Martin walked into the galley for his briefing. He told them Iris had shifted course to the south, and he felt good about their position in Big Creek.

"Since we are so far south, in the morning we will dive at Laughing Bird Caye then work our way back to Lighthouse Reef in the afternoon," he said. "Is everything okay?" He gave them a wide smile. "Are you all happy?"

"Yes!" they said in unison.

"Good," he said, and left the dining area.

Unlike Captain Schnabel, Captain Martin gave his passengers no options and had no plan to get them off the *Wave Dancer* and to a storm shelter. After listening to the captain's briefing, Eloisa, Brenda, and Stanley huddled in the galley.

"Bart, did you hear that?" Eloise asked Stanley. "Did you hear those lies? They won't be diving tomorrow. The water will be too stirred up. He acts like we're in some kind of little rain shower."

"I feel sorry for these people and the bull Martin is feeding them," Stanley said. "I guess we'll just have to cross our fingers and hope for the best."

Nine boats of various sizes, shapes, and styles filled the mangroves. Peter and Marcia Fox boarded the *Talisman* and along with Gagliano and Douglas Young, a small Belizean man, prepared to ride out the storm in its comfortable salon. Prior to leaving Placencia, Gagliano, a gourmet chef, had stocked up on food. For their evening meal he prepared New York strip and sliced mushrooms sautéed in butter with a splash of red wine. Gagliano wanted to eat well regardless of the circumstances. As he cleaned up his galley he heard the wind and rain hammering hard against the boat. This is going to be a bad one, he thought. He wondered if they should have gone to a shelter in Independence, but he quickly brushed away the moment of doubt.

As he read the latest coordinated report from the NWS, Fuller noted the wind gauge holding steady at fifty mph. He knew it probably would climb to seventy-five when the main force of Iris made landfall, just about half of what the people sixty miles south of him would experience.

BULLETIN
HURRICANE IRIS INTERMEDIATE ADVISORY NUMBER 17A
NATIONAL WEATHER SERVICE, MIAMI, FL
8 P.M. EDT, MON OCT 08 2001

LANDFALL OF EXTREMELY DANGEROUS HURRICANE IRIS ONLY HOURS AWAY...

PREPARATIONS TO PROTECT LIFE AND PROPERTY IN THE HURRICANE
WARNING AREA SHOULD HAVE BEEN COMPLETED.

AT 8 P.M. EDT...A HURRICANE WARNING REMAINS IN EFFECT FOR THE
CARIBBEAN COASTS OF BELIZE...GUATEMALA...AND HONDURAS FROM
THE BORDER WITH GUATEMALA EASTWARD TO LIMON.
A TROPICAL STORM WARNING IS IN EFFECT FOR THE EAST COAST
OF THE YUCATAN FROM FELIPE CARILLO PUERTO SOUTHWARD
TO THE BORDER WITH BELIZE.

AT 8 P.M. EDT...0000Z...THE CENTER OF HURRICANE IRIS WAS LOCATED
NEAR LATITUDE 16.5 NORTH...LONGITUDE 88.0 WEST OR ABOUT 75
MILES...120 KM...SOUTHEAST OF BELIZE CITY, BELIZE.

IRIS IS MOVING JUST SOUTH OF DUE WEST NEAR 22 MPH...35 KM/HR.
ON THE PROJECTED TRACK...THE CENTER IS EXPECTED TO MAKE
LANDFALL ON THE COAST OF BELIZE IN THE NEXT SEVERAL HOURS.
MAXIMUM WINDS ARE NEAR 145 MPH...235 KM/HR...WITH HIGHER
INTENSITY. SUSTAINED WINDS ARE NEAR 145 MPH...235 KM/HR...WITH
HIGHER GUSTS. SOME FLUCTUATIONS IN INTENSITY ARE POSSIBLE
PRIOR TO LANDFALL... BUT IRIS IS LIKELY TO MAKE LANDFALL AS
A CATEGORY FOUR HURRICANE. HIGHER WINDS MAY OCCUR OVER
ELEVATED TERRAIN AS IRIS MOVES INLAND.

IRIS REMAINS A VERY SMALL HURRICANE. HURRICANE FORCE
WINDS EXTEND OUTWARD UP TO 15 MILES...30 KM...FROM THE
CENTER...AND TROPICAL STORM FORCE WINDS EXTEND OUTWARD
UP TO 145 MILES...230 KM.

ESTIMATED MINIMUM CENTRAL PRESSURE IS 954 MB...28.17 INCHES.

STORM SURGE FLOODING OF 13-18 FEET ABOVE NORMAL TIDE LEVELS...
ALONG WITH DANGEROUS LARGE BATTERING WAVES...ARE LIKELY
NEAR AND TO THE NORTH OF WHERE THE CENTER OF THE HURRICANE

CROSSES THE COAST.

RAINFALL TOTALS OF 5 TO 8 INCHES...LOCALLY HIGHER...
ARE LIKELY ALONG THE PATH OF IRIS. THESE RAINS COULD CAUSE
LIFE-THREATENING FLASH FLOODS AND MUD SLIDES OVER
MOUNTAINOUS TERRIAN.
REPEATING THE 8 P.M. EDT POSITION...16.5 N...88.0 W. MOVEMENT
TOWARD...WEST NEAR 22 MPH. MAXIMUM SUSTAINED WINDS...145 MPH.
MINIMUM CENTRAL PRESSURE...954 MB.

THE NEXT ADVISORY WILL BE ISSUED BY THE NATIONAL HURRICANE
CENTER AT 11 P.M. EDT.

FORECASTER JARVINEN/RHOME

Fuller knew this would be the last report before Iris made landfall. The storm was closer than the NWS report indicated, and he expected reports from his southern substations to substantiate his observations within the next hour or two. Satisfied he had done all he could to prepare his country for Hurricane Iris, Fuller went to his office and prayed for the safety of his people.

In the salon of the *Aggressor* the passengers watched a slide show of a local cave system taken by their photo pro. As the show concluded, the wind and rain intensified. Something banged incessantly on the topside, perhaps one of the lockers swinging free. The storm pounded harder at the boat, and as much as the passengers looked for ways to relax, the weather worried them. The marine glass windows, though rated to withstand 150 mph winds, seemed like they could be a hazard. Most of the large objects around the dock and banana warehouse had been removed earlier by Zabaneh and his men, but a lot of small debris cluttered the area and could become lethal projectiles.

Mowrer suggested that everyone go below to be safe from flying glass if a window broke. One by one they filed down the narrow stairs to the cabin area. The hallway clogged with people who, while they would've had more room in their cabins, did not want to be isolated in case they needed to evacuate. They reassured each other that the hurricane would pass soon and everything would be all right. "Stay calm," they said. "Don't panic."

Mowrer went to his cabin on the portside of the *Aggressor* and peered out his window, which was below the top of the dock. From his position below the path of the rain and wind, he clearly saw the graffiti on the concrete wall several feet from him. A few moments later a loud thud jolted the boat, and he looked out the window to see what happened. He saw nothing—no dock, no graffiti. He flipped off his cabin light and tried again. He saw pure black, as if on a night dive at a hundred feet without a light. Trying not to panic anyone, he told the group to go to their cabins, get life jackets, and put on shoes.

On the *Wave Dancer*, the guests gathered in the salon, drinking after-dinner coffee while trying to ignore the relentless pummeling of wind and rain. Unlike the *Aggressor*, the *Wave Dancer* did not have the banana warehouse to shield it from the 140 mph horizontal wind and rain. The boat was fully exposed to all the elements an angry Mother Nature could throw at it. Captain Martin, wearing his green hooded parka, slogged into the salon dripping wet. He flipped back his hood, shook off the rainwater, and told them he had just come from the wheelhouse, where he was monitoring the storm. He said he and Stark periodically went to the dock to check the lines, which were holding fine. He assured them that Wouters was at the helm using the diesel engines to counter the force of the storm, relieving the pressure on the mooring lines and keeping the boat close to the dock.

"Everything is under control," he said, but his earlier composure had evaporated. He looked worried. "We're going to be okay," he said, and then yanked up his hood and left for the wheelhouse.

Lisa went to the boat's computer and typed a message to her father, hoping that sending "her favorite bud" a message would calm her. She didn't want him to worry about her, although she knew he would anyway. Before she left he had insisted on buying a new battery for her car so it would start when she got back from Belize. She wrote that she and Mary Lou were having a great time. They had done four dives the first day. The diving had been great, the visibility excellent, and she had seen a lot of sharks. Tomorrow, she wrote, they would do their morning dives at Laughing Bird Caye and then have a picnic on the beach. She signed it "Love, your favorite daughter, Lisa."

Prillaman's eyes darted around the room, and the smile under his thick moustache curled mischievously. He wanted a little stress relief of his own, and he naturally wanted an audience too. He stood up and announced he would perform, for the group's delight and mystification, a bit of magic. He picked "the lovely Brenda" to assist him in a sleight-of-hand trick.

Shy at first, Brenda refused. "No, no," she said with a giggle. "Pick someone else."

"Don't worry," Cheryl said. "He's harmless."

"Mostly harmless," Christy added.

When Brenda reluctantly agreed, the group applauded.

Prillaman said, "Watch and be astounded," as he put a cloth napkin in his left hand and stuffed a piece of it between his thumb and first finger. He then had Brenda pour a packet of sugar into the napkin. When she finished, he said "abracadabra" and pulled the napkin away to show that the sugar had disappeared. "And now, my lovely assistant will kiss my hand."

Brenda shook her head and took a step back, giggling nervously, but after much prodding from the audience, she agreed. As she gave his hand a quick peck he let the grains of sugar fall from his cupped hand into the palm of her open one. She squealed with delight, clearly astonished by the magic. Prillaman stooped into a low bow, thanking the audience and his lovely assistant.

After the magic show, Mary Lou, Christy, and Cheryl decided to go to their cabins. Webb waited at the door of the salon with an umbrella and one-by-one escorted them through the rain to the stairway that led to the deck below. The boat heaved up and down as the wind stirred the waves beneath it. As Mary Lou huddled under Webb's umbrella, the roar of wind and the boat's engines startled her. Though in the salon the noise had steadily increased, outside it was deafening. When she arrived at her cabin, she thought a shower would help her relax. She also would feel better after washing off the mosquito repellent she used during her afternoon stroll around the dock.

The sound of pounding wind and rain grew louder, filling the salon to the point where the passengers had to shout at each other. Baechtold stood outside the salon door shooting footage of the hurricane, the curtain of rain, and the flags stretched so tightly they seemed to be starched. As Captain Martin walked toward the camera he looked like a mime mimicking a person trying to walk into strong wind without moving forward. The affect was both funny and frightening.

He had just been on the dock and saw that two of the *Aggressor's* salon windows had blown out. He headed back to get some duct tape, planning to make a big X on the exposed salon and cabin windows of his boat, grabbing DeBarger and Patterson along the way and asking them to help.

After her shower Mary Lou sat down on Lisa's bed and opened a book. Then she noticed the water sloshing against the porthole. It reminded her of looking through the door of a washing machine. She grabbed her mini-Maglite from the nightstand and slipped it into a pocket of her shorts. Too edgy to concentrate on the book, she walked into the hallway and toward the emergency exit, where she ran into DeBarger and Patterson.

"What're you guys doing?" she asked.

"Trying to tape the windows, to keep them from breaking," DeBarger said. "But the tape won't stick. Everything's too wet."

"Where are you going?" Patterson asked her. Though they stood close to each other, they were nearly shouting.

"Back to the salon," she said.

"It's getting really bad," Patterson said. "You're better off in your cabin." They hurried down the hallway to continue trying to tape the cabin windows. Mary Lou headed back to her cabin.

DeBarger and Patterson had taped the odd-numbered cabin windows one through seven and were working on the emergency door when the full force of Hurricane Iris hit the *Wave Dancer*. The sustained winds pushed the storm surge toward the low shelf peninsula of Placencia, driving the water up the Big Creek channel. Pressure built from the Caribbean Sea to Big Creek channel like a ten-inch water line funneling into a two-inch pipe. At seventeen hundred pounds per square yard, the weight of the water forced into the small channel with pressure behind it increased every inch of the way.

The fourteen-foot storm surge slammed into the exposed hull of the boat, which listed fifteen degrees into the dock, banging into the concrete while lifting only as high as the taut lines would allow. The impact against the dock knocked DeBarger away from the emergency door and sent him sprawling down the hallway.

"What the hell was that?" he shouted. He scrambled to his feet, picked up his roll of tape, and looked at Patterson, who shrugged, his eyes wide. The boat had canted to one side. They stood in the hallway feeling more of their weight on one leg than the other. They froze in that position for a moment as they tried to collect their bearings.

When the *Wave Dancer* listed and then hit the dock, the large appliances not secured to the deck—including refrigerators, stoves and ovens—slid to the port side of the galley. In the engine room, the free-standing water-maker pump, air compressors, nitrox compressor, and spare parts also shifted toward port, as did the two freezers, two washing machines, and dryer in the laundry room. The combined weight of these appliances created a transversal shift in the center of gravity, causing the boat to list even more.

With the wind howling, appliances sliding in the galley, and loose chairs grinding across the salon, the passengers could barely hear each other. Someone screamed, "The boat is going to tip!"

Stanley shouted to Eloisa and Brenda: "Stay close to me."

The boat stabilized and Baechtold hollered, "Get your life jackets."

Patterson yelled, "Get two" to DeBarger, who rushed to his dark cabin and felt around for them.

The storm surge raised the *Wave Dancer* almost six feet, extending its mooring lines to the point where the hull was level with the topside of the dock. Then a full-force wind slammed at the same time as a storm surge into the exposed side of the *Wave Dancer*, ripping the weld and yanking the stern cleat from its bit. The cleat shot out of the hull, and the bow lines popped free. The boat had nothing to hold it upright in the face of the raging storm.

Wouters gunned the engines, desperate to stay against the dock. But with nothing left holding the boat, the storm quickly won the battle. A powerful gust of wind whipped under the canopy of the sky deck, turning it into a large kite, and picked up the *Wave Dancer*, spun it 180 degrees, and tossed it across the raging waters of Big Creek.

The *Wave Dancer* blew 150 yards across the lagoon, almost parallel to its original position at the dock. Then, as if tired of carrying the burden, Iris simply flipped the boat over. It landed hull up in twenty-five feet of surge-swollen water next to the mangroves.

The passengers on the *Wave Dancer* screamed as the boat flew across the water, but the roar of wind and rain buried their cries for help. No one heard them or knew that soon there would be a tragedy in paradise.

The inverted *Wave Dancer* became a death trap. Water rushed into all open doorways, broken windows, through the air-conditioning louvers, down the halls, and into every room. Every orifice poured water. And fast. The storm shredded the blue canvas of the sky deck's canopy, and tossed it aside. The cross-ribbed Bimini top, which a few hours earlier had provided shade and a place to congregate for the divers, buckled under the weight of the boat now resting on top of it.

The four-level yacht was now a three-level mass of inverted mayhem with the salon on the bottom, guest cabins in the middle, and mechanical room on top. The engines and generators shut down, leaving the *Wave Dancer* with no power. Without functioning emergency lights, the boat, within thirty seconds, went dark. The passengers fought blindly for their lives.

With the hurricane now at its peak, neither moon nor stars lit the night. The churned-up saltwater immediately filled with silt from the channel's floor, while the boat's ruptured diesel fuel tanks added yet another hazard for the dazed and struggling divers. Survival seemed impossible.

As the boat capsized, it pitched Baechtold, Webb, Topping, and Stark into the mangroves. Captain Martin and Wouters hunkered in the wheelhouse, grabbing the wheel and a railing. When the wheelhouse landed on the bottom of the channel they opened the submerged door and escaped.

Mary Lou immediately slipped into her life jacket when the boat tipped and braced herself against the walls of her cabin with her hands and feet in the Vitruvian Man position. Within seconds, she flipped upside-down. She rolled to her feet, realizing in the darkness that she now stood on the ceiling of her cabin.

As water poured in, she said, "Dear God, I don't think I'm going to survive." She had only minutes—maybe seconds—to save herself. Trying not to panic, she reached into her pocket for her three-inch penlight and flicked it on. She stuck it in her mouth and opened the cabin door, following the small shaft of light into the hallway, traversing the beam in all directions, trying desperately to orient herself. The light fell on the front of her cabin door where number six now read nine. She focused the beam in the direction, she hoped, of the emergency exit door. She stumbled down the hallway, placing one hand on each wall, using the ceiling as her footpath. The path led to an inverted staircase, where she sloshed across the partially submerged and slippery treads to get to the emergency door. She pulled on the door but couldn't budge it. Water pressure on the submerged other side had sealed it shut. Rapidly running out of escape routes, she realized the capsized boat would kill her if she didn't come up with something quick.

Meanwhile, Patterson, who had been spun around and tossed upside-down, groped his way from a cabin into the pitch-black hallway. Struggling to get his bearings, he looked to his right and saw nothing but darkness. Then he thought he saw a flickering light.

"There," he told himself. "That's where I have to go." He scrambled toward the small beam, and when he was within a few feet of it, he saw Mary Lou. She pulled with all her strength on the emergency door. He grabbed the handle, and they pulled together, but either it was blocked or had too much pressure against it.

Waist deep in rapidly rising water, out of options and almost out of time, Patterson kicked at the door's glass window. With his bare foot he kicked once. No movement. He reared back, and with a superhuman strength sometimes given to people in moments of crisis, kicked it again with all his might. The rubber gasket holding the window in place gave way and the glass fell out. They looked at each other, took a deep breath, and first Mary Lou then Patterson swam through the submerged window and surfaced in the murky, diesel-fuel-saturated water next to the overturned *Wave Dancer*.

As horrible as the water smelled and tasted, it was a welcome relief to be above it. They hadn't died, at least not yet.

DeBarger had been feeling around in his closet for a lifejacket when suddenly he pitched hard against the wall of his cabin. As he collected himself, a gush of water poured across his stomach. Crawling toward his cabin door, he saw that it was now below him. The bunks stood vertically, and the mattresses flopped off them with a thud. He could not see in the dark but resisted the urge to panic. He vowed that he would not die on the boat.

He yanked hard on his cabin door, but it would not open. Suddenly the boat shifted, and the door popped open a few inches, just enough to wiggle out. As he moved into the hallway, more water rushed in around him, quickly filling up the area. He soon found himself running out of air space and almost completely under water. Half clawing, half swimming, he realized he wasn't making much progress. He thought, "Is this how it's going to end?" He figured he had a minute before he would drown.

Then he saw the dim glow from Mary Lou's penlight light and swam toward it. The light shone from an emergency door. He heard Patterson call his name.

"Get out," Patterson yelled. DeBarger felt around the window frame of the emergency door and sensing his path was clear took a deep breath. He dove through the window, swam under the walkway, and as he was about to surface several pairs of hands lifted him out of the water. Still confused, he looked around to see Mary Lou, Patterson, and Wouters sitting next to him in a small raft made out of a solid cork floatable ring with an open mesh bottom. It did not have paddles or a motor, but it did float, and that's all that mattered. Bananas, Styrofoam, and all sorts of debris littered the water around them. The horizontal rain fell so hard it felt like nails pounding through their skin.

Mary Lou rubbed her burning eyes, fearing the diesel fuel had blinded her. She couldn't see, and the fuel covered everything. There was no escaping it. "I can't see," she screamed.

"Look up," Wouters yelled over the roar of wind and rain. "Hold your face up and let the rain wash out of your eyes."

It worked. Her eyesight somewhat restored, Mary Lou scanned the area with her small flashlight, looking for someone, anyone. She hoped they would see the light and come to it. They all sat trembling—from the cold and from fear. They kept telling each other, "We're going to be okay."

Captain Martin wobbled up and down the blue hull of the *Wave Dancer*, slipping on the slick surface while shouting into the howling wind. His voice shook with fear as he yelled, "Are you out there? Can you hear me? This is Captain Martin! Can you hear me?" A few minutes passed before Baechtold splashed soaking wet from the mangroves, holding his video camera over his head.

While Patterson, DeBarger, and Mary Lou made their escape, the *Wave*

Dancer's salon filled with shrieks and screams as the boat blew violently across the water.

"The boat's broken away."

"We're tipping."

"Bart, help me!"

"Please, someone help me!"

Books, chairs, the slide projector, cups and saucers, everything that was not anchored soared across the salon as the *Wave Dancer* went down. Some of the passengers flew like rag dolls into the wall, many landing against the anchored dining tables. Some were injured, some knocked unconscious. A few painful moans rose from the dark salon along with pleas for help.

"I'm over here."

"I'm hurt. Please help me!"

"I can't breathe."

Within thirty seconds water filled the salon, and the cries for help ceased.

In the dark confusion, Stanley could not reach "the girls," to protect them as he had promised. Their screams resonated in his ears. With lungs ready to burst, he believed he would drown with the others, but he forced himself to picture the inverted room and swam to a door. Chairs, cushions, books, Venetian blinds, and tangled debris floated around him, bumping his head and arms. He swam hard in the dark foul water and thought of his two young daughters.

Suddenly—an opening. He kicked and pulled and grabbed and paddled and felt flesh. A hand. He grabbed it. Lost it. Then felt clothing, grabbed a handful, and held on tight. As he and his passenger tried to surface, he bumped the bottom of the inverted walkway that extended from the hull. Realizing something blocked his ascent, he dove down, touched the sediment bottom of the lagoon, re-acclimated himself, and pushed off.

Stanley and Chico broke the surface together, gasping for a breath they thought might never come. The battering waves and whirling wind made it hard for them to orient themselves, but within a minute Stanley secured

Chico to the side of the *Wave Dancer*. With his eyes already burning from diesel fuel, Stanley breathed deeply and dove back to the salon.

In the pitch-black boat, he could see nothing. He groped around, hoping to feel someone, until his breath ran out, and he knifed up to the surface. Without good lighting and diving gear, there was nothing more he could do, so he and Chico held on to the hull. A few minutes later he heard Captain Martin yell, "Is anyone out there?"

Stanley shouted, "It's Bart Stanley and Chico."

Captain Martin directed Stanley to the life raft, where he and Chico joined Mary Lou, Patterson, DeBarger, Baechtold, and Wouters.

Wind and rain lashed them as they huddled on the far side of the hull. DeBarger, confused by what happened, thought he was still at the dock. He couldn't figure out why the greenery and mangroves stood next to them. Wouters started to tie the life raft to the bottom of the *Wave Dancer*, but DeBarger told him to stop.

"If the boat rolls again," he said to Wouters, "we could be dragged under." After giving themselves a few moments to recover, they paddled by hand around the blue hull, and for the first time looked across the expanse that lay between them and the Big Creek dock. DeBarger said, "Good God, we're clear across the lagoon. How the hell did we get over here?"

Captain Martin, desperate to find more of his crew and passengers, continued to shout into the stiff wind, intermittently banging on the hull, listening for a response from anyone trapped in an air pocket. The storm raged on, making it almost impossible for him to hear. No one replied to his calls. After twenty futile minutes, he decided to seek help. Against the hurricane-force wind, horizontal sheets of rain, and pounding waves he swam 150 yards to the *Aggressor*.

Chapter Thirteen

"*The sea is mother-death and she is a mighty female, the one who wins, the one who sucks us all up.*"

Anne Sexton, *The Poet's Story*

Under orders from Captain Schnabel, the *Aggressor's* first mate ran the engines and monitored the storm from the wheelhouse, which faced the stern of the *Wave Dancer*. He wanted to keep close to the dock, but if the boat broke loose the captain told him to run it into the mangroves. The *Aggressor*, like the *Wave Dancer*, listed fifteen degrees into the dock from the initial storm surge. As the lines stretched to their limit, a flying projectile shattered a wheelhouse window and knocked the first mate to the floor. Rain whipped into the wheelhouse, soaking the console, so he rushed into the adjoining captain's quarters to get a towel. When he returned and finished drying the console, he looked out what had once been the window.

The *Wave Dancer* was gone.

In the *Aggressor's* salon, two of the passengers, Joe and Linda Burnworth, along with Captain Schnabel had been holding out, not wanting to go below. The Burnworths liked their chances better above the water in the salon than below in the congested cabin area. After the storm blew out three windows in the salon, however, they decided to go below. Crawling on their hands and knees through broken glass they nearly reached the stairway when Joe looked out the window and saw the lights from the *Wave Dancer's* salon.

He said to the captain, "It looks like the *Wave Dancer* is moving to a different position." As Joe and Linda descended the ladder, Captain Schnabel went outside to check the *Aggressor's* ropes.

Dave Mowrer paced his cabin on the *Aggressor*. From his window, he couldn't see anything but the black night. Finally, he bolted out the door, scrambled to the staircase, up the ladder, and out onto the dive deck, where he saw a group huddled together. The group included Captain Schnabel, Juan, a dive master, and the *Aggressor's* second mate, Steve, who was putting the boat's dingy into the water. Pitching and swerving in the harsh wind, they shouted through the deafening roar.

"What are you doing?" Mowrer yelled at Steve.

"There's a boat over there," he shouted back.

"Over where?" shouted Mowrer.

"Over there!" Steve jabbed a finger at the far side of the lagoon. Blinded by wind and rain, Mowrer rushed to his locker and grabbed his halogen dive light. As he struggled to hold steady the only light that could cut through the darkness, he watched Steve in the dinghy move toward a big blue object in the water.

What the heck is that, thought Mowrer. He panned the object with his light, wondering what boat had come into Big Creek harbor after the storm began. Then he realized the *Wave Dancer* no longer floated in front of the *Aggressor* and that the big blue object was the *Wave Dancer's* exposed hull. Scarcely able to believe his eyes, he took a deep breath and walked back inside the *Aggressor*. He calmly asked Rob Salvatori, a skilled diver with rescue and recovery experience, to come topside. Mowrer explained to Salvatori that the *Wave Dancer* had capsized. He asked Salvatori to get his wife, Jennifer, who was a registered nurse. Then he went to the dive deck to see what else he could do.

After a few minutes Steve arrived in the dinghy with three survivors from the life raft. As he threw a line to the *Aggressor*, Steve yelled through the storm, "There are three more over there. I have to go back and get them."

"Only three?" Mowrer said.

"Captain Martin is looking for more but hasn't found any yet."

Mowrer nodded but wasn't sure he truly understood.

"It looks bad," Steve said. He helped his passengers aboard and headed back to the *Wave Dancer* to get the other three survivors. As Mowrer and the others waited, the wind and rain softened a bit, beginning to feel more like a heavy downpour. Steve returned with the remaining survivors, who boarded the *Aggressor*. As Steve headed back again, Captain Martin swam up dragging Glenn Prillaman.

The group lifted his motionless body, still in the clothes he'd worn at dinner, out of the water and onto the dive platform. Under the lights of the dive deck they worked furiously to resuscitate their good friend and leader. Mowrer knelt beside Prillaman and cleared his airway of the regurgitated saltwater and particles of food. He then began compressing Prillaman's chest while Mary Lou blew air into his lungs. Mowrer yelled, "Do we have any oxygen?" The second mate scurried around looking for the first aid kit. Finding the oxygen, he set it up for immediate use.

News about Prillaman spread quickly among the guests of the *Aggressor*. Since hearing about the *Wave Dancer*, they had worried about their friends. Voices rang out,

"Is there anything I can do?"

"Do you need any help?"

Mowrer, Mary Lou, and Jennifer struggled to save Prillaman. Again,

Jennifer checked his pulse. None. They systematically relieved each other, just in case, using their combined rescue training skills. From the moment Prillaman had been placed on the deck, DeBarger held his best friend's hand.

"Come on, Glenn," he said over and over again. The team continued to work on Prillaman—not wanting to give up. They loved the guy. He couldn't be dead. He was their leader. And if their leader died, that meant others might be dead too. They all thought, we can't let that happen. We just can't.

After ten minutes, Jennifer pronounced Prillaman dead. Mary Lou and Jennifer cried while the men, choking back their tears, stood over the lifeless body of their friend and fellow diver. Together they said a silent prayer.

Realizing they could do no more for Prillaman, they collected themselves and focused on the others aboard the *Wave Dancer*. They decided to move Prillaman's body from the dive deck of the *Aggressor* to the banana warehouse. Meanwhile, Captain Martin and Wouters borrowed gear from the *Aggressor's* divers and along with Mowrer and Salvatori took the dinghy to the *Wave Dancer*, hoping their mission would be one of rescue not recovery.

By now, the storm had lightened. The winds and rain had almost stopped.

"Looks like the worst is over," Salvatori said as he paddled across the dark water.

"Or maybe we're in the eye of the storm," Mowrer said.

"It's a relief, whatever it is," Salvatori said.

Two local men showed up in a pick-up truck, having heard the call for assistance from the *Aggressor's* radio transmission. Captain Schnabel asked them to take his passengers and crew along with Mary Lou, Patterson, and DeBarger to the bank building. He told all non-essential passengers, for their own safety, to stay at the bank building until the storm passed.

On the half-mile trip the truck wove around downed utility poles and palm trees. When they arrived at the concrete building, local people greeted them sympathetically, having heard of the tragedy, and squeezed next to each other to make room. People and pets filled the building, and with the doors and windows sealed, it offered the Americans a warm, stuffy haven. They sat on the concrete floor or leaned against the service counter and thought little of their discomfort, focusing instead on the fate of their friends. Reports phoned in by listeners crackled over the radio, while the locals talked to each other about what they'd seen and heard. The Americans mostly waited in silence.

Fifteen minutes passed. Then thirty minutes. The wind and rain didn't pick up. Someone gingerly opened the door and looked outside to see starry skies. Hurricane Iris must have passed. The Americans gathered as a group and, carefully stepping over fallen power lines, walked back to their boat.

Arriving at the *Wave Dancer*, the rescue divers broke into groups. Captain Martin headed to the bow of the hull, Mowrer took the mid section, and Salvatori and the others checked the stern side of the hull and mangroves. The surge water began to recede, and the mangroves now stood four to six feet out of the water.

Mowrer thought his powerful light would penetrate the main body of the ship, where he hoped to find at least a few survivors still alive in air pockets. He used a rebreather instead of a standard first stage, which allowed him to stay under longer, freeing him from checking his pressure gauge and being concerned with running out of air.

The boat had settled on its port side, exposing the salon windows. Good news and bad news—they had access to the salon but only three inches of air between the windows and water level. There was air in the boat, but not much. He submerged, and as he entered the boat his mask blurred and his light dimmed. He surfaced and tried without success to rub away the film of diesel fuel on his mask and light. Without functioning gear, he couldn't enter the boat.

"How can I help these people?" he asked himself. "What can I do?" At least, he thought, he could break out the salon windows. Someone safe in an air pocket would have a way out. So he broke out all the windows until nothing would impede either his entry or their exit.

He extended himself through one of the openings and attempted to look around. Still too dark. Still too much diesel fuel and sediment. Frustrated, he took off his swim fins and dangled his lower body through the opening. He could feel the stationary tables and window shades. Then, moving around a little more, he felt it. A body. Definitely a body. He paused. It was stuck—trapped by the post of a stationary table. He moved the body with his feet until it came free.

"Help me," he called to Captain Martin. "I've found someone." Captain Martin hurried to him, and together they lifted out Brenda Wade.

Recognizing Brenda, Captain Martin broke down and cried. It wasn't supposed to end this way, he thought.

Mowrer swam Brenda to a rescue raft at the back of the boat, where he saw Salvatori lifting Aaron Stark's body into the same raft.

"Where did you find him?" Mowrer asked.

"Mangroves," Salvatori said.

Mowrer nodded and returned to the salon area to find a body floating at the window's opening, waiting to be lifted out. Mowrer signaled to Captain Martin, who had penetrated the wheelhouse window adjacent to his cabin.

Martin said, "Everything I owned was in there," as he clamored over to Mowrer. Together they lifted out Christy McNiel. This time Mowrer broke down. He sobbed uncontrollably before pulling himself together.

Through his tears, he said a prayer for Christy, the trip's organizer and a good friend. They loaded her body into the "death raft," now containing three occupants.

The *Aggressor's* dinghy took the inflatable raft with three bodies to the dock, where they were carried to the banana warehouse that served as a makeshift morgue. Dwarfed by pallets stacked with crates of bananas, they lay side-by-side on the bare concrete floor. Lacking blankets to cover the bodies, the recovery team used shredded cardboard boxes as well as beach towels from the *Aggressor*. For the moment, there would be little dignity for the dead.

Aboard the *Aggressor*, Captain Schnabel called the American Embassy in

Belize but got no answer. Curious local people milled around the dock. A small boat appeared, circled the lagoon for a few minutes, then left. No help arrived. With the Phase III National Hurricane Warning still in effect, most citizens of Belize still huddled in shelters. The Americans at Big Creek, isolated in a Third World country, miles and hours from significant help were, for now, on their own.

Stanley, who had refused to go to the shelter with the others, joined the rescue efforts. He and Baechtold borrowed dive gear from the *Aggressor's* lockers and insisted on making the next trip with the dinghy. When it returned, they saw three bodies in the in-tow raft. Stanley immediately recognized Brenda. He had hoped to get to the *Wave Dancer* in time to save "the girls," but realized he was too late. Undaunted, he climbed on the dinghy and rode to the blue hull lying on its side in the lagoon.

When they arrived at the *Wave Dancer*, a male body bobbed in the water. One of the crew had found the body in the mangroves, where he had landed after being tossed from the *Wave Dancer*. As Stanley started toward the salon Wouters swam toward him dragging a female body.

Stanley said, "Who is that?"

Wouters just looked at him.

"Who is it?" Stanley said again. "Tell me."

Wouters finally said, "Eloisa."

Stanley couldn't believe his ears. When he looked down to see her, sorrow and frustration swept over him. He just couldn't do this, couldn't help anymore. Eloisa's death sapped the last of his energy. After loading her on the raft and discovering the dinghy had broken down, Stanley swam back to the *Aggressor* and made himself a stiff drink.

When the passengers and crew arrived from the bank building, they had expected to see some of their friends walking around the salon of the *Aggressor*, talking about their close encounter. Instead, they saw four bodies lying on the banana warehouse floor. Their anxiety quickly turned to grief and then to doubt that any of the others remained alive.

The women talked among themselves, trying their best to stay hopeful, telling each other, "Any minute they'll walk through that door. Just wait and see." One would say, "They're good swimmers. They have good dive skills." Another would say, "They know how to survive. Remember, we were all taught not to panic." Finally someone said, "If there is a way, some of them will make it."

The men tried desperately to keep busy any way they could. When the dinghy failed, they foraged around the banana warehouse grounds and found a half-submerged sixteen-foot boat, bailed it out, found a functioning motor, and created a craft to transport people to and from the *Aggressor*. They sent their assemblage to the *Wave Dancer* to help the rescue and recovery team. The team came back to the *Aggressor*, bringing three more bodies with them.

Mowrer and Salvatori were exhausted. Their bruised and scratched limbs ached from the beating of the waves and whipping mangroves. Their wet suits partially shielded them from the elements but not the diesel fuel, which had permeated every inch of their bodies, burning their eyes and small scratches in their skin. They suffered from the odor with every breath they took.

After rinsing off as best they could and getting a cup of hot coffee, Mowrer and Salvatori reported to their friends what they'd seen and done on the *Wave Dancer*. Despite the difficult conditions, they planned to go back right away.

They said that pounding on the hull sparked no response, giving them little hope. The mangroves offered a better chance for finding survivors, but since the surge water receded the going was more difficult.

"We think there are some people alive," Mowrer said. "We just haven't found them yet. We will."

They discussed their concerns about what happened, agreeing that the captain had not prepared the passengers. Not one of the bodies they'd found wore a life jacket or shoes.

"I don't know what their captain was telling them, but it must have been full of 'blue sky,'" Mowrer said. A few of the bodies showed signs of severe trauma. Two of the women suffered crushed rib cages, probably from hitting the stationary tables in the salon when the boat capsized. Another woman had a large gash on her head, and one of the men's heads had a large bruise, leading them to believe they hit something pretty solid.

"They were probably knocked out on impact and drowned immediately," Salvatori said. "But one of the men was in a struggling pose, so he was alive when the boat overturned. He'd tried to reach the surface when he died."

Mowrer shook his head, his lips tightened. "Most of them never knew what happened. It was over as soon as it started."

DeBarger knew he had to pull himself together enough to make some crucial phone calls. When the boat capsized, he had lost his glasses and Daytimer with all his phone numbers. So he asked Mary Lou to dial for him. After calling directory assistance, he called his oldest son, Scott, in Palo Alto, California, to assure him he was okay. He knew it wouldn't be long before the media started broadcasting the devastating news.

Then, he made the toughest call of his life. He called Margo Minter, Prillaman's long-time girlfriend. DeBarger cared a lot about Margo, and he felt they made a great couple. Margo accepted Prillaman's boyish ways with wry humor, giving him space to be himself. They had talked many times about getting married, but she insisted he quit smoking first, which he seemed unable to do. Nevertheless, they were very happy. When Margo answered the phone, DeBarger talked for a couple of minutes about the storm, easing his way toward the dreaded news. Finally, he said, "Margo, there's been a bad accident. The *Wave Dancer* capsized. Glenn is not among the living."

"You're joking," she replied.

"No," he said. "I wouldn't joke about something like that."

She immediately started crying, trying to ask DeBarger between sobs what happened and was he sure about Glenn.

For ten minutes he recounted what happened to ears that really weren't listening. Finally, he said, "Margo, you have to do something for me. You have to call Jenny Chappell. She's the membership chairman of the dive club. Have her call the families of the members on board the *Wave Dancer* and tell them there's been an accident. Tell her that Mary Lou, Patterson, and I are the only ones accounted for right now and everyone else is missing."

He heard her weeping and didn't know how much she heard of his instructions. Still, he went on: "Tell Jenny to tell the families not to pay attention to the news reports. Someone here will call her to give her accurate information when I have a list of who is alive and who isn't. Then the families of the deceased can be notified by the Red Cross."

He listened for a response but heard only silence. "Margo," he said, "can you do that for me?"

She said, "Yes." And they hung up.

Margo sobbed hysterically when she called Jenny but conveyed DeBarger's message. Jenny, in shock, told her husband, Tim, about the accident, located the emergency notification forms filled out by each diver prior to leaving for Belize, and prepared to make the calls. They decided to wait until five in the morning, knowing this might be the last good night's sleep some of them would have for a long time.

As they motored back to the blue hull of the *Wave Dancer*, Salvatori hoped to find at least one survivor in the mangroves. Mowrer did not feel optimistic. Despite the air pockets in the *Wave Dancer*, he doubted that anyone was alive inside the boat. But he would not give up until they found the last of his friends.

Diluted diesel fuel still coated the hull and part of the mangroves but far less than earlier. The wind had calmed and stars shone in the sky, giving the rescue team more light. But time was running out. They needed to find the other passengers, and fast. Salvatori expanded his efforts in the mangroves, periodically stopping to call out. During the next two hours they found two more male bodies in the mangroves and sent them to the banana warehouse. At 2:00 a.m. the rescue team decided they could make no more progress in the dark. They loaded the dinghy and started to leave when Mowrer swam up to them and said, "There's a female body tangled in some debris next to the dive deck. I'll need help to free her." It was late, the team was exhausted, and it was obvious that nothing could be done without an extra trip back and forth, so they promised to return for her at first light.

On the nearby *Emerald Isle*, Gagliano, Young, and Peter and Marcia Fox slept through most of the rescue efforts. The storm had taken its toll on them, too. During the peak, the fourteen-foot storm surge launched *Miss Pamela*, the beached tugboat. The rusted vessel that seemed to be waiting for the scrap collector skimmed into the water and rammed her way down the narrow horseshoe cut in the mangroves. She hit the *Lady Jane*, tearing her spring lines from her mooring but causing minimal structural damage, and then plowed into the *Toucan*, snapping lifelines off the deck and cracking the hull in two places. Next, *Miss Pamela* pitched her way through the water until slamming into the *Miss Lou*, which was dismasted in the collision, and sank *Miss Nancy* before crashing into the *Talisman*.

Gagliano and his guests reeled from the impact of *Miss Pamela*, and the *Talisman* took a dangerous list. Gagliano clambered up the ladder to see the large black iron boat resting against the hull of his sailboat. The mast of the *Talisman* was tangled in the mangroves and the boat nearly capsized. Gagliano ordered everyone up the ladder and told them to jump on the black boat next to theirs. In the brief time it took them to get topside, *Miss Pamela* moved on to claim other victims, leaving the *Talisman* on the verge of sinking.

Knowing they had to abandon ship, Gagliano and Douglas Young prepared to launch the *Talisman's* lifeboat, but before they could get it in the water the hurricane-force winds swept Young, like a feather in a breeze, off the deck and into the mangroves. In the swollen raging water he found a mangrove tree and clung to its root, trying desperately to raise himself out of the water while screaming between gulps of saltwater for Gagliano to save him. The waves, wind, and rain lashed at him as he crawled and clawed his way into a mangrove channel, where he was shielded from the waves. Gagliano struggled to finish floating his motorized lifeboat. He pulled and lifted with every ounce of his energy, knowing he held Young's life in his hands.

Hand-over-hand, Peter Fox worked his way to the stern of the *Talisman* to Gagliano and helped push the lifeboat in the water. Gagliano steered the little boat slowly, clinging to the edge of the mangroves, trying not to let the storm push him past Young's position. If he went too far, going back would be difficult, if not impossible. Finally, he got to the half-drowned Young.

Gagliano took Young fifty yards to the *Emerald Isle*, which had been spared from *Miss Pamela's* wrath, and deposited him on the deck of the luxury vessel. Against the wind and waves he worked his way back to the *Talisman* to get Peter and Marcia Fox, who clung desperately to the severely listing boat.

Upon arriving at the *Emerald Isle*, they found a door unlocked so they made themselves comfortable. They all were soaking wet, as well as battered from the collision, not to mention in shock from their near miss. They took full advantage of the *Emerald Isle's* hospitality, knowing that if the situation were reversed they would offer the same comforts. They grabbed dry clothes from the closets and broke the lock on the well-stocked wet bar. Gagliano, Young, and Peter Fox took full measure of the liquor cabinet and drained several bottles before passing out on the sofa. It had been a rough night, one that perhaps enough liquor would help them forget.

Chief Meteorologist Carlos Fuller reported that Iris made landfall around 8:00 p.m. near Monkey River Town. Maximum sustained winds had been measured by dropsonde several hours earlier at 146 mph. The Dvorak estimated the strength at landfall at 150 mph. There were very likely higher gusts. After landfall the hurricane jogged to the southwest, and by 9:00 p.m. maximum sustained winds were estimated to be 140 mph with higher gusts. The eye passed near Big Falls and exited the country near Otoxha around 10:00 p.m. The last radar position was at 11:00 p.m. when it was well into Guatemala.

At midnight the center of Iris was near 16.3 degrees north and 89.8 degrees west, moving west at twenty-two mph. Winds had decreased to eighty mph. At 1:00 a.m. on Tuesday, October 9, Fuller advised NEMO officials that the winds had subsided enough to begin search and rescue operations. He told them that at 3:00 a.m. Belize should discontinue its hurricane warning. At 3:00 a.m. Tropical Storm Iris was centered near 16.0 degrees north and 90.8 degrees west or about one hundred miles north of Guatemala City, moving to the west at twenty-one mph with maximum sustained winds estimated at near forty mph.

After Fuller's report, search and rescue operations began. A Belize Defense Force team led by Sgt. Emmett Richardson left for Big Creek to assist in the rescue and recovery of the victims of the capsized *Wave Dancer*. Sgt. Richardson heard about the tragedy on LOVE 95 while in the Belize Defense Force hurricane shelter, so he knew his rescue boat and team would be dispatched to the accident site as soon as the all-clear signal was given. When Sgt Richardson received his orders he told his engineer, Serapio Chun, to prepare the thirty-six-foot fiberglass rescue boat for immediate departure to Big Creek. Fortunately, the British Army had been conducting their annual jungle training exercises in Belize at the time, so their five-member scuba diving team added their skills to the efforts at Big Creek. Help soon would arrive for the *Wave Dancer*.

At first light, Mowrer and Salvatori met on the *Aggressor* to discuss how to find the nine people still missing. Mowrer said, "Get any sleep last night?"

"Not much," Salvatori said.

"Stanley and I are going to go through the salon and every cabin looking for air pockets or signs of life," Mowrer said. "It's probably fruitless, but there's a chance."

Salvatori nodded.

"I think our best bet is in the mangroves, don't you?" Mowrer asked.

Salvatori said, "It's going to be difficult getting in there without a boat and machete. But maybe some of them rode the surge over the mangroves and are wandering around waiting for someone to find them."

The team from the *Aggressor* went into the water, swarming around the hull and the mangroves looking for any signs of life. During the night the diesel fuel had diluted, and the morning sun shone brightly in the clear sky. With the improved conditions, Mowrer and the others allowed themselves to hope.

Salvatori and his team scoured the mangrove area, sometimes taking off their swim fins to walk into parts of the thicket. Even in the daylight the mangroves were too dense and too tall to walk through or see over. "Is anyone out there?" they yelled. "Can you hear me?" They heard only silence in return. On several occasions they came to a small water inlet, which allowed them deeper into the aquatic jungle, only to reach a dead end.

On the hull Mowrer and Stanley faced obstacles too. While the diesel fuel mostly had drifted away, the water remained murky with floating sediment. They could see nothing. To be safe they attached ropes to their ankles before submerging into the dark water. With their lights on they could see only two feet ahead. They went first to the cabin area, which seemed the likeliest place to find survivors. Half swimming and half crawling, Stanley went to the bow cabin area, using his hands more than his eyes, relying mostly on familiarity to maneuver up the stairs and into the hallway.

In the cabin area he opened a door and ascended to the floor to check for an air pocket. He found one—a good sign. Anyone who stayed in this area when the boat capsized could have survived. He vigorously searched one cabin then a second but found only mattresses, luggage, and floating debris. He pushed on the third door and slithered through the small opening. Inside he checked the air pocket. Nothing. Then he slowly submerged and groped around in the murky water. He checked the bathroom, closet, the vanity, and the bed area but found only more debris.

When he swam to the door he discovered it closed, sealing him in the small room. He pushed against it then pushed harder but the door did not move. Something had fallen against it. He was trapped. Trying not to panic, he squatted down and analyzed his situation. He had enough air to last another thirty or forty minutes if he was conservative. He had the rope tied to his leg, so Mowrer could find him. But when? Then he remembered the porthole. Maybe he could break it and get out. He felt around, found the small glass opening, and realized he could not fit through it. Relax, he told himself. Stay in control. He breathed slowly and focused on the murky water around him, trying to think clearly. After a few minutes he felt a slight settling of the boat and tried the door again. This time when he pushed, the waterlogged mattress that had settled against the door gave way enough that he could take off his dive gear and, keeping his regulator in his mouth, crawl through the opening, dragging his tank and BC behind him. That was way too scary, he thought.

Having searched all of his cabins, Mowrer tugged on Stanley's rope, and they met at the stairway and surfaced together. Resting next to the hull, Mowrer said, "I didn't find anyone, didn't see any signs of life."

Stanley said, "I don't think anyone's alive on the boat."

Mowrer nodded. "I prayed the whole time, thought maybe we'd find somebody."

"We need to search the rest of the boat," said Stanley. "If we find any bodies at least we will have accomplished something."

"You look in the salon, and I'll check the dive deck," Mowrer said. "Meet me back here in half an hour."

Mowrer submerged to the dive deck area and discovered that the gear had not been properly stowed before the storm hit. Dive suits, regulators, and tanks with attached BCs hung down like neoprene and steel stalactites, which he pushed aside to move into the area. As he floated into the dive deck, his gear tangled in the debris. He struggled to free himself, moved deeper onto the deck, before getting snagged again in the tentacles of jumbled equipment. Unable to see through the brown cloudy water, he felt his way north from one end of the dive deck to the other then moved a couple of feet west and went south to north, traversing the area in a grid pattern. Even in the dangling mess this method allowed him to cover the entire area.

On his second pass through, he felt a body tangled in the dangling equipment. The female body had an arm caught in a dive suit and a leg tangled in a regulator hose. He focused his light on the body, freeing the arm and then the leg. He shone the light into the face of the victim but couldn't recognize her. The bloated body would need to be identified in some other way. Did she die trying to escape only to get tangled up, or was she already dead and floated into her snare? He figured no one would ever know.

As he swam the body to the end of the blue hull, he saw five people huddled on the stern. Three of them wore scuba gear and two had snorkels and fins. Next to them, in a long in-board boat, three uniformed soldiers and four police officers talked to Salvatori. Help finally had arrived. One of the men in scuba gear took the body and put it in the death raft next to a male body found by Salvatori's team. Another man, obviously in charge, sat down on the hull next to Mowrer and introduced himself as Sergeant Jinks of the British Army.

"Are you Mowrer?" the sergeant asked. When Mowrer said yes, the man said, "My men and I have been assigned to this rescue and recovery mission. I would appreciate an update on whom you have found and who is missing."

Mowrer told him, "I don't know who we've found, but I can tell you how many bodies we've collected."

"Good enough," said Sergeant Jinks. "Give me a sit-rep on this site— what you've done, anything we should know."

Mowrer told him that they'd found twelve bodies, and eight people were missing. He outlined the locations he and Stanley had searched, noting the obstacles the team would face. "I suggest ropes, lights, and no fins," Mowrer said.

With that he boarded the dinghy and along with the other members of the make-shift rescue and recovery team headed back to the *Aggressor*.

They hoped the professionals could do something they had not and would find survivors.

As Mowrer and Salvatori peeled off their dive gear, a British Army helicopter assigned to assist the rescue team circled the Big Creek area waiting for orders from its ground control unit. On a frequency monitored by the *Aggressor*, Sergeant Jinks told the helicopter pilot, "We've got the boat covered. Circle the mangrove area. If you find anything, radio me and we'll do the grunt work."

The helicopter flew directly west of the hull into the mangroves. Two minutes later the pilot reported he had found a body. Jinks told him to hover above the body until the recovery crew could get to it. The pilot replied that the mangroves looked thick, and recovery would be difficult. Jinks told him he had a thirty-six-foot boat with a half dozen men who would use machetes to cut their way through the brush and retrieve the victim.

Sergeant Richardson navigated his boat as close to the overhead helicopter as he could get. Then his men hopped into the mangrove thicket, machetes in hand. They slowly hacked their way through the swampy mangrove jungle and twenty minutes later reached the bloated naked body of a very large man.

Serapio Chun of the rescue team saw the man then looked away. Mother Nature is cruel, he thought. Not only is the poor man dead, but his dignity has been taken away too. I'm glad his family won't see him this way. Chun said a silent prayer for the man as he wondered how to move him. They couldn't carry him on their litter through the thick mangroves, so four men took an arm or leg and carried him to Sergeant Richardson's boat, where they placed a tarp over him.

During the next four hours the helicopter pilot found three more bodies. Each time he radioed to Sergeant Jinks with the news, the pilot said he'd found a "victim," a word that stabbed the hearts of those listening to the transmissions on board the *Aggressor*.

By noon the recovery boat brought five victims found by the helicopter and one found inside the blue hull to the Big Creek dock. The helicopter, having completely circled the Big Creek area, radioed that he had not located any other bodies or signs of life. He headed back to his base.

Wouters kept a list of the dead, documenting the names, location, and time of recovery, and the name of the person who found the body. As the recovery mission wound down, officials needed to check the identification of the victims for the list that would accompany the bodies to the Belize City Morgue. Not knowing the victims personally, Wouters asked Mowrer for help.

They went to the holding area, and one by one Mowrer lifted the cardboard or towel covering the deceased's face. All but Doug and Phyllis Cox had been found, and he hoped they had gotten out together and floated through the mangroves into the surrounding area. Of all of the people on the *Wave Dancer*, Doug would know how to survive a disaster and would never leave Phyllis behind. This thought gave Mowrer a glimmer of hope.

After Mowrer viewed the bodies, the recently recovered six victims were laid neatly side-by-side like fallen totems on the concrete pier near the stern of the *Aggressor*. They lay under the scorching sun within six feet of the water that had taken their lives, their bodies covered by the shredded cardboard boxes and beach towels. The British Army unit then moved the victims from the banana warehouse and laid them in line with the other six bodies. The consolidation of the victims allowed the army to keep the gathering media and curious onlookers from disturbing the privacy of the victims.

On board the *Aggressor* the passengers fidgeted nervously all morning while the rescue and recovery efforts went on a mere 150 yards from them. Mostly they stood in silence, sometimes watching, sometimes trying not to watch. They occasionally tried to console each other with assurances that a survivor surely would be found. From the sky deck they looked west and watched the team on the blue hull. When they looked to the east at the Big Creek Dock they saw the accumulating bodies of their friends next to the stern of their boat.

In the salon Baechtold's video played repeatedly. It showed the horizontal rain and wind that had pounded them the night before. The video also revealed the wetsuits on hangers, lashed together in groups of four to six, blowing almost horizontally to the roof of the dive deck. It showed Captain Martin doing his slow walk into the wind then a few minutes later the jolt when the *Wave Dancer's* stern hit the bow of the *Aggressor*. The video panned toward the port side of the *Wave Dancer*, out the window openings of the dive deck. The *Aggressor* could clearly be seen through these windows as the *Wave Dancer*, having broken free of its moorings, moved farther astern and almost next to the *Aggressor*. The video kept running, but the flowing frames jerked as Baechtold struggled to hold the camera steady. Then the footage showed the dive deck spinning, and suddenly a sound of glub, glub, glub and the video stopped. Mary Lou watched it twice then said, "Please turn it off. I can't watch it anymore."

A helicopter landed next to the banana warehouse. A Belize Defense Force officer tromped to the dock to inspect the efforts. After fifteen minutes, satisfied his men were doing all they could, he left. An hour later, Said Musa, the Prime Minister of Belize, surveying the aftermath of Hurricane Iris, landed in his helicopter to see first-hand the mission underway at Big Creek. To that point the only known fatalities inflicted in Belize by Iris had occurred on the *Wave Dancer*, and Prime Minister Musa wanted to inspect the site and show his support to the American visitors. He conferred with several military authorities and police personnel and asked if they needed additional help. He spoke briefly with Captain Schnabel, conveying his sympathies and offering his country's support. Having been assured that the situation was under control, the prime minister boarded his helicopter, which circled once over the blue hull of the *Wave Dancer*, and flew to Placencia.

At 11:45 a.m. Mary Lou, DeBarger, and Patterson were told a plane would fly them to Belize City, where a representative of the Peter Hughes Company would take them to the US Embassy to secure replacement passports, which they would need not only to leave Belize, but also to re-enter the United States. With all of their clothing lost in the *Wave Dancer*, they also needed something other than borrowed shorts and T-shirts to wear home.

A chartered twin-engine light airplane landed on the grass runway and rolled to a stop in the field adjacent to the banana warehouse. The door opened, and a tall thin man with a neatly trimmed beard descended the ladder. Though he knew all about the situation, including the loss of life on one of his company's boats, without so much as a glance in their direction, Peter Hughes walked by three survivors of his ill-fated *Wave Dancer*.

"How rude," said DeBarger in disbelief. "That SOB knows who we are. At least he could've stopped to offer a word of sympathy…or something."

At noon, the passengers aboard the *Aggressor* ate a buffet lunch. After dessert, Captain Schnabel entered the salon to tell them, "We've done all we can do here, so we're heading to Belize City in about an hour. We've been in contact with the US Embassy, and they're trying to cut through red tape and get you home. When we get more information I'll update you."

With Robert Robinson singing The Lord's Prayer over the sound system, at 1:30 p.m. Tuesday, October 9, 2001, the *Belize Aggressor III* slowly pulled away from the Big Creek dock. The tearful passengers stood in quiet reverence as they took one last glance at the partially covered bodies on the dock. They saw the bare feet sticking out, knowing that seventy-two hours earlier their friends had been told to leave their shoes and worries behind for a vacation trip of a lifetime. For all, in one way or another, it was.

Chapter Fourteen

"You gain strength, courage, and confidence by every experience in which you really stop to look fear in the face. You are able to say to yourself, 'I have lived through this horror. I can take the next thing that comes along.' You must do the thing you think you can not do."

Eleanor Roosevelt

Prime Minister Musa's helicopter circled Placencia, surveying the devastation to the small resort town. The pristine beach that attracted visitors from all over the world remained intact, but the palm trees that provided shade for the sunbathers were toppled and strewn haphazardly. Many of the resort buildings along the coast had been raised off their foundations by the storm surge and deposited a hundred feet inland. Other wooden structures lay smashed to pieces. A few had been flipped upside down and flung in a heap. Musa estimated that 95 percent of the buildings in Placencia were destroyed. He felt a deep sympathy for their owners, knowing most of them had no insurance. After completing his survey, he told the pilot to land on the sports field adjacent to BJ's Restaurant. The concrete structure of Percy and Betty Neal's establishment had survived the storm and would be a center for food, water, and clothing distribution to the citizens of Placencia and Monkey River Town until utilities and supply sources were restored.

Percy and Betty Neal arrived from Belmopan as the prime minister and area representative Dr. Henry Conton walked from the helicopter toward their restaurant. From the outside the watermark on the exterior of BJ's indicated eight feet of storm surge had struck the building. Not knowing what to expect on the inside, Percy pried off the sheet of plywood protecting the front door and opened it. To his surprise only six inches of water had penetrated the interior but drained off leaving a thin layer of mud, which easily could be scraped off the floor. Percy told Prime Minister Musa, "I can have this place ready in a few hours. Tell me what you want me to do and consider it done. My family has been spared. We'll help others any way we can."

Having not slept a wink, Wende Bryan decided at six o'clock it was light enough to begin the trek back to Placencia to check the storm damage. Like other residents of Belize she had listened to LOVE 95 during the night, getting the call-in damage reports. One of Wende's friends, Andrea Villaneuava, had stayed behind in Placencia and after the storm phoned LOVE 95 to give her account of the damage to her town. Wende used her cell phone to call Andrea.

When Andrea answered, Wende said, "Can you hear me? Are you okay? How does it look back there?"

Andrea, almost in hysterics replied, "I'm fine, but everything's gone."

"What do you mean?"

"You don't understand. Everything's gone. The houses, the trees, the Pickled Parrott, everything. It looks like an atomic bomb went off here. It's hard to walk around because the trees and parts of houses are everywhere. Electric lines are down. The road just before you get to Verlie's Market washed out. It has a four-foot-deep hole that must be twenty feet long."

"I guess I'm not surprised. The radio has been giving a lot of bad reports."

"When you come back, be careful," Andrea said. "You may get stopped by the defense force. They're setting up roadblocks and checking IDs to keep looters and sightseers out."

Though slightly shaken, Jan Neel and her family survived Hurricane Iris in their category-five home, experiencing just a few minor roof leaks. Though their home had stood up well, taking a direct hit from Iris, the Neels vowed never to stay there during another hurricane. The anxiety caused by the threatening winds and rain was not worth it.

Shortly after dawn Jan made her way to the Turtle Inn to see how much damage Francis Ford Coppola's resort had suffered. Negotiating around fallen trees and debris, driving through streets still covered by a foot of water, Jan arrived at the site that once housed the Turtle Inn Resort. The land sprawled nearly vacant, wiped clean. Not a cabana in sight. The thatched roof office building stood alone. As she arrived, five people poured out of the office, excited to see someone, anyone. They had been through a harrowing experience.

"Maria, Juan, and I were sitting in a corner of the office, and the storm was blowing like crazy," Rosa, a housekeeper, told Jan. "We were scared, Mrs. Neel! Ellye came looking for us. She was by herself at the Mariposa and too afraid of being alone. So just as we opened the door to let her in, Palo drove up, and his car was on fire. He jumped out of it. We thought it was going to explode. Just as he got inside a wave hit the office real hard. The car washed into the lagoon. All the cabanas were blown away. We looked out and didn't see anything. The office was the only thing left. What are we going to do now, Mrs. Neel?"

"I'm glad you're safe," Jan said. "Things will work out."

Frank Gagliano woke up to the smell of fresh coffee, but needed a few minutes to clear the cobwebs and realize he was on the *Emerald Isle*. The liquor had done the trick. He had, in some fashion, managed to sleep until eight o' clock, but realized he needed to get moving because he wanted to inspect the damage to the *Talisman* and *Mariposa*. Marcia Fox handed him a cup of coffee and said, "LOVE 95 said the eye of the hurricane passed right over us. The storm did the most damage in this area, and one of the dive boats tied up to the banana dock capsized. Several people died. They don't know how many yet."

"We were lucky then," Gagliano said. "For a little while I wasn't sure we were going to make it. I mean, the water was rushing so fast I could've surfed on it. You might expect that on the open ocean but not back here."

From the deck of the *Emerald Isle* they could see that the storm surge had subsided, freeing the tangled mast of the *Talisman* from the mangroves and uprighting the boat. Upon closer inspection, Gagliano noticed the broken mast, but the rest of his boat was virtually untouched, making it a perfect place to stay for a few days while he and Peter worked to refloat the partially submerged *Mariposa*.

Curious to see what happened at the dock, Gagliano, Fox, and Young took the dinghy to the accident site. They saw a member of the rescue and recovery team resting on the blue hull while two others loaded two bodies into a raft. A large motorboat with several Belize Defense Force soldiers passed them and cut into the mangroves.

With the scene under control, they went down the mangrove channel to see where *Miss Pamela* had come to rest. They passed the damaged *Lady Jane*, *Toucan*, *Miss Lou*, *Miss Nancy*, *Talisman* and *Mariposa*. When they stopped in front of the *Lady Alexandra*, an eighty-foot yacht, they saw a large gash on the port side. Next to the yacht floated *Miss Pamela*, the culprit of the pinball-like ride down the mangrove channel. As Gagliano steered his dinghy around *Miss Pamela's* black hull, he noticed a streak of blue paint. He pointed to it and said, "That's the same color as the *Wave Dancer*. I wonder if she hit the *Wave Dancer*, too."

*   *   *

During the evening meal, Captain Schnabel addressed his guests, a look of grief and determination on his face. Though he had weathered hurricanes before, none had touched him in this way. "Our office and the US Embassy have been making arrangements to get you home as soon as possible. The next flight out of Belize is tomorrow afternoon, and we have arranged to get you all on that plane. We'll arrive in Belize City in about an hour, and our office has set aside rooms at the Radisson if you prefer not to stay on the *Aggressor* tonight. In any case, breakfast will be served tomorrow morning on the boat, and at noon we'll transport you to the airport. I'll have more information for you at breakfast."

Though a somber mood hung over the group, the captain brought them a bit of relief. During the six-hour trip from Big Creek, they had speculated on what would happen to them. Were they going to be sent home? If so, when? They did not want to be in Belize and have the bodies of their dead friends arrive in Richmond ahead of them. They worried about their families and the families of their dead friends. The passengers wanted to be home. They wanted the security of being someplace safe and familiar. The St. George Radisson was a good start.

DeBarger caught up with Mowrer in the lobby of the Radisson and told him he, Mary Lou, and Patterson had spent the day in Belize City with one of the Peter Hughes agents getting their passports. "I don't know that I have ever felt this lost," DeBarger said. "I'm walking around in a foreign country with no passport, no identification, no money, and no ticket home."

"Did they take care of you?" Mowrer asked.

"Everyone was pleasant. The lady from Hughes took us to get photographs for the passports and back and forth to the US Embassy a couple of times. She also took us to the airline so we could leave Belize tomorrow."

"That's good," Mowrer said. He wanted to say more but could think of nothing.

"Do you know when you're leaving?" DeBarger asked.

"Tomorrow afternoon, on the same flight as you."

DeBarger nodded.

"Are you doing okay?" Mowrer asked. They had lost good friends, but Mowrer knew that DeBarger, who had already lost his wife, now had lost his best friend.

DeBarger said, "I'm blind as a bat. If it weren't for Mary Lou I don't know if I'd ever get out of this place. She's helped me with every bit of paperwork. Other than that, I guess I'm okay."

"Good," Mowrer said. "That's good."

"There's one thing that's really beginning to piss me off though," DeBarger continued, hardening his face in anger. "I've heard people mumbling behind my back all day saying that those people who died on the *Wave Dancer* were having a hurricane party and if they hadn't been drunk they wouldn't have died. Dave, that's just not true. There was no party. We were concerned about the hurricane just as much as anybody. But Captain Martin assured us we were in a safe harbor. What the hell are we supposed to do, tell him he's crazy?"

"Don't listen to that stuff," Mowrer said. "It's crap. We all know it."

"Well, I hope no one says anything to my face. I'm just about at that snapping point."

Mowrer nodded. "The simple fact is our friends were murdered by Captain Martin and Peter Hughes. There's no other way to look at it. They made all the decisions, and now our friends are dead."

DeBarger agreed, recalling the way Hughes had walked right past the survivors at the runway, offering not a word of consolation.

"They can claim all the remorse they want for the media, but they know they're the ones who screwed up," Mowrer said. "They killed our friends, and they should pay for it. And if someone says anything about a hurricane party to me I'll knock them on their ass."

DeBarger asked Mowrer if he'd heard anything about Doug and Phyllis Cox. No one had heard anything about them, Mowrer said.

*   *   *

At nine o'clock on Wednesday morning a car from the US Embassy pulled up in front of the St. George Radisson to take Mary Lou and DeBarger to the Karl Heusner Memorial Hospital morgue in Belize City for positive identification of the RDC victims. The process had to be repeated at the morgue with the proper officials present and the corresponding paperwork completed. Shipping human remains internationally involves conforming to several treaties and has strict physical and legal requirements, which had to be met. Mary Lou and DeBarger volunteered to identify their friends to accelerate the return of their bodies to the states.

Before leaving their hotel, they decided that if they both did not agree there would be no positive identification of that individual. When they arrived at the hospital, instead of being escorted to the morgue they were taken behind the building and shown a large refrigerated truck, which contained their friends' bodies. The medical officials apologized for the lack of formality but said, "Belize is a small country and not equipped to handle such a large tragedy."

As they entered the truck they could see that three-tier racks had been specially built to accommodate the bodies. Crude as it was, it was efficient, with three bodies laid out on each tier for easy observation. They confirmed identifications on most of the bodies, though it took second and third looks in a couple of cases. The diesel fuel-laced saltwater; intense heat, and Belizean sun had not been kind to many of their friends. It was nearly impossible to recognize faces, which by then were black and bloated. They used things like a distinctive belt, earrings, or wristwatch, which a particular diver was known to wear. They identified one woman by her nail polish, another man by his tattoo. They looked at hair length, mustaches, and clothes. Two males could not positively be identified, so the embassy had to send to Richmond for their dental charts.

The human body is slightly heavier than saltwater. Consequently, when unconscious, the body sinks. Fat bodies are slightly more buoyant than thin ones, but all bodies will sink in saltwater. Clothing, shoes, and any other weight on the body, such as things stuffed in pockets, renders the body considerably less buoyant. The question is often asked, "When a body sinks, how far down will it go?" There is some dispute on this point, but evidence indicates that a body will sink to the bottom regardless of the water's depth, unless some obstruction or upward current prevents it. As a body sinks into deep water, the pressure of the water tends to compress gasses in the abdominal and chest cavities, so the body displaces less water as it sinks deeper and consequently becomes less and less buoyant the farther down it goes.

Almost without exception, a dead body lying on the bottom of a river or lake will rise to the surface again. This is due to gas formed in the body tissue during decay. When enough gas forms to inflate the tissues and distend the skin, the body becomes lighter than water and rises to the surface. This process is due to the action of bacteria within the body. Consequently, the length of time that elapses before the body rises depends not only upon the amount of fat contained in the tissues but on the temperature of the water. In warm water, gas forms rapidly and the body may rise to the surface in a day or two. However, if the water is cold, bacterial action occurs very slowly, and the body may take several weeks to appear on the surface. When a body is fully distended it is almost impossible to sink even with counter weights.

When someone drowns in a river, the most common mistake is to search for the body far downstream. Sinking takes place immediately, which results in the victim reaching the bottom close to the point he was last seen on the surface. When the body begins to rise, it will appear on the surface not far from where it disappeared.

If someone drowns when a river is swollen, the supposition is that the rapid current will carry a body along before it strikes the bottom or encounters an obstruction. The fact is that the current on the surface is entirely different from the current on the bottom. While the speed on the surface may be ten knots, current speed will decrease with depth. There is virtually no current on the bottom. Consequently, the deeper a body sinks, the slower the current acting upon it until it reaches the bottom where it will stay. It is rare to find a victim more than a few hundred yards from the point of entry. It is true that when the body begins to rise to the surface after several days it may drift a considerable distance from the site of the death.

When the *Wave Dancer* capsized, Doug Cox escaped, injured and dazed, from the salon, fighting through the raging surge-swollen water of Big Creek. Disoriented, he saw the lights of the *Aggressor* and began swimming toward them. But the wind-blown, white-capped waves quickly overwhelmed him. Upon submersion he held his breath until he was forced to inhale. Then he gulped a mouthful of diesel fuel-laced saltwater. The water induced spasms of his larynx, which closed his trachea to protect his lungs. Only a little water entered his lungs, but with his trachea blocked by laryngospasms, no fresh air entered his lungs, and the supply of oxygen to his brain began to fail. The lack of oxygen, anoxia, affected his brain and within thirty seconds the laryngospasms began to weaken, creating imminent brain failure. Cox then inhaled again. This time he aspirated water into his lungs before a fresh spasm closed his trachea again but for a shorter duration. With each successive inhalation, he aspirated more water; anoxia increased, and laryngospasm duration decreased until they were finally abolished and his lungs filled with water. Less than two minutes after he submerged below the raging water at Big Creek he was dead. His body lay concealed under the water for two days until Wednesday morning. Then it emerged in the channel a quarter mile from the blue hull and half way between the Big Creek dock and the open Caribbean Sea, where the receding storm surge had deposited it two days earlier.

At the same time as Doug Cox's body was being retrieved, a few members of the Peter Hughes staff were recovering personal belongings from the hull of the *Wave Dancer* when a body emerged among the floating rubble. They hurriedly informed their supervisor, who pulled the body of Phyllis Cox onto the blue hull. After two days of being apart and an hour after their mutual discovery Doug and Phyllis Cox were reunited on the dock at Big Creek. They had come to Belize together and now would leave together. The last victims of the *Wave Dancer* tragedy had been recovered. The vigil of hope was over.

With DeBarger's many years of experience working at a television station, he knew a media frenzy would erupt around the survivors, so he, Mary Lou, and Patterson agreed on how they would handle inquiries about the accident. First and foremost, their friends who died had families back home, and so maintaining the dignity of the deceased was the number one priority. Next, they wanted to be sure correct information was released. Finally, there would be no sensationalism of the accident. Little did they know their pact would be put to the test before they left Belize.

At the Philip Goldson International Airport in Belize City, the former passengers of the *Aggressor* and Mary Lou, Patterson, and DeBarger reunited in a private waiting room as they prepared to make their painful journey home. Outside their lounge, Gene Cox, a special reporter for WWBT-TV in Richmond, waited patiently to talk with someone about the accident. Reluctantly, along with Reid Bennett, his cameraman, Cox stepped into the waiting room, where he met uncooperative indifference until DeBarger and Mary Lou, acting as the ambassadors for the group, agreed to talk with him.

Cox began by saying, "I know this is very difficult for you, but the people of Richmond, the victims' families and friends, need to know what happened at Big Creek."

DeBarger explained about Iris and the capsizing of the *Wave Dancer*.

Cox asked, "How did you manage to survive?"

DeBarger spoke first and said, "I swam into what had been a corridor. I went one way, and Patterson went the other. I wound up in a blind alley in another cabin. It was completely filled with water. I turned around, went back, got to where there was some air above me, and got my head above the water. I saw a light. The light was coming through a window that we had been unsuccessful in taping. The other passenger had kicked out the window, and he was outside shouting my name. I did a surface dive, went out the window, and a bunch of hands pulled me up into a lifeboat outside. I was the last one out."

Cox then turned to Mary Lou for her response. She said, "It happened incredibly quickly and the three of us have talked about this. We don't know why we were able to survive, except that Rick Patterson, with a superhuman force, was able to kick through the window of the emergency door, which wouldn't open, probably because of the water pressure, and I happened to be there. I had a small flashlight, and this is the light that Dave was able to find."

She held up the small Maglite and Cox asked, "That is the light?"

"That is the light," Mary Lou responded. "That is the light that saved my life."

Cox thanked them then panned the room looking for someone else to interview. Unable to make any positive eye contact with anyone in the room, he got the idea and left.

At 1:30 p.m. the Continental airlines flight lifted off the ground from the Belize City airport with the survivors aboard. Thirty members of the RDC had arrived a few short days earlier, excited and happy about enjoying the best diving holiday of their lives. Now, thirteen were leaving, mournful and filled with despair. What had started out as a promising week of scuba diving on the world's second largest barrier reef, in the country often advertised as "Mother Nature's Best Kept Secret" ended with profound sadness and loss.

Emily Bradley sat in the chartered bus as it rumbled east on interstate 64 toward Norfolk and ultimately her father, David Mowrer. She had spoken to him during a frantic, five-minute phone call the day before and had been assured he was okay. "I'm not going to believe it until I see him tonight," she said. Bradley, twenty-six, sat next to her half-sister, Megan Mowrer, and across the aisle from their grandmother, Lois Kohler. Five relatives and friends of Richmond Dive Club members sat nearby.

Bradley described her father as hard as nails and said she had seen him cry only once, when the family had to put down Humphrey, their English mastiff. Bradley said her father sobbed when he called her Tuesday morning after he searched for survivors but found only bodies. Because of transmission problems, Bradley and her father spent most of the call trying to determine whether each could hear the other. "I just kept telling him I loved him," she said. Those sitting silently around her in the dark bus nodded, too weighted by their own worries to offer much more.

The bus, chartered from Martz Richmond, had plenty of empty seats, but Jackie Bush didn't want to be alone. Once the bus bumped onto the highway, she moved closer to other passengers. She had joined the dive club about three years earlier, after separating from her husband. She knew all of the victims of the *Wave Dancer* and was close to a few, including Shirley Johnston. She didn't know those returning from Belize as well. "I'm here to help whoever, support whoever," she said.

At times the mood on the bus turned light. Bradley chattered about her daughter, Hannah, whose first birthday had been the day before. "She walked clear across the room last night," Bradley said. But mostly a somber pall hung over the bus. Jim McNeal, who owned The Dive Shop in Richmond for nineteen years, reflected on Jim and Kim Garrison, dear friends now gone. "Things were working out great for the two of them," he said. "I still can't believe it." Those listening to him murmured that they understood his confusion.

The bus rolled into Norfolk International Airport around ten o'clock. With a dozen or so reporters hovering nearby, the group waited about an hour outside a concourse area before Continental Flight 136 arrived from Houston. Soon after, Dave Mowrer, Don Trice, and other survivors stepped through a clear security door and hugged their families and friends. Many of them clung to each other, unwilling to let go, as if needing assurance that the person they were hugging was really in their arms. They said little more than that they were all right. They didn't mention the accident or the victims left behind. That would come later, if at all. Workers for the American Red Cross rushed them to a private room and down a back stairway to the bus. Mary Lou, DeBarger, and Patterson walked down a long dark hallway with a lot of lights at the end of it—walking, Mary Lou thought, as if to judgment.

They emerged into bright white camera lights shining in their faces. Reporters from local as well as national television stations, along with print journalists and radio reporters gunned questions at them about what happened at Big Creek, how they survived, who was to blame for the accident, did they know Hurricane Iris was threatening them, and a list of other questions they barely had the energy to answer. After ten minutes they left the terminal and joined their friends in the bus.

On the way back to Richmond, the bus remained dark and quiet. Several passengers talked one to one. Some slept. Others stared blankly out their window at the lights running by in the night, seeing their own dim reflections looking back in the glass. They all were relieved to be going home. The bus returned to Martz Richmond's garage on Commerce Road around 1:30 in the morning. The survivors rose slowly from their seats, collected their bags, and hugged each other one last time. Then they stepped off the bus and walked toward their cars.

Mowrer paused for a moment and said to his daughter, "It's real eerie to be here and see these cars." They looked around at the cars hunkered under the lights of the lot, knowing the owners would not be returning. Mary Lou called a friend to come and get her. She had an empty feeling as she drove past Lisa's car. Just five days before, Lisa had assured her the new battery she and her father installed would start her car when she got back from the trip.

DeBarger, sensing the possibility for chaos, asked several active members of the RDC to meet him at his office. Most of the club's officers died aboard the *Wave Dancer*, so he wanted to establish a committee to handle the problems they were about to encounter. The bodies had not been released from Belize, so no burial arrangements could be made. The Red Cross offered assistance, the deceased members' families begged for information, there were minor children left behind, and the national and international media were reporting about the tragedy, sometimes incorrectly.

DeBarger asked for ideas and volunteers. Jenny Chappell, who had called the families after the tragedy, said, "We have dive buddies when we're diving, why not set up a 'buddy person' for each victim's family so they'll know what's going on? We can tell them their buddy will make sure they get correct information. Right now there are so many stories in the media I can't imagine what these people are thinking." Everyone liked the idea and felt an acquaintance or friend of the family would be the ideal buddy.

DeBarger agreed to be the central figure through whom all information would be disseminated. He said, "Get me all the buddy e-mail addresses so when I have something, I can send it out to everyone at the same time. That way the buddy families will be informed correctly and simultaneously." Steve Glenn, the volunteer attorney for the RDC said, "In tragedies like this there's always someone looking to find fault and someone to sue. I want to caution you to be careful what you say, because your comments could be used against you and/or the RDC."

The group discussed the idea of having a combined memorial service for all the victims after their funerals. Many people called to volunteer their services, and while their help was greatly appreciated, it needed to be channeled in a productive manner. Much effort was needed and many questions left unanswered, so the group decided to meet the next day and every day thereafter until they felt prepared to handle the situation.

As the meeting ended, DeBarger said, "I've talked with Mary Lou and Patterson, and we want to personally visit each of the families to answer any questions about their loved one's death. They have a right to know what happened from us, not a second-hand source. By now some of them have heard or will hear the "party boat" rumors. I can tell you all emphatically, there was no excessive drinking and certainly no hurricane party. Captain

Martin was in charge of the *Wave Dancer*. He told us everything was okay before and even during the storm. We had no reason to doubt him. We were all concerned and careful, and the memory of our friends will not be tarnished. They will be glorified. See you all tomorrow."

The club received and declined requests from *The Today Show, Good Morning America* and a few others for the three survivors to appear and tell "their story." DeBarger, Mary Lou, and Patterson kept to their pact, agreeing not to bring any extra stress to their friends' families while maintaining the utmost dignity for all involved.

Within a few days, the bodies of the RDC victims arrived from Belize and were sent to the designated funeral homes for burial preparation with the exception of Christy McNiel. When DeBarger arrived home, he received a call from Christy's parents, requesting information about her, the circumstances of her death, and her personal appearance. DeBarger explained how she died and said he had seen her body shortly after it was recovered. He confirmed to Christy's mother that her daughter looked like she was taking a nap—as lovely as ever. With that level of comfort, her parents acceded to Christy's wishes and left her body in Belize where it was cremated. Then, in a small private ceremony, her ashes were sprinkled over Lighthouse Reef.

DeBarger, Mary Lou, and Patterson decided they would attend as many funeral services as possible, appearing at nine funerals in seven days. They could not be at two local funerals that occurred at the same time or at the out-of-town services of Ray Mars in Maryland, Jimmy Topping in North Carolina, and Cheryl Lightbound in Canada. But several RDC members attended the funerals in their place.

On November 17, 2001, a memorial service for all twenty victims of the *Wave Dancer* tragedy was held at the Grove Avenue Baptist Church in Henrico County, Virginia. In the foyer of the church the club set up twelve tables, one for each deceased diver and married couple. They covered each table with a white tablecloth and a large dive flag. To personalize their table, each family displayed photographs or other memorabilia, as a remembrance of their loved ones. They gave markers to those who wanted to write something about the person or to simply sign the dive flags.

Then, much like a military funeral, the flags were folded and given to the families following the ceremony. The service itself was simple but appropriate. A video presentation showed photos of the divers at different stages of their lives while a soundtrack played music. DeBarger, the new president of the RDC, set the tone for the service by saying, "All those people up there," he said, pointing toward the sky, "they're wearing shorts and T-shirts. What the heck am I doing in a tie?" He took off his sports coat and tie, instructing the other men in the audience to follow his lead. They all did. He then read the names of each of the seventeen divers and the three *Wave Dancer* crewmembers who were killed, as another club member lit a purple candle for each.

DeBarger continued, "In the last five weeks we have been to many ceremonies of loss. Today, we celebrate life. We are all survivors." Panning the audience and making eye contact with many of the victims' families, he said, "What we have lost cannot be measured, but what we still have far exceeds that loss."

Reverend Mark Jenkins, the outreach minister of the church and an avid scuba diver, offered a prayer and a few comments. Mary Lou read a poem, songs were sung, and vice president Mike Carr ended the ceremony by invoking the RDC slogan: "Let's Go Divin'!"

Chapter Fifteen

"*If I can endure for this minute whatever is happening to me, no matter how heavy my heart is or how dark the moment might be…If I can keep on believing what I know in my heart to be true, that darkness will fade with the morning and that this will pass away, too…Then nothing can ever disturb me or fill me with uncertain fear, for as sure as night brings dawning, my morning is bound to appear.*"

Unknown

In the weeks following the *Wave Dancer* accident, the victims, their families, the survivors, and the Richmond Dive Club received overwhelming support. Scuba divers, dive clubs, friends, and caring people from all over the world sent their condolences. At a time when the RDC teetered near collapse, the remaining members pooled their energy to keep the club, which meant so much to the victims, moving forward. The club served as the focal point around which everyone rallied. DeBarger, out of necessity, became the president, delegating responsibility to the many eager members intent on keeping the club, and the memory of their dive buddies, alive.

Jenny Chappell, former RDC President Gary Kinsler, and volunteer

Mary Ann Klisch created a memorial pin to show support for the departed loved ones. The pin incorporated a small American flag, a scuba diving flag, and a looped, flowing purple ribbon. It featured the words "Continuing Their Dive." Jenny, Gary, and Mary Ann made six hundred of the memorial pins, but demand for them burned through the supply of safety pins. Friends in New York, New Jersey, and Florida supplied more, and in the end the club distributed over four thousand memorial pins.

Gary Kinsler's son Chris designed a page dedicated to the victims and attached it to the RDC Web site. The page, which included a photograph along with personal information about each of the victims as well as details about the accident, told a poignant and compelling story of the lives of the victims—their accomplishments, diving experiences, families left behind, and causes for which they worked. More than 381,000 hits were recorded on the memorial page of the site.

New memberships to the RDC poured in from around the world. Individual membership requests came from almost every state as well as from Canada, England, Argentina, Australia, and Mexico. Cheryl Lightbound's kayak club joined as a group, as did a dive club from California.

The club set up a memorial fund to benefit the families of the victims. Groups and individuals from around the world sent donations to the victims' designated account. The staff of the *Richmond Times-Dispatch* won a first-place award for their coverage of the *Wave Dancer* tragedy and donated their monetary prize to the fund. At its April 2002 meeting, the RDC Board of Directors voted to disperse the $20,384.25 fund among the underage survivors of the victims. DAN [Divers Alert Network], at the request of Peter Hughes, set up an individual account to benefit the families of the all the victims on the *Wave Dancer*, including the three crew members.

In Virginia Beach, the V.B. Hammerheads Dive Club purchased a memorial reef ball from Eternal Reefs in Decatur, Georgia. The artificial reef, designed to serve as a living legacy to the deceased members of the RDC, was emblazoned with a bronze plaque featuring each victim's name.

The Lynnhaven Dive Club placed the memorial reef ball in the Atlantic Ocean off Virginia Beach. It now serves as a lasting tribute to their fallen dive buddies.

Jenny Chappell honored her good friend Buddy Webb by visiting one of his favorite dive sites at Lake Rawlings. She dove to the deepest and coldest part of the lake and spent a moment at the headstone marked Herbert "Buddy" Webb, which had been created originally as a memorial to Buddy's grandfather but now served as a memorial to both men.

In their own way the twenty million certified SCUBA members worldwide acknowledged their fellow divers through moments of silence, financial contribution, memorial tributes, or words of sympathy. The members of this close-knit, if far-flung community would long remember and talk about the tragedy at Big Creek.

Although still stunned by the tragedy, the Richmond Dive Club thrives with more than seventy active members. In the months that followed, DeBarger and the other leaders struggled to generate interest in club trips. For the most part, however, the problem stretched throughout the industry and had more to do with the economic condition of the country and political instability around the world than with the tragedy. More than half of the current active members joined the club after the Belize trip, so most did not know the lost divers. Among the members who were on the *Aggressor*, a few gave up diving. Some left the club and pursued other interests. The rest remain members, attend meetings, and dive regularly. The club moves on.

Several months after the tragedy, the *Wave Dancer* survivors returned to diving. As a group, they spent a week in Cozumel in January 2002, and—to their great relief—had no difficulty feeling at ease in the underwater world that had claimed their friends just a few months earlier. Since then, each of them has enjoyed many dive trips, though none has been on another live-aboard dive boat. Dave DeBarger has logged more than seventy dives since the accident. He returned to Cozumel in 2003 and also dived in Bonaire, the "Graveyard of the Atlantic" off Cape Hatteras, and in Nassau, as well as made several trips to Lake Rawlings.

The years since the accident have been a mix of pain and joy for DeBarger. His father passed away in 2002, and his father-in-law in 2003. His son Terry and his wife made him a grandfather in 2002, repeated the honor in May 2004, and added a third grandchild in 2005. His son Scott married in the summer of 2004. DeBarger served as president of the Richmond Dive Club for two terms following the accident, stepping down in the fall of 2003. He continues to be involved with the club but not in a leadership role. With mixed emotions he says, "The accident at Big Creek was the club's biggest tragedy but finest hour."

Rick Patterson, Mary Lou Hayden, and Dave DeBarger remain close. In the past couple of years Patterson has focused on his job and new family, but he still attends dive club meetings and exchanges e-mails with the other two survivors. Mary Lou and DeBarger grew close while spending so much time together meeting with the victims' families and attending funerals in the days and weeks after the accident. Within the local diving community their names often were mentioned in the same breath. The friendship evolved into a romantic relationship, which continued for a number of months. However, the tragedy that brought them together ultimately became too great a burden to overcome, and in 2003 they returned to being close friends. They dive together and occasionally share a lunch or dinner to keep in touch.

Since the accident Mary Lou has spent a good deal of time coping with the tragedy and continues her work in a private medical practice in the Richmond area. She regularly presents programs in her specialty at national conferences and received the 2004 Recognition Award from her national professional society. She plays tennis several times a week and is a member of a competitive league. The Belize tragedy has refocused her priorities to family and friends as well as to improving the quality of life of her parents. She recently celebrated the birth of her first grandchild.

Immediately after the accident, Captain Martin and Frank Wouters filed their obligatory accident report with the Belizean authorities and within forty-eight hours Martin flew back to New Zealand. Wouters, as a representative for Peter Hughes Company, attended a few of the funeral services and the memorial service. At Brenda Wade's funeral he told Angela Luk that he supported her decision to get off the boat. A few months after the accident Angela married her long-time boyfriend, Egbert Hislop, and the couple purchased a home in Belmopan. In May 2003 she gave birth to a baby boy, Nathan, and is happily a stay-at-home mom.

Having lost his worldly possessions and his employment opportunity, Thomas Baechtold left the US and went back to Switzerland. Chico continues to live in Belize City.

The years since the accident have not been kind to Bart Stanley. His anger at Peter Hughes and his representatives for not listening to him, and his grief from the deaths of Eloisa and Brenda, dominated his conversation for almost three years. He suffered nightmares involving Eloisa's and Brenda's screams for help and his inability to save them. He carried a heavy psychological burden of survivor's guilt over the death of "the girls." Damage from exposure to the fuel-laden saltwater blurred his vision. Unable to overcome his fear of night diving, he couldn't get a job as a full-time dive master. Then in 2004 he landed a job as a part-time dive master at the Lighthouse Reef Resort. His wife, Brenda, is pregnant with their third child, and his life, at last, moves forward.

Captain Jerry Schnabel continued on as captain of the *Belize Aggressor* for a few months, but the memories of the accident soon became too much for him, and he left the employment of Wayne Hasson. He is writing a book about Belize and its above-water ecological environment. Rob Salvatori continues to dive, remains active in the RDC, and has served as the club's chairman of education.

Dave Mowrer has temporarily given up his position as an instructor at Dallas Weston's dive shop to pursue another hobby—traveling the professional barbeque circuit. In 2003 he and friend Kim Walker purchased three Kamado cookers and perfected their skills. In their first year they ranked as the number one team in Pennsylvania and fifth nationally in their specialty, brisket, and were selected the International Iron Chef Grand Champions. They tripled their honors in 2004, and toured the southeast giving cooking classes.

It didn't take long for the families of victims to level accusations of neglect and wrongdoing at Peter Hughes, his company, and Captain Martin. Within forty-eight hours of the accident, Nelson Ayala, admiralty investigator for Huggett & Watford Law firm in Miami, flew to Belize to investigate the tragedy and enlist clients for what his firm knew would likely be a major lawsuit against Peter Hughes and his company. The firm, known for specializing in maritime disasters, handled the case for victims' families of the *Fantome* disaster, quickly signed an agreement to represent the survivors of Eloisa Johnson. On October 19, 2001, they filed a ten-million-dollar lawsuit in Miami-Dade County, Florida, against Peter Hughes, Peter Hughes Diving, Inc., Wave Dancer, LTD., and Captain Philip Martin.

The suit contended, among other things, that the *Wave Dancer* was the last boat to head for shore as the hurricane approached; the boat's captain, who was in contact with Peter Hughes via satellite phone, continued to head for Big Creek despite warnings that the storm had changed directions and was heading that way; the 120-foot boat was moored to a dock with a substantial portion of its bow exposed in the Big Creek Channel; those aboard the craft were not told to go ashore; scuba gear was not made handy in case of disaster; and the boats lines were not properly tended.

To support their claim of wrongdoing and negligence, the Huggett firm hired Ocean-Oil International Corp., a company of naval architects, marine engineers, and marine surveyors based in Palm Harbor, Florida, to inspect the *Wave Dancer*, which had been refloated at the request of the insurer, Lloyds of London. On December 18, 2001, Hector V. Pazos, P.E. naval architect and marine engineer, inspected the *Wave Dancer*, checking every space from the stern toward the bow, recording the inspection with photos and video. He submitted the following report.

His inspection of the steering compartment:

a. Rudders are positioned for a turn to starboard.
b. There are 14″ of liquids and mud indicating that the bulkhead is watertight.
c. The bit that was pulled out of the vessel's port side was "sitting" on a horizontal aluminum bracket connecting the upper side and upper transom stiffeners, without damage to the bracket, indicating a bad welding or no welding at all between the bit and the horizontal bracket.
d. There were several loose items such as large batteries, paint buckets, and miscellaneous items, and substantial mud; indicating that the hatch[s] were either open or they became opened during the capsizing.

His findings in the space forward of the steering compartment included:

a. The compartment was dry, hence the watertight bulkheads are okay, and found almost no mud, indicating that the manhole covers were secured.
b. This compartment contains a black water tank and a freshwater tank.
c. The main engine and generator exhaust pipes crossing this compartment appear to be undamaged.

His findings in the engine room:

a. Several large pieces of equipment were not secured [welded or bolted] and are in disarray, indicating that most of these items ended up on the underside of the deck during the capsizing. The loose equipment would have contributed to the capsizing by increasing the eccentricity of the transversal center of gravity. To be specific; the water maker was found loose just under the main deck at centerline. The water maker pump is loose against the starboard side. The air compressors are loose close to the centerline. The nitrox compressors are loose. Many spare parts and some spare pumps are displaced from their original location.

The floor plates are all displaced.

b. The E.R. has about 15" of liquids at the forward bulkhead.

c. The E.R. appears to have five sea chests: one for each engine, one for each generator [they have rubber sleeves], and one for the water maker.

d. There is a 1¾" to 2" diameter aluminum pipe that has been cut and it is open at centerline.

e. There are two intake air blowers on the port side and one exhaust blower on the starboard side. It is not known why the bolted cover for the "box" for the blowers [above main deck] on the port side was not in place, but it is assumed that salvors may have removed it. Also, it appears that the intake louvers were not covered by "hurricane panels" because the engines were running and because there is substantial mud in the engine room, which may have entered the engine room thru the intake and exhaust louvers. Also, mud in the engine room may have entered thru the starboard escape hatch in which the dog [a lever-like security door lock] is missing. The hurricane panels found in the storage rack have no rubber gaskets.

His findings in the laundry room:

a. There are two bilge pumps on the starboard side and a bilge manifold with 8 valves on the port side.

b. The water in the bilges of the laundry room was all the way up to the floor. We measured the depth of the bilges [at about 4' off centerline], which was found to be 25" [depth of water].

c. There are several pieces of equipment missing in the laundry room [most probably removed by salvors], with their foundations and/or retaining plates indicating that the missing equipment was not secured: i.e.: 2 freezers, 2 washing machines, one clothes dryer and several loose pumps. All this loose equipment may have contributed to the 180 degrees capsizing by leaving their retaining plates and sliding to one side creating a transversal shift of the center of gravity.

d. On the starboard side the A/C equipment is located, with intake louvers that most probably were covered by hurricane panels.

e. Mr. Albert Hall, Eloisa's boyfriend attended the inspection and indicated that he suspected that the laundry room and engine room are somewhat connected because there was always some oil in the bilges of the laundry room. Nevertheless, we could not confirm this without pumping both spaces to inspect the bulkhead between the engine room and the laundry room. The opening [if it existed] communicating these two spaces may be plugged with rags and mud.

f. There was substantial mud in the laundry room indicating that the louvers for the air conditioning equipment had no hurricane panels, but also indicates that the watertight door used to access the laundry room from the main deck was most probably open or became open because it has only one dog.

Findings in the under-deck passenger quarters:

a. The bilges in this space extend side to side of the vessel and were full of water, up to 4" below the floor.

b. On the starboard side, there is a photo lab, which also has two electric fans or blowers [besides other pumps], piped up to flexible 6" hoses and piping going from the bilges to the side shell, presumably to remove odors from the bilges under the quarters. This indicates that the vessel was operating with substantial volumes of gray water in the bilges, as well as possible leaks of black water, which required the installation of two blowers to reduce the smell.

c. There are two broken windows on the starboard side, covered by salvage patches.

d. According to Mr. Hall, at one time there was a transducer installed in a recess in the bilges that was eliminated by covering the recess with a bolted plate. This detail can only be inspected in drydock by a diver.

e. There is a substantial amount of mud throughout the under-deck-passenger quarters, which indicates that the watertight door separating the laundry room from the under-deck-passenger quarters was open, and the mud that entered the laundry room also flowed to the under deck quarters.

Findings in the crew quarters under the main deck:

There is an escape hatch in the aft-port stateroom, located on the main deck without means to climb to the escape hatch from the crew quarters. The hatch was apparently covered by carpets of the main deck, making it difficult or impossible to open if a means to reach the hatch existed. This is an infringement of USCG Rules, which requires two means of escape.

Findings in the forward peak:

a. There were loose mooring ropes of various sizes spread thru the forepeak.

b. There is a freshwater tank and a pump, which was apparently dislocated from its foundation.

c. A second anchor could not be found in the forward peak.

Observations of items above the main deck, starting at the stern:

a. The aft bitt is 39" height above to the main deck. The circumference is 17½".

b. There are two 20" x 20" one dog square hatches to access the steering compartment, which were most probably not secured during the capsizing.

c. The black water space has 2-20" diameter flush manholes with covers.

d. There are two-engine room escape hatches which are: single dog type and have 20" x 20" x 10¾" coamings, but the dog of the starboard hatch is missing. Hence, most probably was open during capsizing.

e. The access door to the laundry room is a two-dog door, but has one dog missing. The coaming of this door is 16" high.

f. The access door to the centerline passageway in the main cabin is a light, non-watertight door [has no dogs], and has only a 7" coaming [joiner door construction-half glass style].

g. The emergency sliding door, just forward of midship on the starboard side of the main deck has a 7" coaming. The latch system is extremely light and is activated by gravity.

His general comments:

The gaskets in all watertight doors were either damaged [had gaps], or were over compressed. The vessel had several appliances [refrigerators, ovens, etc.] that were distributed as several locations [pilothouse, galley, main deck, under deck, etc.], which apparently had no means of restraint or securing fittings, and therefore, most probably were dislocated during the listing of the vessel creating a shift of the transversal center of gravity and therefore, accelerating the 180 degrees capsizing. The vents on deck had floats. The vessel had several plugs installed by salvors on the deck, transom and sides. The hole where the port bit was pulled out is about 5½" in diameter. Mr. McPherson, from 3-D Marine indicated that there was a second anchor on board, located under the skiff, close to the stern. This second anchor should be in the Peter Hughes Warehouse in Belize. It should be noted that the fact of the existence of the second anchor is important because, having two anchors available, the *Wave Dancer* should have been positioned some 20 to 30 feet away from the dock, using one anchor forward-starboard and the second anchor aft-starboard. This would have allowed the necessary elasticity of the port mooring lines to the dock bollards and pile, and therefore, permit the vessel to move up with the storm tide. The lack of flexibility of the mooring lines resulted in the failure of the aft-port bit, an event which initiated the sequence of events that ended with the capsizing.

In essence, Mr. Pazos's report states that the *Wave Dancer* had several large pieces of heavy equipment in the engine room and galley that were not secured and moved from their positions when the boat first began to list. This loose equipment caused a transversal in the center of gravity of the boat. As the *Wave Dancer* broke away from the dock the flat bottom boat that didn't heel well [slow to return to its upright position] was unable to fully stabilize. Without a keel on the bottom of the *Wave Dancer*, there was no counter balance to compensate for the transversal and listing. Thus, the continuing pressure of Hurricane Iris's wind and storm surge forced the

Wave Dancer, at its will, to capsize. Once in an upside-down position the boat took in water through unsecured vents and doors. One escape hatch had been covered in carpet, impeding any effort to get out of that area. The report observed that the *Wave Dancer* had two anchors. The boat, according to the report, should have moved away from the dock, dropped the anchors fore and aft, giving the lines enough flexibility to move up with the storm surge.

As a result of this report, along with facts already known and other information gathered during the discovery process, Lloyd's of London agreed to pay five million dollars, the full amount of their exposure, to the victim's families and the three RDC survivors. The *Wave Dancer* had been set up as a separate legal entity within the global Peter Hughes Company and as such shielded Peter Hughes from any personal liability. Thus, the only money that would be paid to the victim's families and the three survivors came from the Lloyd's of London insurance settlement.

Legal fees and the cost of refloating the *Wave Dancer*, which later was sold for scrap, amounted to nearly two million dollars, leaving approximately three million dollars for the twenty victims' families and three survivors. On September 18, 2002, the twenty-three claims were arbitrated by retired Circuit Judge Robert L. Harris Sr., who apportioned the money, giving the largest sums to the victims who had minor children.

DeBarger, although on the low end of the financial settlement list, felt the apportioned settlement was fair, saying, "Those who lost the most got the most." He had entered the suit to "get the truth" and recover enough money to replace the dive gear and clothing he had lost when the *Wave Dancer* capsized. He was, however, very upset that Peter Hughes did not offer any of them the same refund or voucher for the ill-fated trip that Wayne Hasson had given to his *Belize Aggressor* passengers. DeBarger felt he was at least entitled to reimbursement for his loss, as much for the gesture of compassion as for the money itself.

Already suffering from a backlash following the 9/11 attacks, the live-aboard industry took a major hit from the *Wave Dancer* disaster. Scuba divers around the world canceled live-aboard trips, and all operators felt the repercussions of the accident at Big Creek. Add a weak economy to the mix and the live-aboard industry struggled through the worst time since its inception. It has since recovered as time has passed since 9/11 and the Big Creek tragedy, and the economy has strengthened.

The *Wave Dancer* tragedy polarized the diving community. Immediately after the accident, divers and organizations used the Internet to express their opinions on the liability of the Peter Hughes Company and the responsibility of the RDC divers who stayed on the boat. Many divers felt that magazines supported by advertising from live-aboard operators accepted too easily the explanation from Peter Hughes that the tragedy was a freak accident. Divers called for justice and accountability. Bitter arguments exploded in chat rooms as some people blamed Hughes and Martin, others faulted the divers themselves, and still others pointed to the unregulated live-aboard industry as a whole. "Scuba Forum," a feature on the Cyber Diver News Network [CDNN] Web site, became a popular battleground for the on-going argument. CDNN offered extensive and candid reporting on the accident and in March of 2002 launched a campaign called "Act Now" to rally support for a full investigation.

The International Merchant Marine Registry of Belize [IMMARBE] headed by Angelo Mouzouropoulos did not have all of the witness reports, which were held up by attorneys representing their clients. As a result, for a long time no official public report had been filed. Furthermore, it appeared none was forthcoming, fueling accusations and speculation.

Teresa Mars, wife of diver Ray Mars, and Tom Stark, father of dive master Aaron Stark, gave interviews to CDNN that sparked thousands of responses. Both were frustrated by the many questions surrounding the deaths of their loved ones, and they reached out to the only avenue of hope they thought was available to them. Teresa became particularly vocal in her quest to find out what happened to her husband of thirty-three years. She wrote to Dave DeBarger and Rick Patterson and solicited the support of the RDC. She received sympathy cards from President and Mrs. Bush, and Tommy Thompson, Secretary of Health and Human Services, Ray's boss, but received no information from the RDC. By that time the lawyers entered the situation and closed the channels of communication, which frustrated her even more. She ran into one brick wall after another and wondered if she ever would find out what happened to her husband.

She wrote to the author of this book to say, "All I have ever wanted was that the truth of what really happened that night be known. I am not pointing fingers, nor do I expect Peter Hughes to change his official statements that they did nothing wrong. However, I knew Ray better than anyone else possibly could have, and there is absolutely no doubt in my mind that he was not aware of the severity of the storm, or he would not have been on that boat. I can say the same for many of the other victims, because I had met them on a previous trip the year before. They were mature, safety-conscious adults, not the drinking, party animals that have been reported." She asked that a fund be set up in Ray's memory at Divers Alert Network. She continued, "I decided that we would request that people not send flowers, but instead send contributions to the Ray Mars Memorial Chamber Fund. I wanted to use the money to repair dive chambers on some of the smaller, less prosperous islands, because I thought Ray would really like that idea. He visited the chambers everywhere we went. They set up this fund, and many, many people [actually everyone who knew about it] made contributions. At the Memorial Service in Richmond in November, Joel Dovenbarger from DAN was there, and came over and talked with me. He told me there was enough money already in Ray's fund to make an inspection trip in the spring of some of the chambers. Since Ray had been an investigator for many years for the FDA, an inspection trip seemed so very appropriate. I had the comfort of knowing that he would be very pleased with that idea." Teresa has since become an activist for increased safety on live-aboard dive boats.

CDNN conducted a poll on its Web site regarding hurricane awareness and safety. The question read, "Should live-aboard operators keep guests onboard when a category four hurricane threatens?" The poll received twenty-five yes votes and 5,956 no votes.

Undercurrent, a monthly magazine self-described as "The Private, Exclusive Guide for Serious Divers," received and published reports from divers, victims' family members and former Peter Hughes employees. Divers were both supportive, touting their many good experiences with the Hughes Company, and critical, citing, "safety first, profits second." In one issue of *Undercurrent*, Publisher and Editor Ben Davison remembered Ray Mars as a person who had submitted excellent articles to the chapbook section of the magazine for many years.

After a few months of heated debate over responsibility and accountability, Peter Hughes, feeling the pressure had been relieved and not wanting to pass up the lucrative opportunities offered on the Belizean reef, moved his *Sun Dancer II* to Belize. With the exception of being black instead of blue, the *Sun Dancer* was a spitting image of the *Wave Dancer*. To allay any anxieties divers might have about his operation and safety procedures, Hughes adopted a "hurricane plan" for the company: "In the event any Dancer Fleet vessel is within the predicted track of any officially named hurricane or tropical storm, [as predicted by NOAA] all passengers will be disembarked from the vessel in question at least twelve [12] hours prior to the predicted landfall of the hurricane or tropical storm. Passengers will be accommodated ashore, at the discretion of the captain and at the expense of Peter Hughes Diving, Inc., at a place determined to be a safe haven depending upon location in question."

In the summer of 2003, having received the final necessary witness reports Angelo Mouzouropoulos and his IMMARBE staff prepared a preliminary official report on the accident at Big Creek. Satisfied that all questions had been asked and answered, the formal official report would soon be made public. As it was about to be released, the Peter Hughes

Company sued Wayne Hasson and his Aggressor Fleet. Hughes alleged that at the peak of Hurricane Iris the *Aggressor* moved forward on the dock and bumped the *Wave Dancer* and that the bump caused the stern cleat to pull out of the boat, which led to its capsizing.

Incensed at the accusation, Hasson contacted Mouzouropoulos, who met with Bart Stanley to get his second formal statement. Stanley's written statement read: "I, Bartholomew Alexander Stanley, Dive Master and Photographer onboard the *M.V. Wave Dancer* further declare that I assisted in the mooring of the vessel at Big Creek on 8th October 2001, specifically in the aft and midships areas. There was no aft breast line as described in Captain Philip Martin's corrected mooring line plan. The contact with the *Belize Aggressor III* occurred shortly after the *Wave Dancer* had broken loose from the dock. At that time, I was in the salon and saw the aft section of our boat drifting away from the dock. I also saw that the *Belize Aggressor III* was still in place and secure. Thereafter, our boat collided with the *Belize Aggressor III*, the sound and impact of which I heard and felt. The *Belize Aggressor III* remained secure in the same position."

On Hasson's behalf, Captain Jerry Schnabel stated that when he and his crew tied up the *Belize Aggressor* they used "spring lines" fore and aft to prevent the boat from moving forward during the storm. He also stated that the *Wave Dancer* had no such lines, and it was his opinion that the *Wave Dancer* moved back into the *Belize Aggressor* causing damage to the bow of his ship. Before Iris hit Big Creek, Captain Schnabel and Mowrer walked along the dock and inspected the *Aggressor's* mooring lines. Hasson contacted Mowrer to get his written statement as well.

All of the statements were for naught as Mouzouropoulos was forced to delay the release of the IMMARBE report until the litigation between Hughes and Hasson was settled. In August of 2004 Hughes dropped the suit, and the officials said the formal report would be released in mid-November. The release of the IMMARBE report was delayed until January 2005. It can be accessed on the Belize Web site.

The extensive report exonerates Peter Hughes but finds fault with Captain Martin and Second Captain Wouters. Captain Martin is banned indefinitely from service on any vessel in Belize while Frank Wouters is banned for five years. The officials found fault with the tie-up of the Wave Dancer but did not believe that the position of the bow, jutting in excess of thirty feet into the channel, played a role in the accident. The report recommends that boat operators follow a specific plan of action during hurricanes as well as annual inspections by Belize authorities.

As Forrest Powell, Lisa's father, sorted through her belongings following her death he found a paper she had written for a college English class. It was written from the point of view of Lisa's mother, mourning the death of her daughter—an unusual assignment for young college students but one that Lisa took to heart.

Lisa Powell, April 21, 1989   English 102

Remembering Lisa

I still can't believe she's gone! There are so many things that we never got to share. She was my oldest daughter. I wonder if she can see me now? Lisa was nineteen years old, and yet, I still don't really know who she was. I wonder if she even knew? Maybe sifting through a few of her things before I pack up I can learn a little about my lost baby. What's this? Oh! A photo album of friends. Lisa always did like to be surrounded by people. I'll just take a peek through here...Hmm...I don't remember hearing about this party...there sure was a lot of beer drinking!! I guess it is a little late to ground you for this one, Lee. Let's see what else you have saved in this closet of yours. I must admit one thing, you sure were organized. I never would have been able to find anything in here if things were not so neat. Gosh! This is almost too neat, this is sick. I'm only kidding, honey! I'm glad somebody could find what they were looking for in this family! How am I ever going to stand your dad's forgetfulness without you being there to make fun of him? Remember the time he told you to put your chair up—when he meant to say down—at the dinner table, and you put it on the table? I will never forget what a smart ass you were! Okay here's something. Oh, your bank books. You have saved more than I thought you had! I was always proud of you for saving your money. I wish you could have taught your brother a few things about saving money. That reminds me, who is going to be the referee to your brother and sister when I am at work? They will probably kill each other without you around.

I don't want to get in your real personal things. I respect your privacy. I think I'll check your closet. Did you leave me any clothes to wear? I doubt that I can fit into any of this stuff? You are the only person I know that has a new jacket for each week. No wonder you don't have any other clothes! You sure got a lot of wear out your shoes, except for those black Reeboks you just had to have. Did you ever wear them? Oh, well…maybe your sister can wear them. This purple vest with the glitter on it sure is…interesting! What am I going to do with all this stuff?

What else did you leave behind for me to sort through? All these tapes and records…The Police, The Eagles, Led Zeppelin, Motley Crüe, Steve Miller, The Jane Fonda Workout...Hey, this is mine! I wonder what else you have of mine? You always did have a habit of borrowing things without asking, like your dad's Randolph Macon sweat shirt: I think he is still mad about that!

Would you look at that mirror? I will never be able to clean that up. Your dresser has enough junk on it to open a small gift shop. Hey, now that's an idea. Baskets, restaurant coasters, make-up, perfume, telephone, souvenirs. You saved bows from flowers, a Cayman Island sticker, and ticket stubs galore! You must have been to at least twenty concerts. So where is all the valuable stuff? I didn't really mean that. I know that all this stuff was important to you and in that case, it is all valuable. If you can hear me I want you to know that everyone really misses you.

I think I will keep all of your stuff just the way it was. That way we can remember who you really were.

He felt an odd comfort while reading the essay, as if Lisa herself were consoling him, telling him how to grieve. He felt close to her again. Exactly what happened on that terrible night aboard the *Wave Dancer* may never be fully known, and no one has accepted full or even partial responsibility. The sad fact remains that the tragedy was entirely preventable, and if anything positive can come of it, perhaps owners and crews of live-aboard boats have learned some valuable lessons.

But no official, legal, or financial resolution will bring closure to those who lost loved ones and friends far away in a distant country. For them, peace will come from remembering the victims as they "really were," by remembering them in moments unclouded by doubt or blame or anger at the cruelty of circumstance. In those moments, their laughter and strength, their tenacity and spirit of adventure will shine through—and guided by that light, they will find their way home.

Acknowledgments

At Big Creek, prior to the hurricane, I met and visited with several of the victims of the *Wave Dancer* accident as they gathered aboard the *Belize Aggressor* to enjoy good cheer with their friends. Then, heart-wrenching as it was, a few hours later Jeff Clark and I carried their lifeless bodies from the dive deck of the *Aggressor* to the floor of the nearby banana warehouse. The shock at the loss of their friends and the hurricane party rumors caused the survivors of the tragedy to close ranks and not talk with the media in order to preserve the dignity of their lost friends and their families.

The tragedy and its aftermath haunted me. I read several online discussions blaming the victims for partying during the storm, for not taking safety precautions, and for staying on the *Wave Dancer* when they should have gone ashore. A year after the accident, I hesitantly called Dave Mowrer. He remembered me from the *Aggressor*, agreed to be interviewed, and invited me to come to Richmond. We scheduled a date that coincided with the monthly Richmond Dive Club meeting so he could introduce me to Dave DeBarger, Mary Lou Hayden, and Rick Patterson. He also introduced me to Dallas Weston, Tara Williamson, and several others. He opened many doors.

Dave DeBarger, Mary Lou, and Rick were reluctant to talk with anyone about the accident because they had been misled by a previous journalist. However, since I had been on the *Aggressor*, Dave felt I had credibility and would write an accurate version of what happened at Big Creek. He wanted the truth to come out about the accident and met with me on each of my several trips to Richmond. He shared his photos, news clippings, and personal insights with me. He also arranged for me to meet with Mary Lou. He is a true gentleman and professional.

Mary Lou Hayden reluctantly carries the badge of heroine in the tragedy. She spent several hours describing her conversations with Bill and Sheila Kelly, Byron and Shirley Johnston, and Lisa Powell. Her recollections of the time leading to and the aftermath of the accident were as insightful as they were emotional.

I met with Bart Stanley on three occasions in Belize. He provided me with his memories of the days prior to and immediately following the accident. He also enlightened me on the many meetings he had with the Belizean crew and gave me invaluable information about the *Wave Dancer*, Captain Martin, and his crew.

I also want to thank Teresa Mars for sharing her innermost feelings about the pain of losing a life companion before his time. She also provided me with the Naval Architect and Marine Engineers report, which described what happened internally to the *Wave Dancer* when it listed at the Big Creek dock.

Forrest Powell wrote to me about some of the special memories he had of Lisa and provided me with her college theme, which is included in this book.

Heather Johnston and Scott Kelley each shared fond memories of their parents, and I thank them.

I received moral support and huge assistance from my personal editor, Marilyn Olsen, who transformed my rough draft into an acceptable manuscript. Once done, Jack Heffron at Emmis Books took over to polish the manuscript to its final form. These were two major operations, and I thank them both for their advice and insight.

I want to thank my good friend Steve Meyers, who was going to assist me in offering suggestions, but due to health problems was unable to do so. Nevertheless, he has stood firmly by me, encouraging me along the way.

Last but not least, I want to thank my wife, Linda, who spent many hours reading my manuscript, offering suggestions and showing a great deal of patience that only a wife of thirty-three years can possess.